GERMANY
The Empire Within

GERMANY

The Empire Within

Amity Shlaes

Farrar, Straus & Giroux

NEW YORK

Copyright © 1991 by Amity Shlaes
Maps © 1991 by Farrar, Straus and Giroux
All rights reserved
Printed in the United States of America
Published simultaneously in Canada by HarperCollins*CanadaLtd*
Designed by Tere Lo Prete
First edition, 1991

Library of Congress Cataloging-in-Publication Data

Shlaes, Amity.
Germany : the empire within / Amity Shlaes. — 1st ed.
p.   cm.
Includes bibliographical references.
1. Germany—Civilization—20th century.   2. Nationalism—Germany—
History—20th century.   I. Title.
DD257.S47   1991   943—dc20   90-42999

Population figures on map showing the number of Jews in Germany before the
Second World War taken from *Atlas of the Holocaust* by Martin Gilbert, © 1988,
Pergamon Press PLC. Reprinted with permission

Contents

	INTRODUCTION	3
1	Home Through Friedland	17
2	The Lost House	43
3	Serving the Empire	71
4	A Prince in Bavaria	103
5	Barbara's Work	133
6	The Empire Abroad	161
7	A Jewish Place	183
8	One Family's Berlin	217
	ACKNOWLEDGMENTS	247
	NOTES	249
	BIBLIOGRAPHY	251
	INDEX	255

GERMANY
The Empire Within

Introduction

As for the Germans, they need neither freedom nor equality.
They are a speculative people, ideologues, before- and after-
thinkers, dreamers who live only in the past and the future
and have no present.

The words come from Heinrich Heine, and they are more
than a hundred and fifty years old. The poet produced them
in his disappointment that his countrymen, unlike the heady
French, could not manage to make a revolution. But Heine's
description also fits some more recent Germanys—the West
and East Germany we have known since World War II.
Economically, the two states certainly lived in the "present."
West Germans, a people so hungry after the war they fought
over single potatoes, built themselves into the strongest economy in Europe. East Germans, too, produced their own
"economic miracle," albeit one within the gloomy con-
straints of the socialist system. Culturally, though, the two
half-nations lived in a kind of nervy suspension. Germans
themselves often used fairy-tale language to describe their
state. "We are like Sleeping Beauty," they told visitors. During that sleep, Germans felt safe, safe enough to dream up
their own, private Germanys. Now events outside Germany—the disintegration of the Soviet empire—are forcing
Germans awake. It is the difficulty of matching those dream
Germanys to the new, real one that this book seeks to describe.

When I first started traveling in Germany, at a time when the Berlin Wall seemed a fixture as unchallengeable as the moon in the sky, the "after-thinkers," the reflective Germans, were the ones I encountered. I was a student, and these Germans were as young as I was—sixteen, or twenty, or twenty-four, or twenty-eight. But they lived in an odd landscape marked by some very old dates. 1848, the year dreamers like Heinrich Heine watched German kingdoms and principalities try to become one democratic nation and fail to do so. 1871, the year unity came—but unity brought through war, and unity under a bossy Kaiser. 1918, when the Kaiser left and Germany launched into the shaky Weimar Republic. 1933, when Hitler took power and broke that republic. 1945, "zero hour," the year "history" ended and the German division began.

These were not dates Germans spoke of with affection, or even the respect other peoples accord their own history. They were dates that obsessed them. At my newspaper we liked to joke that the youthful West Germany was the "anniversary country," even the "funeral country," because of the steady flow of publicity we received announcing various commemorations. 1983 was "Hitler's anniversary," fifty years since the National Socialists seized power. I was living in West Berlin then and spent a whole week in January attending "Hitler" events—an exhibit where red banners with black swastikas floated in halls to show the frightening power of Nazi propaganda, a colloquium in the battered Reichstag where a tribunal of historians wondered aloud how Hitler could have been prevented. 1985 brought the anniversary of Hitler's Reichsbürgergesetz, which said only Aryans were Germans. 1988 brought yet another sad commemoration: the commemoration of Kristallnacht. In an odd way, all these tic. She talked about a mystical city that no longer existed, Reval, and still thought of those faraway parts as her "Germany." At the university I met someone else: an architect with a "von" before his name who complained bitterly that his Germany used to be bigger, that where his family came from was now Poland, and that now they had nothing left to rule. Yet another student had a different story—he carried the burden of being a "Sudeten German": he felt guilty about being German because his family was from the Sudetenland and the only time the Sudetenland had been part of Germany was during the Third Reich. The last was someone I met downtown at West Berlin's Jewish Community Center, a volleyball player. He was Jewish, a Zionist who felt Jews should move to Israel. Yet he stayed on in Germany, although he argued that "no Jew can be comfortable here."

What I had to go to history books and outdated maps to discover was the size and cultural magnitude of this "lost" Germany. When, at Potsdam, Churchill, Truman, and Stalin rearranged the map of Central Europe, they did more than divide Germany into zones of occupation. They also expanded the Soviet Union and moved Poland westward, so that Polish cities became Soviet and German cities became Polish. To me and, I suspect, to most people who are not scholars of modern history, this came as a surprise. Gdansk, Lech Walesa's home and the birthplace of Solidarity, had once been the free port of Danzig portrayed in Günter Grass's *Tin Drum*. The Allies wanted to clear Central Europe, once and for all, of ethnic Germans who might cause the kind of trouble that had led to the Second World War. "A clean sweep will be made," Churchill told Parliament. The sweep *was* made; more than 12 million Germans were driven and fled westward as a result of this transposition. Some 2 million died—mostly of the cold, or disease, or malnutrition—on the trek. The survivors and their children were some of the "war ghosts" I was encountering in West Germany.

The second surprise was that, even after this rearrangement, pockets of Germans still dotted the map at points far to the east of Communist East Germany. Ethnic Germans still live today in Romania, in Czechoslovakia, and, in larger numbers, in Poland; there are German speakers who make their homes in the Soviet Union, in Baltic Riga, and in spots as far east as Siberian Novosibirsk. These Germans are the living traces of the old Habsburg empire and of Germany's historic expansion eastward. Today, like Armenians in the Soviet Union, or Albanians in Yugoslavian Kosovo, these Germans and their problems are coming to the fore as nationalism emerges; they are some of the sources of the great ethnic unrest now putting pressure on political lines that have for decades shaped Central and Eastern Europe.

It was the pressure history put on West Germany, though, that became my focus. A few years after my studies, I returned there, this time as a journalist, to take a look at the groups that had occupied a place in the Kaiser's empire, or even in the Third Reich: ethnic Germans from points far to the east, East Germans who had fled the Communist German Democratic Republic, Jews who lived in Germany but still seemed outsiders, Berliners who thought of themselves as citizens of a capital but lived in a city that was no longer one. The groups I sought out were very different from one another—I even met with officers from the army to find out what kind of person still chose, after this nation's troubled history, to make a profession out of fighting for "Germany"—but they shared one characteristic. They seemed, in their way, anachronisms in the then relatively ahistoric life of West Germany. As a starting point for this reporting, I picked the group that seemed to stretch the definition of

"German" to its oddest extreme: families from the Soviet Union who were "returning" to Germany and thought of themselves as Germans but had been away from German territory since the time of Catherine the Great.

These were not groups that interested Germans. Why study relics, they wanted to know. Why glorify fossils? The guest workers, Turks and Italians who had come to help the West German economy but lived uncomfortably in its culture, would be a better subject. Or, they suggested, how about the growing Green movement? The reaction seemed odd: the same people who lectured on those old totemic dates were doing their best to steer me clear of the living links to those dates.

More than a few people—often people from the university world—pointed out that there was one postwar date worthwhile studying: 1968, the year the thunderstorm of revolt that shook many Western nations threw its lightning bolt on German campuses. But, they hastened to add, the " '68 movement" was an international one, not a German one. In fact, it can be argued that socialism, a goal beloved of many of the sixty-eighters long after the year 1968, had such a hold on West Germany precisely because it was safely international. For many sixty-eighters, however, the revolt was a reaction to their parents' history of Nazism. One of the most colorful exponents of this view was Christof Wacker-nagel, a friendly man I found seated next to me on a British talk show one evening. He turned out to be a former terrorist—an ex-member of the Red Army Faction, a murderous team specializing in kidnapping and killing people it regarded as the linchpins of capitalism. He had since abandoned terrorism for writing and acting. But there, before the cameras that night, he stuck to the same reasoning that had once made him shoot a policeman: "I thought I had the duty

to make resistance if I didn't want to be like my parents."
Wackernagel was born after the war but, he said, he still felt
"shame to be a German"—and waved a Swiss passport
wildly at the camera by way of proof of his serious commitment to this sentiment. Even more conventional young Germans, though, often tried to avoid the label "German."
Abroad, asked their nationality, they usually ducked the
question by responding, "I am a European." This "European" cover held so long because it was comfortable.

The more I studied these "borderline," disparate groups,
the more evident it became that their problems and projects
were the clearest reflection of the problems and projects of
German society. The German reunification program—or
unification program, as some like to put it—emerged as
prime evidence of this; only a few years ago, Germany's
spokesmen, the journalists and politicians who showed up
at think-tank conferences, were close to unanimous in de-
scribing the hoary "German question" as irrelevant. Only
the marginal outsiders spoke of a national longing for "one
Germany." Now the entire nation is bent on realizing the
outsiders' dreams. The problem is that these dreams differ;
Germans nurse varying fantasies of "one Germany." Some
dreams even conflict with each other, so much so that, ironically, they occasionally presented formidable obstacles to
reunification. Some Social Democrats dream of a Germany
that guarantees equality—that guarantees security—and
fear that the fast pace the West German government set in
1990 will give them instead a cold capitalist giant. The question of the new Germany's eastern border with Poland has
popped into the headlines just over the past year, but it is a
question that has obsessed these marginal groups—the exiled Silesians, in particular—for decades.

It is no accident that the German reunion comes so late

in the train of events. Mikhail Gorbachev had to appear, Hungary's border with Austria had to open, Poland had to push aside Communism before Germans on both sides of the Wall dared to begin talking seriously of "one Germany again." Even the official reconciliation, the meetings between heads of states and the old Allies, is merely a reaction: Erich Honecker, the East German leader, fell, the Wall opened, but only after the refugees washing into West Germany were already providing a de facto reunification.

The reluctance comes, of course, from fear. How can Germans build what seems to be a new, empire-sized Deutschland when the last empire they built was Hitler's Third Reich? "Germany," as such, has no strong traditions of freedom or democracy. Germany had no revolution like France, and the only successful democratic Germany has been the provisional postwar Federal Republic. The historian Golo Mann reports a joke that circulated in 1949, the year the Federal Republic was born—that the Allies needed a West German fortress in the deepening Cold War so badly that the Federal Republic would have been forced into life even if it had to be called the Emergency Association of German Länder. Germans liked that imposition because it absolved them of responsibility. Konrad Adenauer, a Rhinelander, turned away from the Prussian vision of Germany and pressed his choice for a capital, the Rhineside university town of Bonn, on his colleagues. Germans liked to joke about the humdrum nature of this choice—they called Bonn the *Bundesdorf*, the federal village. Nevertheless, Bonn has suited those who have worked there—it is pleasant, it is on the water, and, save for the Hotel Dreesen, on whose covered terrace Hitler chatted with Neville Chamberlain, it is relatively clean of that bugaboo, history. Germans fear that a new Germany, like its predecessors, will value freedom too

Introduction

little, and their fear is legitimate. The reconciliation taking place now was triggered by the absence of freedom—in East Germany—but it is principally a nationalist event. In fact, both Konrad Adenauer, West Germany's first Chancellor, and Walter Ulbricht, East Germany's first leader, headed their states for a period longer than Adolf Hitler controlled his "thousand-year" empire. But in German national memory both men stand in the shadow of that screechy giant.

Today the two Germanys are setting about making Berlin their capital again, but the precedents for their project spook them. The heart of their city, the logical place for a new government to site its bureaucracy, contains the rubble of the old diplomatic Wilhelmstrasse, where in 1933 Hitler created Angriff Haus—Attack House—a name prophetic of his international ambitions. In the same quarter lay Prinz-Albrechtstrasse, where the Gestapo kept a small prison with thirty-nine cells to house Resistance members before sending them off to the noose in Plötzensee. Beside the same lake, the Wannsee, where sunbathing Berliners today spend their weekends, Hitler's team thought out the Final Solution.

For outsiders, especially Jews, the prospect of a unified Germany is often even more frightening. Throughout the fall and winter of 1989–90, when German unity was suddenly becoming a genuine possibility, they voiced their concern. To them, the breakdown of the Wall provided the first alarming signal. November 9 had gone down as a black date in history, for on that day in 1938 the Nazis took their anti-Semitism to the streets in a nationwide pogrom, burning and destroying Jewish homes, shops, and synagogues. West Germany itself took care to commemorate the fifty-year anniversary of Kristallnacht with a 1988 ceremony of mourning in the Bundestag, the West German Parliament. When, on the same date a year later, East Germans pushed past border guards and broke the Wall, November 9 became a new and important symbol whose strength instantly threatened to overpower the date's old significance in international memory. In fact, the November 9 of Kristallnacht itself overshadowed yet another November 9—November 9, 1918, when the hopeful, nervous, Weimar Republic was born. That three such different events in German history took place on the same day was sheer coincidence. Even so, many have argued, the most recent November 9 will obscure the memory of the Holocaust, and perhaps even permit the construction of a threatening Fourth Reich.

Nevertheless, the Germans are building Germany. They are reestablishing a connection which for forty years was cut. It is precisely the odd groups from the old empires, my "relics" who seemed so much beside the point, who are providing much of the continuity that makes that reconnection possible. My Berlin friend who for years felt herself isolated in a backwater now walks me through the city's newly crowded subway stations to show me how "Berlin is becoming itself again." East German refugees, a group that began to dry up after Walter Ulbricht put up the Wall in August 1961, were the ones who traveled via Hungary or Poland when the borders opened there and so forced their own regime to take down the Wall. Bearers of old noble names from Central Europe may not see their confiscated family estates returned, but some of these people are taking leading roles in shaping the new states of Hungary and Czechoslovakia.

My "relic" groups are also the ones to feel most strongly the disappointment these events bring. Everyone in Germany, even those who don't like to admit it, has his own dream of Deutschland, but not all those dreams can be fulfilled. A bigger Germany won't console the nation's remaining Jews: their dream of life here is set entirely in the past. Another unfulfilled dream will likely be that of West and East Germans whose families come from Silesia or the Sudetenland. Both these groups, in particular the Silesians, always included their old homelands in *their* vision of Germany. The Silesians had some historical justification for this. Silesia was not cut out of Germany and handed to Poland until the end of World War II. Before that, Silesians traced a past in Germany dating back to Frederick the Great. Yet the Germany being built now is unlikely to claim Silesia back from Poland. The bitterness of disillusioned groups like the Silesians will have political consequences in the new Germany. Some argue the most troubling outlet for nationalist sentiment may be the neo-Nazi skinheads showing up in Dresden and Berlin, or the young far-right party, the Republikaner. Others argue that the danger comes not in nationalist sentiment but from the far left, in the utopian and redistributive goals of the Green movement.

Even for those Germans who are getting their wish, the reunion bears some element of bewilderment, even sorrow. The punchy crowds at the Brandenburg Gate may have celebrated, but they celebrated with mixed emotions. In part, this is because Germans have so long been a nation of mourners. What happens when, in mid-elegy, the beloved returns?

For Germany, the greatest emotional difficulty in this untimely return is reconciling the old Germany with a new, modern nation-state. Unlike Britain, or France, or even the United States, Germany has not been through the decolonization that defined recent decades, simply because Germany, during that period, did not exist. Readers may well question an implicit and unmodern equation that runs through this book, the equation of empire and nation. The equation, however, still lives in the minds of the German people. What we can expect to observe in coming years is Germany's mental decolonization, a racing effort to reshape the old Reich into a simple nation.

The prospects for the new Germany, half Reich or nation, are not dark. In the raw East German territory, Germans from all over are finding an exciting frontier, their own Wild West to the east. The new Germans recognize, too, that they do have forty years of democratic tradition in West Germany to build on. Germans from the fading Democratic Republic were raised in a different tradition, but they have demonstrably rejected it. The united land the rest of the world will now face, however, will still be Heine's reflective one, and it will trouble us with its ghosts. In the same pages in which he concludes that Germans need neither equality nor freedom, Heine modifies his own judgment. "It cannot be denied," the genial poet adds, "that the Germans, too, love freedom. But in a different way from other people."

1

Home Through Friedland

NORTH SEA

DENMARK

BALTIC SEA

POLAND

Berlin

EAST

GERMANY

Friedland

Düsseldorf

Bonn

WEST

GERMANY

CZECHOSLOVAKIA

FRANCE

Stuttgart

Munich

AUSTRIA

THE GERMANY THAT MADE FRIEDLAND

The ugliest monument in all of Germany stands atop a hill in a village called Friedland. Here, from a field waving with dandelions, four giant concrete walls jut out at odd angles into the sky. Travelers who start climbing the hill and come closer to the monument soon see that the walls aren't solid: tiny rectangles, like prison windows, dot its gray surfaces. When the travelers reach the top, they find a stark message scraped on one wall: "People, Forswear Hatred." The sculpture is ugly because what it commemorates is ugly: the years after the war in which millions of Germans were driven from the new Poland, or Romania, or the Soviet Union, to the Western zones of Germany. Friedland stands just a few miles west of the East–West divide; many of the settlers first set foot in their new homeland when they stepped off a train here. To house the arrivals, and start them off on their new lives, the Allies set up a refugee camp after the war. By the 1960s, Europe had hardened into postwar blocs and the flood of Friedland refugees slowed to drops. In 1967, West Germans built their Friedland monument. When they finished it, they thought—perhaps in relief, perhaps in sorrow—that they were closing a chapter in history.

Now, more than twenty years later, small Friedland finds itself busy making history of a cheerier variety. Monument visitors who stand long enough at the bottom of the hill see buses whish past, buses headed for the same collection of low buildings that once housed the postwar refugees. This time, too, large families are arriving at Friedland, and this time, too, they are coming from Poland, or Romania, or the Soviet Union. When a bus's door sighs open, grandmothers in kerchiefs, grandfathers in fur caps, grandchildren in old-fashioned overalls stumble out. Within minutes, Red Cross workers in white-and-red uniforms zip them into a long hall and hand them cups of red hibiscus tea. Within days, the Red Cross and camp workers complete what would seem a daunting task: they convert these strangers into German citizens.

Friedland performs its prestidigitation on a specific group, known in the official jargon as *Aussiedler*—"settlers." At Potsdam, the Allies who reshaped the map of Europe also tried to make sure that local nationalism, local ethnic division, would never cause another world war. In the name of this goal Churchill and Roosevelt agreed to allow Stalin to force some 12 million souls of German descent out of the section of Central Europe east of the two Germanys. When the number of arrivals started to drop, around 1950, young West Germany, for its part, promised to continue to welcome any refugees who might straggle in later. For many years, this promise was largely a symbolic one, for Stalin soon reversed his policy, and eastern borders, including the border of East Germany, became lines designed to keep people *in*. The ethnic Germans remaining in Poland, the Soviet Union, or Romania spent decades applying for exit visas, but they, like Soviet Jews, saw these applications denied. Like the Soviet Jews, too, these Eastern-bloc Germans were exploiting an ethnic heritage in the forgivable hope that it would get them to a part of the world where they could live a better life. When, a few years ago, new "settlers" did get exit visas and started showing up by the hundreds in Friedland, it was the first sign that the postwar European order was beginning to crack. In 1989, the crack widened—377,055 "settlers" showed up in West Germany, a greater number even than the number of East Germans arriving the year the Wall came down. Most of those "settlers" passed through Friedland.

At heart, Germans don't like strangers. East Germany may have had no choice in the matter, but for years it nevertheless seemed to take pleasure in controlling its own borders, hosting mainly sibling socialists and whatever Western visitors could bring hard cash. West Germans, too, welcomed tourists, and themselves flew in chartered hordes to Agadir, Florida, or Bali at Easter. In the 1960s, West Germany also invited laborers from Italy, Turkey, and Yugoslavia to fill jobs created by its *Wirtschaftswunder*, its economic miracle. In the 1970s and 1980s, the Federal Republic took in thousands of candidates for political asylum from places as far away as Ethiopia and Sri Lanka, in the conviction that Germany, with its record of political persecution under the Nazis, now ought to serve as a model of political tolerance. But West Germans accepted most of these arrivals only warily; they didn't like the idea of new faces showing up for a prolonged stay on home territory. The moment foreign four-year-olds crowd their kindergartens or foreign workers fill jobs, citizens react with a uniform phrase: Germany is not an immigration country. Even after decades in the Federal Republic, the arrivals still felt like strangers. From the German point of view, this land has room for only one exception: other Germans.

"Settlers" of the kind who pass through Friedland are evidence of how far this principle can stretch. They are not "brothers" from East Germany—they come from points farther east. Some of them don't even speak German. Officially, their classification as Germans is based on a law enacted in the early 1950s under which most candidates of German extraction from the Eastern bloc were given the right to automatic citizenship and benefits. Emotionally, their inclusion is a form of consolation: Germans in the West wanted to help a group of distant kinsmen who faced decades of discrimination under Eastern bloc governments because of their German roots. Philosophically, the "settlers" exception comes from an old, odd commitment to the notion of race —the commitment that found its nastiest expression in Hitler's Third Reich. But it is also akin to Israel's definition of what makes a Jew. A baby born in America is an American, and, to a great extent, the same holds true for Britain. In Germany, blood is what counts, and the settlers are German because they are of German blood.

In later days, as the Germanys became one, citizens from Cologne and Munich would tire a bit of subsidizing the "settlers," just as they tire of subsidizing East Germans. But in these early times—1988, 1989, early 1990—the attention camp officials gave settlers at the Friedland stage of their odyssey reflected the care with which Germans—in this case, the West German government—fulfill their "blood" commitment. The encounter starts south of Friedland, when a mini-van bearing two Red Cross volunteers pulls up at Frankfurt's International Airport. The young men wave special passes at the customs guards and march to a terminal gate to meet Lufthansa flight 1373 from Moscow. Soon their charges emerge: 107 tired grandfathers, parents, and children, blinking and muttering in German. The Red Cross team is accustomed to this scene, for it undertakes the same mission every morning and evening. Now they get busy, directing their charges toward buses to Friedland. A pair of business travelers halt their race to the gate for Munich to pause and stare at the pilgrims. Amid the glass and glitz of the airport, the arrivals look like visitors from not another planet but another century. A young man in white jeans standing by a store window takes fright when a babushka starts trundling toward him. Before the young man can move, the grandma in her green kerchief closes in—and plants both hands and her nose beside him on the glass to inspect a cellular phone.

Friedland literally means "Peace Land," and to the settlers staring through the bus windows as they pull up at this small complex of prefab dormitories and geranium beds, the place does seem to have almost a holy connotation. To an outsider, Friedland merely looks busy. Piles of luggage with names in large Cyrillic letters overflow at its bus stop. Polski Fiats packed with men, women, babies, and cartons of diapers back into Friedland's already crowded parking lot. One by one, a cheery bus driver helps his passengers down onto new ground. After many such excursions, the driver has picked up a bit of Russian, and he kisses the prettiest passenger in the busload. "*Maya zhenzhina*," he jokes, and the arrivals laugh—"my wife."

The pilgrims' first station is a few steps away, a long Red Cross hall lined with pine chairs and pussy willows in vases, where thirty pale adults, yesterday's arrivals, are passing the evening hours watching *Die Schwarzwaldklinik*, a German soap opera that's a cross between *General Hospital* and *Dallas*. "Here they come," a Red Cross sister calls, and everyone in the hall moves toward the windows to inspect the arrivals, wondering where they come from. "You can tell by their clothes," says one of the volunteers as she arranges star-shaped cookies on a platter behind a counter. "Poles always wear denim." A glance at the earlier arrivals, all from Poland, seems to prove her right: dark blue denim jackets, tie-dyed denim skirts, denim backpacks, even a denim quilted vest are in evidence in the hall. Twelve of the new arrivals sport fur hats—three black, four brown, one tan, one leopard, and three that move into the shadows before there's time to classify them. "That means they're from Russia," guesses the Red Cross lady, correctly. Seen from Friedland, Poland is the land of denim; the Soviet Union, the land of fur.

Inside the Red Cross hall, all is action, as Friedland staffers get to work assigning dormitory beds. The Soviet arrivals hand in their papers in groups—five red passports, united by a paper clip. Almost no passport sits in the pile alone—the "Russia Germans" are a clannish people. Within an hour, most of the families have gone to dormitories to sleep their first night in Western beds under white-and-blue-checked duvets. Friedland is overcrowded: this week, the camp registers 2,535 arrivals, 1,090 of them from the Soviet Union, almost all the rest from Poland. To the organizers' relief, most of the arrivals accept their bunk spots without complaining. Earlier in the day, a representative from one unhappy team came to complain that eleven people were quartered in a room with only eight beds. Through an interpreter, a Red Cross lady communicates the solution in telegraphic Russian: "Mother, child, together, sleep."

Weekday mornings at eight, Red Cross workers and state officials begin transforming foreigners into Germans. After so many bureaucratic encounters in the Soviet Union, the arrivals are afraid that Friedland, too, will be an ordeal. Lidiya, a pretty blonde from Kazakhstan who keeps a hand over her mouth to cover a set of gold-capped teeth, is in tears ten minutes after the preliminary interview has started. She has told the official she wants to settle in Neustadt, West Germany. But she's afraid that because she's arrived before her brother, and didn't fill out the right forms early enough, she may not get her wish. Her siblings, seated by her at a table stacked with yellow German–Polish dictionaries, watch as her shoulders begin to shake. Friedland does entail serious paperwork, but, as it turns out, this paperwork will work in the family's favor. The Red Cross worker soon sets about the first order of business: establishing the family's German name. Government offices in Moscow transliterated from Russian to French, so the passports read "Chnaider." "That's Schneider," says the West German worker. The family nod in unison. "Schneider is correct."

The next step is an interview with state officials who will determine whether the families are "really" German. The Schneiders, including Lidiya, show up at 8:15 on a Monday and stand in a crowded, smoky hall full of other would-be German citizens. A bit later Iris Karsch, a lawyer, reviews their case. "Are you a German family?" Always, we spoke German at home. "How did you show you wanted to leave?" At their home in Kirovsky, Kazakhstan, the family had applied for visas. "How many times was your application rejected?" asks Iris Karsch. Six times. "How much did you pay for passports?" Two hundred and one rubles each. "Where has your family lived?" The Schneiders, typically, have a disjointed history. They once lived in the Ukraine, were resettled in Poland, were deported to Siberia when Stalin took back Poland, and lived in Omsk, Kirovksy, and Yakutsk before coming here. Both Lidiya and Rosa have children with them; both are divorced. Rosa got divorced in order to come to West Germany: the Soviets required that her husband's parents sign the departure papers and they refused. So she ended the marriage and came alone—in the hope that her ex-husband would come later.

Francis Josef, a thirty-six-year-old, is not such a clear-cut case. He is a miner and comes from Poland; he speaks, reads, and understands only Polish. In the space after the question "Nationality?" on the German form, he has written "Polish." A German interviewer crosses out this faux pas and prints in the word "German" instead. Three lines on the miner's forehead come together. But the West German government is so eager to help the settlers that it overlooks such infractions. Francis Josef has Germans in his family—he has passed the test. "There," the official says, and dismisses him. "Now your name is Franz."

The same morning brings two simpler problems, brothers from the Katowice area in Poland. The pair hand over blue Polish passports, but what determines their future is another document: a disintegrating brown booklet whose cover features a Prussian eagle clawing into a swastika over the words "*Deutsches Reich.*" The official fingers the Nazi document. It is a record of the men's father's employment—he was a noncommissioned officer in the Wehrmacht, promoted in the last weeks of World War II. The pages give his blood group and his gas-mask size. This evidence satisfies the official, since only those of German ancestry served in this section of Hitler's Third Reich. At least one of the brothers, Edward, wants to settle near Karlsruhe. It is a burdensome request—there are already so many Eastern-bloc citizens camped out on the state dole there. Edward, too, at least initially, will have to go on the dole. The amiable official nevertheless is willing to have a go at selling Edward. "Good morning," he chirps into the phone. "I have a special sale offer for you—young man, capable of work, vintage 1950."

Of the long line of nervous refugees behind the Schneiders and Edward in the hall, each one with a plastic bag full of documents in his hand, very few will fail to pass this morning's test. (A social worker does take a visitor into a corner to whisper the story of one exception: a "refugee" whose Third Reich papers the local police had investigated—and discovered to be forged. "Imagine," clucks the storyteller in disapproval. "It turns out he bought them. They were prepared for him in Katowice—a small counterfeit ring!") On most routine mornings, though, case workers process three or four or five cases, then close their doors and take a ten-minute break to peruse files over a cigarette. Many of them are new to the job. They are unemployed law-school graduates whom the government recruited to help in this "*Aussiedler* emergency." "This isn't what I expected to be doing," says dour Frau Karsch, who feels that her two law degrees entitle her to a fancier position than that of social worker. "But everyone in Germany is surprised that there are so *many Aussiedler.*"

That this idiosyncratic affair has reached such massive proportions is due to a change outside German borders, a change stemming from the rise of Mikhail Gorbachev. Not counting East Germans, some 3.2 million people of German ancestry live in countries east of the Iron Curtain. The law Konrad Adenauer's government passed in 1953 guaranteeing first-class hospitality to those who made it back never envisioned arrivals in such multitudes. Ten years before this season, Friedland was a quiet place—for a while, Vietnamese refugees were processed here because so few Germans arrived. Only in the Gorbachev era have Eastern governments begun giving their German populations exit visas in significant numbers. The 377,055 who washed onto West German soil in 1989 and the 200,000 who came the year before add up to a formidable number when compared with, say, the 100,000 Soviet Jews the United States took in between 1972 and 1983. The benefits guaranteed these people have been wide-ranging: a new family may get a small "welcome" check, housing, free language courses, and subsidized loans. With the arrival of nearer cousins, the East Germans, the strain on the Federal Republic's coffers is considerable. To help these kinsmen, West Germans spent $964 million in 1989. In one year the West German government spends more than half a billion dollars teaching "Germans" German.

To handle the wave of settlers, the West German government set up a chain of resettlement camps across West Germany; one farther south, in Nuremberg, handles only Germans from the Soviet Union. Friedland is the central camp, the grand machine that processes this latter-day confrontation with Central Europe's past. It is an odd machine—a machine whose job it is to define what is a German. To that end it accepts documentation from all German history—in particular documents such as the ID papers from the Nazi era. A couple of doors down the hall where families undergo their "German interviews," state workers use an ITT telefax to transmit names and World War II prisoner numbers to a West Berlin archive containing Wehrmacht records preserved since the war. The irony here is this: to establish who is a German, the Friedland machine must turn to the most recent best record, and in many cases it finds that that record is the one kept by the Nazis. If an arrival from Poland can prove that his father, or grandfather, served in the Nazi army, he can also prove his German ancestry, for the Wehrmacht accepted only Aryans in its ranks. The Berlin office is well organized—the Nazis were good record keepers—and within a day or so Friedland receives a response on its candidate. "Germans are still German," a self-conscious government staffer admits when a visitor points out that this efficiency is the beneficiary of a less felicitous period—"even here in Friedland." For all the bonhomie he senses, the outsider occasionally catches a strong whiff of old-fashioned Prussian *Ordnung*. Through a closed door in another building, a state employee can be heard struggling to indoctrinate an arrival in the rigorous requirements of the German language. *"Dem,"* the voice chides. *"Dem,* not *den.* Use the dative!"

The Friedland refugees spend a week or so here. It is time enough for the younger ones to wander into town and listen to the jukebox in the bar down by the train tracks ("Two Hearts, Living in Just One Mind"). It is time for the older ones to drink a beer in the Friedland canteen and tell their families' stories. The ethnic Germans from Poland are a sophisticated bunch, with knowledge of the West culled from previous excursions "over" or even glimpses of Western television. They spend their time at the phone booth outside Friedland's gate, dialing 0-0-48-2-2 over and over again, until they get a connection to Warsaw. Often, they arrive well acquainted with the list of benefits they are entitled to in Germany, having been briefed back home in Warsaw or Katowice. As a result of the Polish government's strict "Polish only" policy since the war, many Polish Germans, even teachers and engineers, often know little more of their parents' language than *ja* or *deutsch*.

The Soviet Germans, by contrast, are generally simple people, truck drivers or factory workers, with little education. Like America's Pennsylvania Dutch or Canada's Mennonites, they are farmers who've stuck together in small Protestant communities. They speak a basic and antiquated German that often causes Friedland bureaucrats to smile and think of Goethe.

Heinrich Peters, a polite older man in a neat brown suit, is one of these relics of history—a relic who wants to be sure the world gets to hear his story. Soon after he completes his stay in Friedland, he spends an hour at a second resettlement camp in North Rhine–Westphalia, telling a Sanyo tape recorder his life. His family may have come from East Prussia—he's not sure—but they eventually settled in the Ukraine. After World War II, his farmer parents were sent to Central Asia, to Leninpol in Kirgizia. "Because of Stalin," he says, and courteously asks the others at a canteen table —have they heard of Stalin? Orphaned early, he was able to complete only four years of school, "a fact of which I am ashamed." "But we wanted to leave Leninpol," he says, "we wanted to be with Germans." (Later his wife, Elsa, gives her explanation for why they didn't like Kirgizia. The Kazakhs, she says, were so dark-skinned. "Like blacks, only worse.") One half of Heinrich Peters's village has already migrated to West Germany in the past two years. The father of eight and grandfather of twenty-three proudly notes that he can read German. Why did he learn? "To read the Bible."

The visitor who sits at such canteen tables long enough, and talks to enough settlers, can begin to piece together the long sojourn behind a story like Herr Peters's. Most of the settlers can tell you precisely when their family's journey started: in the 1760s, when Catherine the Great, herself a German, invited German families to travel east and set up farms on the Volga River. Perhaps the erstwhile Sophie of Anhalt-Zerbst was lonely. In any case, the Czarina knew the value of establishing populations in an expanding empire and invited Jews along with Germans to settle the new lands.

Frei, "free," is the word the grandmothers and grandfathers in Friedland use to describe their pilgrim ancestors. In the bookshops of nearby Göttingen, there are volumes that describe that freedom in detail. The law the Czarina wrote for the German settlers is worth reviewing, if only for the great contrast between its enlightened phrases and the anti-religious and confiscatory order the same families lived under with their later master, Stalin. Catherine's *Ukaz* guaranteed religious freedom: "Let us permit arriving foreigners in our empire the unlimited practice of their religion, according to their churches and customs . . ." It also established the right to property: "All lands transferred to the settlers are their unencroachable property for all time, although not as personal property but as common property of each colony . . ." "The colonists are permitted to buy land from private individuals and to acquire property in general in the interests of spreading and improving their economic situation . . ." Pioneers from Swabia or Hesse paid taxes to the Crown, but they also enjoyed the right "to unlimited travel, wherever they like."

This invitation from the frontier inspired many farmers to travel to Hamburg and sail to Russia, a trip they made in the same spirit in which pilgrims plunged into their hazardous voyage west to the New World. In the Czars' Russia, Germans came to be grand landholders. Germans held 9.6 million hectares of property by 1918. One family, the Falz-Feins, who owned half a million sheep, were the biggest sheep farmers in Europe. In backward Russia, Germans were the strange "educated ones." The first foreign settlement in Russia was the "German suburb" of Moscow in the time of Peter the Great. Germans—like the broken-down piano teacher Christopher Lemm in Turgenev's *Home of the Gentry*—tutored the Russian nobility and turned them westward. Educated Baltic Germans, another group, amassed property and political influence in the territory that is now Latvia, Estonia, and Lithuania. "Our forefathers were important people," says Heinrich Peters, and books document that importance. At one point in the early nineteenth century, 62 percent of the employees in the Czar's Finance Ministry were of German origin.

The refugees in Friedland often don't remember earlier events firsthand, but they report what their parents have told them: that this happy time extended even into the early days of the Soviet Union. In those first years, the sun of self-determination still shined, and an October 19, 1918, decree signed by Lenin proclaimed the "Autonomous People's Commune of the Volga Germans." Lenin was quite explicit about the political effect such a liberation was designed to have on the Volga Germans' brethren farther west: it should contribute to "a rapprochement of the German and Russian mass labor, whose union will be a basis for their victory in the international proletariat revolution." Germans got their own "German town" in the Volga region, called Engels, the name presumably a tribute to the same political hope of a German–Russian revolution. The books contain evidence of this German community: sixteen institutions of higher education, two theaters, and a publishing house that produced a newspaper and 35,555 German-language books.

What most of the grandparents here do remember is how their parents or grandparents suffered when Stalin collectivized farming. Some 300,000 of them died in the famine that followed Stalin's liquidation of the kulaks. It was the first of many deportations. Before Germany and the Soviet Union went to war in 1941, many of them were shipped west—"*Heim ins Reich*"—to man Hitler's new empire in an administrative area that today is part of Poland, the Warthegau. Germans from the Soviet Union also resettled in other cities of the Reich. It's hard to find them among a single day's sample at Friedland, but settlers exist who are coming to Germany for a second time, the first time being during the war. One amazed staffer talks of an old man she'd encountered—a man who'd arrived directly from Siberia but who recalled how he'd spent part of the war in Germany and as a child had seen Hamburg burn. After Hitler attacked the Soviet Union, Germans within the Soviet Union became enemies of the state, suspicious aliens in the same class as America's Japanese. When Stalin reclaimed the Polish lands, he shipped the Volga Germans who had been settled in Poland to internment camps—not near their homes on the Volga or the Black Sea, but far away in Siberia, the Urals, and Central Asian Kazakhstan. When the war ended, the Western allies indirectly helped Stalin in this cruelty: while British, French, and Americans looked on, Soviets rounded up "Soviet" Germans from Berlin to Baden-Baden and packed them into trains headed east.

Next came the period the settlers sum up in one phrase: "Trud Army," the "labor army." Unlike the Japanese in California's camps, Moscow's Germans served sentences long after the war ended. They spent the decade after 1945 under military law in tight settlements, their movement restricted and their days spent chopping wood in the service of a socialist "labor army." The Schneiders' parents, for example, were sent to Krasnoyarsk in Siberia, a frigid site that mainly pops up in Western conversation in the context of controversial radar systems installed there. Mostly farmers or simple laborers, they were rarely offered the opportunity to visit big cities like Leningrad or Moscow, let alone to receive higher education. Many of them were Mennonites and Jehovah's Witnesses, whose faith and its precepts—no alcohol, no television—erected an additional barrier to assimilation into the nearly godless Soviet society. In 1955, Konrad Adenauer traveled east and won concessions that eventually led to their release—along with that of German prisoners of war. Even then, these farmers never made it home to the Volga. As soon as it became clear that they couldn't return to their original farmland, many of the families filed applications to emigrate from the Soviet Union. In 1987 a change in Soviet administrative law made it easier for settlers with relatives in West Germany to leave. Exactly what provoked the shift, the bewildered settlers can only guess. But what with problems from more vociferous national groups, like Armenians or Estonians, Moscow was probably more than happy to get rid of the potentially divisive Germans with a minimum of trouble.

Friedland arrivals from Poland tell a simpler story. Where they come from—cities such as Breslau and Danzig, now known as Wroclaw and Gdansk—was once Germany. When that part of Germany became Poland after the war, they became a minority group—one often discriminated against. As traveling west from Poland became easier over the past decade, more and more of them began taking advantage of the West German offer of immediate citizenship. Why, an outsider might ask, didn't these people just move to East Germany? The answer is simple: while West Germany defines the decision to welcome ethnic Germans as based on blood and family ties, the ethnic Germans from Poland—and those from the rest of the Eastern bloc—see it also as a political decision. Like the Jews who leave the Soviet Union claiming they want to join their co-religionists in Israel and then end up in the United States, the Germans of the East use their ethnic connection as a pretext—a chance to get themselves to a better, yet still German, life.

However they got here, the refugees seem contented with Friedland. "Why shouldn't I be happy here?" asks an old man, resting after his first perusal of a German newspaper. In part this is so because they know that what follows Friedland is more difficult. The German social welfare machine is thorough, and when the settlers leave Friedland, most of them will spend a few more weeks in state camps before town governments set to work finding them homes. The Polish settlers may have problems with the language; for the Volga Germans the cultural shock is worse. As Mennonites, most of them don't smoke, drink, or watch television, and they cover their children's eyes when they pass the bosoms and behinds featured on a cover of the weekly magazine *Stern*. In a classroom set up for children passing through a resettlement center in North Rhine–Westphalia, three little girls in long braids from Kirgizia stand out among the other kids in their Esprit T-shirts and short haircuts. The teacher even brings them forward as an example of "our adjustment problem." Alwina, Lilli, and Helene—even their names are old-fashioned for Germans—curtsy courteously, and then dissolve into giggles.

A classroom for adults in the same town must deal with more serious adjustment problems. The students here have been in school eleven months, the length of the language and orientation course guaranteed them by the West German government. Most of these arrivals had worked in Poland for years—as mechanics, TV repairmen, and engineers—and even on the last day of their course have trouble expressing themselves in German. "In Poland, it was easier," sighs an engineer with bright blue eyes. A seatmate translates for him. "Maybe I will never learn this German!"

An especially difficult challenge the settlers face comes from another group of "foreign Germans"—Germans from East Germany. When the settler wave started, in 1988 and early 1989, the Iron Curtain was still firm, the Wall was still up, and East German arrivals were still something of a secondary group. But with the opening of the Iron Curtain along the Hungarian–Austrian border, the stream of East Germans widened and their numbers began to match those of the settlers. For 1989, the Federal Republic counted 348,000 East German arrivals, only 30,000 fewer than the settlers. Traditionally, the *Aussiedler* had served as something of a pet for West Germany's right wing: as long as it couldn't welcome brothers from East Germany, it was happy to have settlers from more exotic places "come home." When East Germans came to fill the spaces in overcrowded state settlement camps—not to mention the cities' overloaded apartment supply—the settlers suddenly started to look more foreign. The favor accorded this relatively arcane group began to create resentment. Polish Germans and Russian Germans enjoyed privileges, such as the first right to public housing, which outraged many West Germans who didn't like seeing the settlers moving to the front of the nation's long queues for benefits. Voters may have shared the government's commitment to the principle of blood in theory, but in practice a foreigner, to them, was merely a foreigner.

Heinrich Lummer, a conservative West German politician both loved and vilified for his sharp tongue, gave voice to many citizens' sentiments when he publicly attacked the settlers. Some of the ethnic Germans had so little to do with Germany, he charged in a statement reported by the press, that their closest link to this nation was that they "perhaps once owned a German shepherd dog." After 1989, a record year for settlers from eastern areas and a record year for arrivals from East Germany, the West German government sought to curtail the number of arrivals and closed down many transfer camps like Friedland. This step, though, was not an end to the West German commitment. The camps were designed to bring Germans together—to facilitate a practical German reunification. When the West German–

East German border started to break down, the West German government began focusing on the political union of the two Germanys, rather than the reunion of refugees.

As much as the settlers' passage through Friedland and beyond tells about the history of the movement of peoples in Europe, it tells more about contemporary Germans and the way they deal with that history. To the visitor from the outside, Friedland itself presents some unavoidable and unpleasant echoes of Germany's past. Friedland is a mecca, but it is also a *Lager*, with all the word's connotations. The connection between this benign center and the old Nazi death camp is one that foreigners find eerie and Germans do their best to ignore. When I stopped by a sign reading "Bath Hours," a local official read my mind and hurried me on. The Friedland camp is even led by a Herr Adolfs—Dieter Adolfs, the federal official who supervises the placement of arrivals throughout West Germany. Perhaps anticipating a visitor's thoughts, Mr. Adolfs starts out a first meeting on the defensive, explaining how much work it is to keep the camp from falling into chaos. "We don't want any Palestinian situation here."

The link to the bad old time is also and most clearly visible in the efficiency with which Friedland and its daughter transfer points are administered: Germans are still Germans, and they still know how to run a camp. Staffers are devoted to their jobs—they spend hours compiling records and regularizing spellings on questionnaires—but they also keep their distance from the refugees. The arrivals have the run of most of Friedland, but when they stick their noses in staff offices, they are waved away. When the more intrepid of them step in, frosty receptionists quickly back them out. Part of this efficiency is simply the efficiency of the modern social welfare state. Each new arrival receives a *Laufzettel,* a piece of paper on which is listed the itinerary of Friedland posts through which he must pass before leaving the camp, and he is warned that he must stick to it meticulously. Most arrivals are patient, perhaps because they are so accustomed to queues. In many ways, they feel at home. They are merely passing from a poor social welfare state, like Poland or the Soviet Union, to the world's richest one, West Germany.

To lend authority to its classifications, the Federal Republic developed a special "foreigner" vocabulary which has also served the united Germany. The ethnic Germans at Friedland are *Aussiedler*, or, translated literally, "outsettlers." The East Germans who are bringing the two Germanys together are *Übersiedler*—"trans-settlers" or "cross-settlers." Non-Germans from outside West German territory are *Ausländer*, a word closer to neutral than the Nazi-stained *Fremde*—"strangers." Tamils, Cambodians, and Ethiopians trudging through queues would dearly like to be *Asylanten*—candidates for political asylum. But thanks to thinning patience on the part of Germany—and on the part of Third World-weary Europe in general—ever smaller percentages are passing the political asylum test. *Gastarbeiter*, or "guest workers," are Italians, Turks, and Yugoslavs who fueled the second phase of Germany's economic ascent in the 1960s. The term expresses the government's vain wish that these arrivals are here for a visit.

Behind this nice lexicon lies nationalism—unexpressed, often unacknowledged, and serious. The ultimate nationalist leader, Hitler, went to war with Britain but his life's focus was eastward—from his Wolf's Lair fortress in Prussia, he conducted the eastern campaign that was to give Germans their dream of *Lebensraum*. Today the same nationalism, although of a much milder variety, is bringing the two Germanys together into one nation. Some even interpret the devotion to the settlers as the subtle expression of German ambitions beyond Germany. Whether expressed or unexpressed, there is a strong longing among Germans to regain lost influence in their frontier territory, the East. Evidence of this old longing shows up, for example, in the jacket copy of *Die Russland-Deutschen*, a volume about Germans in Russia brought out as the wave of settlers mounted in early 1989. "There is no other example in history of one people having so much influence on another as the Germans have had on the Russians." This exaggeration—one need only compare the influence of Britain, say, in India, or the Anglo-Saxons' disastrous influence on the American Indian, to see its error—is typical of remarks expressed in corners of Germany.

One of the best opportunities to spot these sentiments as they move under the surface is found in West German encounters with the settlers at Friedland. The settlers' vocabulary embarrasses the Germans, mainly because of what it tells them about themselves. Ever since the Allies hurried this nation through denazification, Germans have expunged Nazi-tainted terms from their own language. The practice has become so routine it's easily forgotten—until the old-fashioned settlers open their mouths. Life in their Central Asian or Siberian vacuums kept them ignorant of West Germany's subtle taboo system. Watching modern-day Germans listen to the settlers' words is therefore somewhat like watching a post-Eden Adam meet an innocent one. At the Frankfurt airport, an old man asks who the group's *Führer* is. An embarrassed young guide quickly corrects him—the man meant *Leiter* (an unsullied synonym) or even a second word taken from English, *Leader*. Rueful social workers at Friedland report that settlers say they are happy to come *Heim ins Reich*—"home to the Reich."

The same relations, however, are also an expression of a happier side of the German character: the West Germans' genuine joy at finding what seem like strange, long-lost grandparents. When they meet the old, gentle Volga Germans, the bureaucrats are often so moved that they drop their officious demeanor. In Espelkamp, a town in North Rhine–Westphalia so full of Friedland graduates it already has three Mennonite prayerhouses, the harried head social worker informs a visitor that "Espelkamp just can't take any more." But the same man, clad in green Gore-Tex, also leads guests to a temporary dormitory, a large hall in which "rooms" are divided by curtains. He stops by a room where a nineteen-year-old girl with a pink ribbon in her hair sits on a bench before a Belaruss piano—it accompanied her when she left the Soviet Union. "Listen to that," the social worker says, smiling, as the girl wanders through some Beethoven. "Für Elise."

Friedland itself is something of a symbol of more positive German traditions—a museum of the decades of philanthropy Germans have offered to needy refugees. Here, Germans have really spent decades following the commandment of the stark monument on the hill—"Forswear Hatred." Before the brick church where arrivals say their first "Western" prayers stands a statue of a gaunt man in a long coat, an emblem for the earlier *Heimkehrer*, the "returner home" of the late 1940s and 1950s. In a quiet storeroom not far from the camp director's office—perhaps the only quiet room in Friedland—an album bound in wood lovingly presents a detailed record of those years. From its start, Friedland functioned as a barometer of Germany's confrontation with its past, and in particular its relations with Moscow. Between September 20 and December 5, 1945, 270,000 hungry Germans and their luggage checked in at Friedland; by 1960 the number of arrivals had reached 2,148,003. In 1956, the year after West Germany's national father, Konrad Adenauer, smoothed things over in Moscow, some 1,003 veterans arrived from Soviet camps—ten times the number who had come the year before. When things froze between Kennedy and Khrushchev, during the Cuban Missile Crisis and when the Berlin Wall went up, movement at Friedland also froze. When Willy Brandt set to work writing a treaty with Poland in 1970 and 1971, the number of arrivals, largely from Poland, quintupled. In 1981, when Solidarity shook Poland, 45,061 people came from Poland, twice as many as in the quieter previous years.

Hildegard Prahl, a Red Cross worker in uniform and pearls who welcomes settlers today, remembers the emotional arrivals of the late 1940s. "Bells rang the moment they stepped off the train, and they held earth from their homeland in their hands and sang the *Deutschland Lied*"—the German national anthem. "Then everybody had a good cry."

No one expected such numbers would ever come again, says Frau Prahl. "After all, the war was over." Other staff point out that an odd thing has happened at Friedland over the years: people who were once refugees, or their children, become camp officials or volunteers. Otto Flegel, a civil servant being trained to help out in Friedland's interview department, expresses his wonder at this. His father had passed through here in 1950 on his way back from a stint as a POW in the Soviet Union. The first time his father phoned his family to tell them he was on his way home, Otto recalls, it was from here—he gestures—"this camp."

Whatever happens after Friedland, Friedland is a place

2

The Lost House

DENMARK

Berlin

POLAND

EAST
GERMANY

Bonn

WEST

GERMANY

Prague

SUDETENLAND

CZECHOSLOVAKIA

FRANCE

Stuttgart

Vienna

AUSTRIA

THE SUDETENERS' MAP

Rommel moves to the microphone in a hall lined with 1,000 waiting Germans. A spiky black eagle, symbol of the Sudeten Germans, stretches a claw across a red banner hanging just below his feet. The crowd applauds when Rommel opens his hand to display a pocketknife—a gift of gratitude from the Sudetengau, an important province in the expanding Third Reich, to the Reich's most formidable general.

This Rommel is not the Desert Fox—it is his son, the lord mayor of Stuttgart. And the Sudeten Germans cheering in this hall aren't Nazis. They are among the solider citizens of modern Germany. Two generations after the war's end, some 100,000 of them gather in a Stuttgart convention center to mourn their own losses in that war and to celebrate the new lives they've made since then. "What happened can't be changed," intones the mayor, an amateur orchestra spills out the German national anthem, and Rommel hands the pocketknife back to the clan in a gesture of reconciliation.

The Sudeten Germans meeting here are just one tribe in a quirky league of exiles which wields considerable power in today's Germany. They, or their parents, were part of the original crowd of 12 million ethnic Germans forced out of Eastern Europe and into the zones of Germany between the years 1945 and 1950. More than 2 million Germans died of hunger, cold, and abuse in that evacuation—and they remember it with bitterness as their "unknown" tragedy, a tragedy whose proportion, they say, has been unrecognized in history. Many of the exiles, or "expellees," as they sometimes like to translate the term, came west just as the settlers are now doing, and like them they passed through Friedland. The difference is that the exiles made their trek four decades ago and now stand out as the integration success story among the odd groups that since the war have tried to fit into demanding, bureaucratic Germany. These Pomeranians, East Prussians, Silesians, Balts, and Sudeten Germans arrived poor, set up ethnic associations to defend themselves in Bonn, and got rich along with the rest of the nation in the *Wirtschaftswunder*.

The exiles are a phenomenon unto themselves, but they also provide a fairly useful picture of what the Friedland settlers will be like thirty years down the road: a group at home in today's Germany but still preoccupied with its painful loss. Politically, they are conservative: these ex-victims of Stalin long opposed cooperation with the old Eastern-bloc regimes, a posture that drew a lot of criticism in the conciliatory West Germany of the late 1960s and 1970s. Politicians from all parties, even conservatives, in particular resent it when their delicate *Ostpolitik* gets trampled by what they regard as clumsy political dinosaurs.

On today's shifting Central European stage, these "dinosaurs" play a more important role. They remind that Germany's ethnic problem is not solved with the reunification of Germany. Even though the expulsion of the late 1940s was massive, some ethnic German families remained behind in every Eastern-bloc state. In most cases they faced decades of discrimination; they were the "bad Germans" whom locals associated with Nazis and the war. When the Iron Curtain started to loosen, exiles in West Germany began traveling by bus or private car to Poland, Czechoslovakia, and the Baltic States to visit their old cousins and encourage them to fight for equal treatment. Embattled Communist governments reacted with responses ranging from official indifference to outright frustration and rage; Polish embassies and consulates, for example, regularly denied visas to Westerners who wanted to visit Poland's ethnic Germans.

At home in Germany, the exiles have also made their presence felt. Decades ago, they organized a lobby in Bonn, the League of Exiles, to ensure that no one forgot that lands beyond the two Germanys had once been home to Germans as well. Silesians, exiles from what is now Poland, became specialists in influencing foreign policy. In 1990 they threw a few obstacles in the way of the reunification process by pushing, directly and indirectly, for the inclusion of Silesian territory in the map of the new Germany. It is a battle which, in the long run, they seem bound to lose. But the energy with which they fought is evidence of the strength "old forces" have in Germany. And these old forces don't die out; when oldsters pass from the picture, their children and grandchildren take up their fight. An example of this is the head of the League of Exiles, Hartmut Koschyk. Koschyk is a Silesian—but a Silesian who grew up in West Germany and is less than thirty years old. Whatever the age of the exiles, though, one theme preoccupies them when they gather: imagining a lost Germany.

That act of imagination is particularly tricky for the Sudeten Germans. Other exiled groups have old connections to the German Reich. The Silesians, for example, can claim a history as a part of Germany that stretches back to 1741, when the Prussian Frederick II took their home from Maria

Theresa in a victory so neat people started calling him "the Great." The only Deutschland to which the Sudeten Germans ever belonged, though, was the Deutschland of the Third Reich.

The Sudetenland is a hilly, steeple-filled region that wraps around central Czechoslovakia like a belt. For centuries, it, like the rest of Czechoslovakia, was part of the Austro-Hungarian empire; Sudeten Germans thought of Vienna as their capital. Before Sarajevo, the region was one of the industrial engines of the Habsburgs' realm. After Versailles, the territory became part of a new republic, Czechoslovakia. But many of the republic's 3 million Sudeten Germans resisted the new government in Prague. As its name indicated, Czechoslovakia's new structure was dedicated to two ethnic groups, Czechs and Slovaks. If Czechoslovakia stood for Wilsonian self-determination, the ethnic Germans argued, why didn't it do more for the self-determination of Sudeten Germans? In most modern schoolbooks, the Sudeten Germans are generally portrayed as traitors to democracy—important instigators of World War II. When Hitler wanted to expand his Reich, he found support from Sudeten German leaders like Konrad Henlein. Henlein built a Sudeten German Party so strong that it gave Hitler a constituency within Czechoslovakia. When the moment came, Henlein and the Sudeten German Party swung open Czechoslovakia's door for Hitler—and did so with such convincing appeals for German rights in Czechoslovakia that Chamberlain and Daladier gave the change international approval at Berchtesgaden and Munich. In retrospect, the names Chamberlain, Daladier, and Sudeten Germans were classed in the history books beside the term "appeasement" —the West's early, weak-minded surrender to Hitler's raving program.

For most of today's Sudeten Germans, those names have different connotations. Like other exiles in West Germany, they make no territorial claims to their old homes. Weekend gatherings like this Stuttgart meeting are largely cultural affairs: they sing Sudeten songs, they wear Sudeten aprons and velveteen vests, they meet old friends, and they put together Care packages of auto parts or coffee for poorer cousins in Bohemia or Moravia. Like West Germans of many other groups, the Sudeten Germans are fond of talking about a new Europe—one that has looser or different borders, one that reunites the Germanys. Like many other exiles, Sudeten Germans like to reflect on a time in history when they lived in a grander empire. In the Sudeten German case, though, such musing focuses further back in time. It skips over the shameful Third Reich period to the reign of the Habsburgs and life before World War I. It also focuses farther eastward, in the direction of Prague or, more often, Vienna. When the Sudeten Germans dare to picture an empire, they sometimes picture it *à l'Autriche.*

Money is the first thing that strikes the visitor who arrives to spend a Whitsun weekend at the Sudeten Germans' annual convention—a folksy, confident kind of wealth that is typical of capitalist Germany today. Hilly Stuttgart, this year's convention site, was hit hard by Allied bombing—of the 150,000 apartments and houses in the Swabian capital before the war, only 97,550 were habitable after it. The bombs also destroyed whole halls of Stuttgart's Neues Schloss, a pretty, frivolous mixture of Baroque, Rococo, Classicist, and Empire styles laid out like Versailles. But on this Friday evening in spring in the corner of Stuttgart where Sudeten Germans meet, no sign of war is visible. BMWs and Mercedes-Benz unload stout gentlemen in lacy knee socks and tanned ladies in dirndls and rosy nail polish in front of the Neues Schloss—the first of some 40,000 private cars and 400 buses that will deliver Sudeten Germans from all over West Germany this weekend. Inside the castle, the families settle down on red plush seats under high chandeliers in a cream, white, and gray hall. For a group of strangers that arrived here only two generations ago, they've done well— among the Sudeten Germans speaking at this festive evening are a deputy state governor and two ministers.

When the speakers open their mouths, though, it is to talk of one thing: this group's loss. Franz Wittmann, a Sudeten German and member of the West German Parliament, the Bundestag, starts the mourning with words about "the fate of the exiled" and his own recollections of a town's "last religious service before the expulsion." Gerhard Weiser, deputy governor of the state of Baden-Württemberg, tries to console his audience by joking: "We're doing very badly— but on a very high level." Heads start to nod agreement when he acknowledges the Sudeten Germans' special past: "Man has to know where he comes from in order to know where he's going." An orchestra opens the evening with a divertimento for strings by an eighteenth-century Sudeten composer, Franz Xaver Richter from Holleschau in Moravia, and continues it with a 1974 string piece composed by a contemporary Sudeten exile, Helmut Bräunlich from Washington, D.C. This is the fortieth such Sudeten German meeting, and it is taking place in the fortieth year of the existence of the Sudeten German's new world in the West. But when the guests arrive and when they leave, the dressed-up visitors arch their necks to catch a glimpse across the hall of an old-world guest—Regina von Habsburg, Queen of Hungary.

The next morning at Killesberg, Stuttgart's fairgrounds, more Sudeten Germans arrive to settle down for a thirty-six-hour stay in a mini-version of that old world. Killesberg is the sort of grand complex that's won West German towns international fame as convention venues, and its massive halls are usually filled with the hum of voices and the steady clack-clack of high heels of salespeople doing business for the tourism or auto industry. Now, though, benches in its vast halls are lined with tables under signs bearing names of lost places that today have Czech names: Marienbad, Karlsbad, or the Egerland; Aussig, Reichenberg, or Dux. Older couples crowd benches, sip beer, and chat with their ex-neighbors—sometimes tables are dedicated to individual villages, their names on less official handwritten cardboard signs. In a set of blond-wood offices up some stairs, the Sudeten German Society's press officers are busy handing out green folders on which the red and incomplete ring of the old Sudeten territories stands next to three flags: the black-red-gold West German flag, the black-red-black Sudeten flag, and the blue flag with gold stars of the European Community. Even as retrospective a clan as this one is happy to advertise its support for the borderless Common Market state set to be complete in 1992. A few doors down, before rapt Sudeten Germans, Mayor Rommel is quoting Schiller: "Forward is the way to go, because you can't go back again."

Going "back again" is nevertheless what most of the crowds here do. They spend a lot of time, for example, walking through a photo-and-poster exhibit entitled "The Sudeten Germans: An Ethnic Group in the Heart of Europe." A father shows his son, dressed in white shirt and knickers, a map of Europe with concentric circles enclosing the Sudeten territories. Another family inspects a set of pink-and-black drawings above a caption announcing: "The expulsion of the Sudeten Germans is equivalent to the deportation of the entire population of Bolivia, Ireland, or Tunisia." Signs deliver usable sound bites of Sudeten lore: In 1920, there were more Sudeten Germans in Czechoslovakia than there were Slovaks. The Sudetenland's 27,000 square kilometers amount to more than the area of five West German states put together. The Sudetenland is nearly as big as Belgium. It is three times as big as Lebanon. Long before Christopher Columbus discovered America, the Sudetenland was a cultural center in Europe. Franz Kafka was a Sudeten German. So was Sigmund Freud. The Sudetenland was the industrial heart of the Habsburg empire. In 1938, in northern Bohemia, Sudeten Germans owned Europe's biggest sock factory.

Some of this version of history cuts against the facts of the twentieth century as we have learned them. However Gregor Samsa's melancholy creator saw himself, it certainly wasn't as a member of a down-home, rural, Christian group. Once part of Hitler's Reich, Sudeten Germans participated with vigor in Nazi programs, including the persecution and annihilation of Jews. Whatever Sudeten German connection Freud in Vienna may have had, it certainly didn't prevent Hitler from forcing him and his couch from their dim study at Berggasse 19. The boldest target of such Sudeten German displays, though, is the state of Czechoslovakia as it existed between the wars. Tomáš Masaryk and Eduard Beneš, two fathers of Czechoslovakia, are portrayed as agents of betrayal and injustice. Had they permitted plebiscites in their new country, Sudeten Germans argue, the Sudetenland would have immediately returned to Austria. In March 1919, Czech soldiers fired on German crowds demonstrating in the name of self-determination; from that moment on, Germans were an oppressed minority in Czechoslovakia. There is some truth to this view. But it is also the same view that Hitler and his team shared—and the one with which they justified the return of the Sudetenland *Heim ins Reich*.

Sudeten Germans, for their part, see their account of

things as anti-Nazi—and they love it. At stands before the exhibit, families line up to buy a few Sudeten souvenirs—posters, recipe books, or commemorative stamps. For DM 30 they buy accessories for Sudeten dolls that wear the special Sudeten lady's *Haube*, a construct of woven lace and ribbon that hangs back over the head like a sideways lampshade. Sudeten literature is also a big draw, as is literature by younger generations "remembering" the Sudetenland. At a book stand, a woman leans forward as she reads a Sudeten poetess's elegy:

> In a dream . . .
> I went back home
> The doors opened without effort
> And the faces
> Of my beloved ones were young
> In a dream I found my parents' house
> Not yet plundered
> By memory

One of the most popular items, going for DM 10, or $5.00, is a colorful map of the Sudetenland, surrounded by reproductions of each community's heraldry. Leskau's shield sports a goose arching its neck; two bears climbing a tree represent Pflaumberg; Strzebowitz's sign is an openmouthed fish. A little boy with a long, thin strand of hair reaching his T-shirt—West German kiddie punk, vintage 1989—shows his sister his favorite: Uittwa, a simple rounded red heart.

Kitsch is important to Sudeten Germans, and it's hard to blame them for the weakness. The only kind of return "home" allowed them is a visit to a strange country that, until recently, has usually required a visa, and this narrow opportunity is one they treasure. The Stuttgart stands contain books showing pictures of their old houses—often empty and abandoned buildings with boarded-up windows which the Czechs have never repaired and whose disrepair distresses a people as orderly as the Germans. The Sudeten Germans estimate that 1,000 villages and towns were razed after their departure—and show photos of empty fields to prove their case. It is indisputable, in any case, that much of what was once a thriving region is now underpopulated or even deserted. Only about 200,000 ethnic Germans, they estimate, remain of the more than 3 million who once populated the Sudetenland. The Sudeten Germans are rightly distressed about "farms where no cock crows any longer." Acid rain and the damage it causes is the fault of the Communist regime in Czechoslovakia, at least in Sudeten German eyes: some 20,000 acres of a favorite Sudeten woodland are now threatened.

To maintain their memory of the old world back home, and in some cases that world itself, Sudeten German clubs from the various regions have appointed *Heimatpfleger,* "home caretakers," who travel to Czechoslovakia to inspect and restore old Sudeten properties. Back in West Germany, the *Heimatpfleger* keep archives that document the history of Sudeten towns and villages so Sudeteners here can study their roots. *Heimatpfleger* also lead nostalgia trips, via train, bus, and private car, back to Czechoslovakia. These days, Sudeten envoys speak with leaders of Civic Forum, the resistance movement that broke the Communist government. They work hard to improve relations between Germany and the new Czechoslovakia. When Václav Havel, the Czechs' new President, made his first official trip abroad, it was not to Moscow or to Washington, but to Germany. He even stopped in Munich, a city that is home to many Sudeteners.

Carrying on the Sudeten German cause, and explaining

its more arcane aspects to uninitiated strangers, is the particular task of the Sudeten Youth Group. This organization arranges for folk dancing, sponsors special seminars on Sudeten history, and puts on Sudeten German skits for adults. On Saturday morning young Sudeten Germans descend from Killesberg to announce their presence to Stuttgarters with twirling folk dances in the city's pedestrian shopping zone. In the evening, the Viennese chapter of the Sudeten Youth—boys in white velvet vests, girls with flying petticoats—hop gracefully to the tune of accordion music, while the younger Sudeten Germans in the audience smoke Marlboros, clap, and down Meister Pils. The event is underattended, and a Sudeten Youth Group leader grumbles about it. "There are so few here and even those who are here don't know the songs."

At first it's hard to see why the kids are here at all—beyond substantial parental pressure. The mistress of ceremonies talks about how the memory of the Sudetenland must be kept fresh: "Forty years is not a long time in a human life," she announces, but those in the audience look doubtful: forty years is longer than both she and they have lived.

In a spare moment at Stuttgart, though, four second-generation Sudeten Germans sit down to talk and give other reasons why they've come to the Killesberg convention. Inge Krabler, a student teacher, is twenty-eight and lives in northern Bavaria. "It starts like this," she says, and begins a familiar story. "My parents are both from the Sudetenland." At first her parents "dragged" her to the Sudeten German meetings. "I didn't like it. As a child one doesn't like arriving somewhere to be introduced to a bunch of old people. But then somehow it caught and I felt like I belonged. I started to ask, 'Where do my parents actually come from? Maybe these people [those attending the gathering] can tell me something about my parents that my parents don't tell me.' And then each time a new piece of information was added to the old."

Something amazing happened when Inge visited her father's hometown. "I was there with my sister. We wanted so much to find our father's house. But we didn't know what direction to go in. Then we both searched through our childhood memories and found the house by way of those memories. It was an eerie experience for me. I took a look at the house and thought that I would feel at home there. We photographed it and then went around the back and asked, and it turned out that it indeed was his house." This season, Inge is angry because she can't return. Just recently—although before the arrival of President Havel and his new government—Czechoslovakia denied her an entrance visa, for security reasons: both of her husband's parents work for the West German army.

Inge's research seems a typical case of German "roots" nostalgia, but for Klaus Geisler, seated next to her, the matter is more political. "There are moments when one recognizes that Europe doesn't end at the Iron Curtain. One forgets that Poland, geographically, is not an Eastern European country but is in Central Europe. It has more of a relationship to France, from the point of view of history, than it has to Russia. And Hungary has more connections to Austria than to Russia."

All these young people feel it is important to give visitors details of their families' violent departure from the Sudetenland. In their accounts they often mention Aussig, a town where Czechs killed between 2,000 and 3,000 Germans in a massacre that included throwing German women, children, and baby carriages into the Elbe River. The Joint Relief Commission of the International Red Cross gave this report in general on the fate of the expellees: "These uprooted masses wandered along the main roads, famished, sick, and weary, often covered with vermin, seeking out some country in which to settle . . . On 27 July 1945, a boat arrived at the West Port of Berlin which contained a tragic cargo of nearly 300 children, half dead with hunger, who had come from a 'home' at Finkenwalde in Pomerania. Children from two to 14 years old lay in the bottom of the boat, motionless, their faces drawn with hunger, suffering from the itch and eaten up by starvation . . ."

To the outsider familiar with the story of World War II, it is hard to succumb to the pathos in these accounts. Germans, after all, did worse to their own political prisoners, and they did worse to the inmates of concentration camps. Fifty years later, outsiders ask these young people: What about Treblinka? What about Zyklon B at Auschwitz? But the Sudeten Germans' point is that their loss shouldn't be ignored, and, like it or not, they push on with their argument. Klaus Geisler, a lawyer, likens the expulsion of his parents from the Sudetenland to the kind of brutal scenes portrayed in the film about the Khmer Rouge brutalities in Cambodia, *The Killing Fields.* "The Germans were not the last people who were driven out. You as an American know the problems of Vietnam and Cambodia and what happened there after the departure of American troops, or in South Africa." He tells of an example he read about in *The Times* of London which he considers particularly appalling. "A British MP honestly thought the problem in Ireland could be solved by resettling the Catholics. He said: 'It worked for the Germans.' " He calls the idea that ethnic resettlement can work "the evil in the world."

Over and above these moral questions, another force serves to get young Germans involved in the exile cause: "exile work" is a door to the powerful world of West Germany's political establishment. In Britain or America, a cultural cause like the preservation of the Sudeten heritage is generally a private cause, backed mostly by private funds. In West Germany, helping the exiled Germans is a national responsibility. The state of Bavaria, which shares 213 miles of border with the Czechoslovakia that contains the Sudeteners' old homeland, has assumed the role of official "godfather" to the Sudeten Germans. In Munich, Sudeten Germans operate out of a lovely tall house, finished in 1985 at a cost of some DM 20 million. The state funded the building and supports a large staff who work there for the Sudeten cause. Among the attendants in Killesberg is the "homeland caretaker," a woman named Walli Richter, who looks after the Sudeten Germans' cultural heritage at the expense of the taxpayers of the state of Bavaria. A row of silver plaques by the entrance honors Sudeten Germans or their children who have given more than DM 10,000 to the Sudeten cause. But much of what the Bavarian state can't pay, the federal government kicks in. Conservative politicians babysit the issue in the Bundestag and make certain to show their faces at events like the Sudeten German weekend. Lothar Späth, the governor of Baden-Württemberg, speaks here in Stuttgart at the final ceremony. Hans Klein, Chancellor Kohl's new press spokesman, chaired a meeting on German-Czech relations the afternoon before. Young people, not all of them of exile origin, use this connection to further a political career. One such figure is the personable head of the League of Exiles, Hartmut Koschyk. Even Mr. Geisler, who merely heads the Sudeten Youth Group, gets to rub shoulders with political glitterati. He's already met at least one of the nation's most formidable political figures: Franz-Josef Strauss,

Bavaria's leonine Premier, once invited the young Sudeten German to luncheon.

The mighty Sudeten establishment—both young and old—spends the weekend here pushing three causes. First, they attack an evil they sum up in a single word: "Potsdam." For the benefit of those who don't remember, and even more for the benefit of those who do, Franz Neubauer, a Sudeten German spokesman, storms through the Sudeten argument once more. "The expulsion of 3.5 million Sudeten Germans was determined in Article 13 of the Potsdam agreement," he intones, and pauses. A young man in the audience opens a legal tract to the hated paragraph penned by the Allies in 1945: "The three governments have weighed the question from all sides and recognize that the transfer of the German populations and elements of German populations that remain in Poland, Czechoslovakia, and Hungary shall be undertaken." Mr. Neubauer continues: "This inhumane document bears the signatures of Harry S. Truman, President of the United States, Clement Attlee, Prime Minister of Great Britain, and Joseph Stalin, then the head of state of the Soviet Union." He demands that President Bush, Mrs. Thatcher—he pronounces the name "Thetscha"—and Mr. Gorbachev show their goodwill and "withdraw" the commitment made in the old agreement.

For outsiders, this focus on "wrong done to Germans" is hard to take. Some 40 to 50 million people were forced onto the road as refugees when the war ended in Europe. Only a quarter of them were exiled Germans. Moving west and ceding their homes to Stalin was, in international eyes, less than a fair price for the murderous deportation the regime they supported inflicted on Central Europe's Jews. East German and Czech journalists from the old Communist regimes are—for the last time—among the numerous members of the press accredited at Killesberg, and it isn't hard to sympathize with their reports of the events taking place here. "In order to reach its revanchist goals the organization [of the Sudeten Germans] once again . . . twisted the historical truth and tried to revise the results of World War II," reports East German radio. Radio Prague, for its part, offers this reply to a Sudeten German who claims his countrymen are currently suffering abuse at the hands of the Czech government: "If one started counting up for Mr. Neubauer all the crimes that the Henlein fascists and the Nazis perpetrated against the Czech population before they were resettled, one would never get to the end."

Nevertheless, exiled Germans feel justified in pressing their cause. Killesberg's history exhibit displays copies of forty-five-year-old photos of Sudeten males bent under sixty-six-pound sacks on their trek to the Western zones of Germany—photos that remind the viewer unavoidably of similar pictures of Jews, gypsies, cattle cars, and Auschwitz. A special English-language pamphlet they distribute entitled "Who Are the Sudeten Germans?" puts the case in simple language for foreign consumption. "Everybody who loves his own country and is proud of its traditions will readily acknowledge that we Sudeten Germans, too, have the right to love our country."

Less advertised but just as important to the Sudeten Germans here is cause number two: toppling the myth that the Sudeten Germans were all Nazis. The Sudeten Germans formed their own party in Czechoslovakia, the SdP, which pushed Sudeten German causes in Prague and gradually became hostile to the government there. When Konrad Henlein, the leader of the Sudeten Home Front, was called to Hradcin Castle in Prague by Czech leaders who hoped he would abandon his support of the Nazis, he walked away from the table and turned to Hitler. But the Sudeten Germans don't like to focus on this event. They prefer to spotlight the Sudeten Germans who fought Hitler.

One of the most respected and toughest soldiers in this group can be seen moving through Killesberg's modern halls this weekend. Volkmar Gabert is a wheezy older man who chairs one of the Saturday meetings. West German politicians assume a gray look after years in service, and Gabert is no exception. His faded eyes are concealed behind a pair of heavy glasses and it is hard to catch his attention. Some of this may have to do with the rough-and-tumble of politics in his home state, Bavaria. He served as leader of the Social Democratic Party there in the years when political power belonged to its opponent, the jowly Franz-Josef Strauss. Social Democrats so disliked Strauss that they occasionally even talked of "Nazi-style" oppression by his bossy party. Gabert comes from a hardworking industrial corner of the Sudetenland that produced glass and coal. His hometown was at the foot of the Erzgebirge, a chain of hills on the border of what later became East Germany. Until 1938 the Social Democratic Party won majorities there. It was a German town that hated the Nazis.

Volkmar Gabert's parents were Social Democrats; his father was once mayor of a Sudeten German town. According to Gabert, his father considered himself a German and spoke German to his family. Only German? *"Only* German." The young man himself attended German-language schools, where instruction still followed a curriculum based on that used under the Habsburgs. To the world, the new state of Czechoslovakia represented a victory for the goal of self-determination as expounded by Woodrow Wilson. When they got their new state, Czechs and Slovaks named the main train station in Prague "Wilson Station" in gratitude. But in Gabert's memory, as in the memory of many other Sudeten Germans, there came a day when they discovered that the Wilsonian ideals were not to serve them. On March 4, 1919, Sudeten Germans massed to press for their right to self-determination. Czech troops responded by firing into the crowd and killing fifty-four civilians.

Twenty years later, when the Germans (Nazis) approached his town, Gabert's German (Sudeten) family was in danger. The Nazis were coming—Nazis who put socialists like them into concentration camps! His parents fled to Prague, and Volkmar and his brother followed via Teplitz and Aussig. They took the last train manned by a Czech crew. The Gaberts stayed in Prague for a while, then fled the country, along with thousands of other anti-Nazi Sudeten Germans. Some 25,000, trapped behind, joined homosexuals and Jews in Nazi concentration camps. Gabert himself ended up in London, where he became a classic refugee socialist, joining the Fabian Society, attending Harold Laski's lectures, and studying at the London School of Economics.

For Gabert and other exiled Sudeten Germans, one of the most distressing periods came at the end of the war. They watched the government of Eduard Beneš push for the expulsion of the Sudeten Germans from the Sudetenland. It was particularly painful to Gabert to see that Clement Attlee, a politician on his side of the fence, was the Briton who worked on the Potsdam agreement that made the Sudeten evacuation official.

Back in Germany, one of Gabert's principal missions, and one at which he has succeeded, has been to reconcile the Sudeten Germans who used to sympathize with Hitler with the Sudeten Germans who had been opposed to the Nazis. In Stuttgart, Gabert chairs a panel with Franz Neubauer, a

conservative, and jokes about the fact that the man is sitting
to his right. When a visitor shows up at the Sudeten German
House in Munich, a staffer gives him the names of conservative Sudeten Germans in Munich worth paying a call on,
but also includes Gabert on the list. Gabert acknowledges
that in the early years this reconciliation came hard. No one
welcomed a Social Democratic Sudetener, but "I pushed my
way through everywhere."

Battle three in the weekend war involves the Sudeten Germans' only forward-looking cause: their campaign to expand
the rights of ethnic Germans in Czechoslovakia, conducted
under the banner of "Wilsonian self-determination." Sudeten Germans aren't specific about what they mean by this
goal; certainly, few of them, for example, would call for Sudeten secession from Czechoslovakia. That they choose to
raise this issue is, even so, a bit daring. As a product of
Versailles and Wilsonian idealism, Czechoslovakia was the
world's premier example of this dream. Through their alliance with Hitler, the Sudeten Germans were seen as the
criminals who crushed it. The Sudeten "right" to self-
determination was one of Hitler's principal pretexts for his
military venture. In Nuremberg he told a 1938 Nazi convention: "The poor Palestinians are defenseless and perhaps
abandoned. The Germans in Czechoslovakia are neither defenseless nor forgotten." For most of us such words still
create a nasty echo.

The Sudeten Germans, though, see themselves as victims
of the abuse of this ideal. Some of the people attending this
weekend were also present at a small memorial gathering
in West Berlin a few months earlier, on March 4. About a
hundred of them gathered to recall the day fifty years earlier
when Czech soldiers shot down fifty-four Sudeten Germans.
The principal speaker at this funereal event was Otto Habs-

burg, who recalled the group's "seventy-year struggle for self-determination." He advocated the rebirth of a pan-European movement and told of a jubilant reception he received when he recently traveled to Hungary. He also offered hope for the future. "The Yalta empire is nearly dead," he told the crowd, and praised Wilson, whose name he pronounced "Veel-zin."

That the dapper, bespectacled "Mr." Habsburg should be one of the foremost modern advocates of the cause of self-determination is one of the ironies of contemporary European history. As the man who would have been heir to the multi-nationality Habsburg empire, the Holy Roman Emperor Otto von Habsburg lost more than perhaps any living individual when at Versailles and St.-Germain the Allies broke up his family's empire in the name of that goal. Politically, Otto Habsburg remains persona non grata in Vienna, his old capital, but he has built himself a new, tiny empire in Bavaria—he represents a Bavarian community in the European Parliament in Strasbourg. The Sudeten Germans are also acquiring other odd partners in their struggle for the rights of ethnic minority groups. One of them is the Hungarian government, which sends diplomats to exile meetings in order to publicize problems of ethnic Hungarians in Romania.

To further the cause of self-determination for the descendants of the 200,000 Germans who remained in Czechoslovakia after the expulsion, the Sudeten Germans have produced an artillery of literature. Most of it is available in Stuttgart, and even more can be found at Sudeten centers throughout West Germany. The Sudeten German House in Munich maintains a library of some 100,000 volumes, all of which are designed to remind the world of their claim to their old home. For the most part, they say that their interest in the land is cultural and that their research is a Central European version of American blacks' search for "roots."

This interest in things Eastern however has an unhappy precedent in German history. Under Hitler, military advances eastward were preceded by just such a cultural *Drang nach Osten*. Back in the mid-1930s, while the Führer was still ruminating over his plans for the East, he funded large-scale and often objective *Ostforschung* of a nature not always dissimilar to the exile group's research work. In an excellent volume entitled *Germany Turns Eastwards*, London historian Michael Burleigh details an intensive academic campaign conducted in the 1930s to establish historical claims to land in Poland. Burleigh describes the work of scholars at a Nazi-era think tank known as the *Publikationsstelle* and situated in Dahlem, Berlin's leafy university neighborhood. The *Publikationsstelle* served the Reich by creating a data base that provided vital information for the occupation of Eastern territory and the administration of the Holocaust. The researchers who downgraded Polish (Slavic) culture were working in an even grander tradition. Frederick the Great himself justified his Eastern territorial claims with the assertion that the German race was superior to the Slavs, whom he referred to as "that imbecile crowd whose names end in 'ki.' " This ivory tower became an important fortress in the war Hitler eventually waged in the East.

The echoes of that earlier time that can be found in the Sudeten Germans' proud talk are enough to put off many contemporary Germans. The same Whitsun weekend as the Sudeten Germans meet in Stuttgart, some 3,000 Carpathian Germans—their homeland is on the mountain range that links the Alps with the Balkans—rally in Karlsruhe. Not too far from Stuttgart in Franconian Dinkelsbühl, the Siebenbürger Saxons, mostly from Romania, draw 20,000 West

Germans. When the Sudeten Germans' cousins, the Silesians, meet later in the year in Hanover, the Hanover mayor, a Social Democrat, ostentatiously stays away.

West Germany's conservative publishing house, Axel Springer, regularly gives the exiles prominent play in its newspapers when they meet in various regional capitals. But the rest of the national German press often ignores them, or plays down their presence, to indicate their disapproval. A meeting of the Young Generation of Exiles in Braunschweig attended by many young Sudeten Germans drew a pack of demonstrators who stood outside the door shouting, "Nazi!" To climb a hill for an open-air religious service at a cross called "the Cross of the German East," the young exiles required police protection. "These people talk about *Heimat*," explained one of the protesters, a Volkswagen worker in a leather jacket. "But to me, your home is where you live."

However displeasing the exiled Germans' various campaigns are to many of their countrymen, they have powerful support. Of late, two sources of support have been, surprisingly enough, Moscow and Warsaw. These capitals have helped the exiles by providing them with *Aussiedler* to strengthen their numbers in Germany. The hundreds of thousands of "settlers" who pass through places like Friedland become, from the exiles' point of view, exile constituents. These numbers increase the exiles' influence with the German government. Over the weekend a veritable relay team of important conservative politicians keeps the podium in Stuttgart occupied. This year Chancellor Helmut Kohl doesn't make it to Stuttgart, but his press spokesman, Hans Klein, delivers a hackneyed, if adequate hello from the boss. "Because the Chancellor knew that I would spend this Whitsunday once again with my Sudeten German countrymen, he gave me this greeting to pass along . . . You prove that you were exiled under terrible and unjustifiable conditions."

Which way the old exiles and the new settlers will throw their political clout in the future is hard to judge. The most internationally visible bid for their allegiance in 1990 came from Helmut Kohl. Foreigners who watched the idea of German unity harden from a dream to a possibility over the winter of 1989–90 generally treated the project with tolerance—until Mr. Kohl began arguing that "Germany in the borders of 1937," a Germany that included a good chunk of what is now Poland, should be the base from which to start the discussions or plans for a new Germany. His concession to the idea of this Germany—he never backed a Germany of the future with these borders—was an effort to retain the vote of exiles, specifically Silesian Germans, whose old homeland was at issue. That Mr. Kohl risked international censure and domestic rage to continue talking in these terms is testimony to the political power of the exiles. Even after Tadeusz Mazowiecki, Poland's Prime Minister, expressed his displeasure at Mr. Kohl's mapmaking, the German Chancellor refused to modify his terms entirely: to him, the West German elections set for the end of 1990 were of greater significance than the Pole's anger.

Another eager bidder for Sudeten sympathies present on the Stuttgart fairgrounds is the young ultra-right party born in West Germany, the Republikaner. Politically, the Republikaner stand to the far right of the German political spectrum. When Kohl speaks of "Germany in the borders of 1937," he is trying to prevent Republikaner from shaving votes away from his more centrist conservative party. Young Republikaner stand at the hall doorways and do their best to push fliers advertising "one Germany" into the hands of the pensioners stepping out for cake and coffee. Republikaner like to talk about "Germany in the borders of 1937," a catchphrase that refers to a Germany that includes Silesia—but not the Sudetenland, which the Nazis swallowed later. The Republikaner nevertheless are here in Killesberg in the hopes that an appeal to the memory of loss will also draw Sudeteners. Leaders of the Christian Democratic Union and its sister, the Christian Social Union, also do their best to woo the exiles. And some of the exiles—like Volkmar Gabert and his friends—are dedicated Social Democrats. The last group has traditionally focused on making friends with the Eastern bloc and, in particular, helping Eastern countries to solve their massive environmental problems.

Reconciliation is also a goal for young Sudeten Germans, who often shy away from the Cold War anti-Communist streak in their parents' rhetoric. Klaus Geisler, the leader of the Sudeten Youth Group, works with Czech groups to "build contacts." His conception of an ideal Europe might raise some questions for more national-minded thinkers—like Americans or Mrs. Thatcher. The Sudeten youth's "political task," he says, "is to create a Europe in which all ethnic groups and peoples, not only the Germans but Czechs, too, can determine their own lives and their homelands." What he means by this is hard to say. Nevertheless, he enjoys support for his vague statements from other Sudeten Germans, not all of them citizens of the Federal Republic. A young Sudeten German girl from Vienna announces, somewhat prissily, that "to be a bridge is the job of Austria."

At Stuttgart, signs of these odd bridges are already visible—such as the presence of representatives of one of the most controversial and irredentist groups in the Eastern bloc today, ethnic Albanians from southern Yugoslavia. Guests from this group, the National Democratic League of Loyal

Albanians, draw huge applause when their presence is announced at a Saturday-afternoon meeting. "The Sudeten Germans understand all too well the situation in Yugoslavia," announces a Sudeten German spokesman as he welcomes them. "We wish you the best." Also receiving the stamp of approval from the Sudeten Germans is the Hungarian government, which has done a great deal to recognize the Sudeten cause and for which the Sudeten Germans retain warm feelings left over from the Habsburg connection.

One entirely modern trend to which the Sudeteners legitimately connect their old homeland dream is regionalism. In the Europe of 1992, the Europe in which divisions of the Soviet empire are eroding, regions are gaining political importance. Like the Scottish, the Flemish, or the Slovenes, Sudeteners hope this means new political autonomy for them.

All this Central European talk of brotherhood and ethnic rights doesn't please a Swedish diplomat. He throws cold water on the gathering when he wonders aloud whether a chestnut like the Sudeten cause is still worth discussion. "There are so many new problems in the world." He also questions the exiles' focus on pushing for yet another set of international rights in the world arena. "What," he asks, "do ethnic rights mean in the Soviet Union?" And where, he wonders, will such a program lead? "How much of this can the Soviet Union handle? How many ethnic rights can one give minorities without the collapse of the entire state? I have to say it would be a nightmare for me if the Soviet Union collapsed." To this a Sudeten German leader has a clear response: "It wouldn't be a nightmare for *me*."

A unified Germany may, for a while, mollify even such figures as this one. But it will not ever, entirely, make good their painful loss. After church some 40,000 gather on a damp, grassy hill to listen as exile leaders and politicians close the weekend with promises to return for next year's Sudeten weekend in Munich. As the weekend ends with a thumpy rendering of the national anthem, some in the crowd look a bit disappointed at the prospect of returning to their buses. Green-uniformed policemen with plastic rain guards on their caps surround the departing politicians, but one old man manages to get close to Otto von Habsburg. "Sir," he says, but Habsburg can't hear him. The old man gets worried—what if he has to wait another year?—and tries a form of address he hopes will get him more attention. "Excuse me," he calls. "Your Highness?"

3

Serving the Empire

NORTH SEA

DENMARK

BALTIC SEA

SCHLESWIG-
HOLSTEIN

Free City of
HAMBURG

Free City of
BREMEN

K I N G D O M   O F   P R U S S I A

Berlin

RUSSIAN

EMPIRE

KINGDOM OF
SAXONY

Silesia

Rhine-
land

Alsace-
Lorraine

A U S T R O - H U N G A R I A N

FRANCE

KINGDOM
OF
WÜRTTEM-
BERG

KINGDOM OF
BAVARIA
Munich

E M P I R E

SWITZERLAND

GERMANY IN 1914

succeeded in doing what idealists and politicians had failed to do—unite Germany. In their way, officers and soldiers from West Germany's Bundeswehr, officers and soldiers like Axel, have spent their careers fighting for the same goal. Now that goal is becoming reality, and the soldiers face an irony: this new Germany is one in which they, its loyal advocates, may have no place.

To understand the unnerving revolution that "one Germany" brings for these officers, it helps to review the proud and troubling history with which they have lived. The proud part was the early part. Field Marshal von Moltke's victory on their behalf in Paris gave the German principalities the momentum to unite and form their long-postponed Reich. Known for their adherence to ideals like *Gehorsam* and *Treue*—obedience and loyalty—German armies served as models for the military from the young United States to Czarist and Communist Russia. The German Generalstab, or General Staff, an elite policy-planning team at the top level of the military, so inspired Leon Trotsky that he copied it when he built the Red Army. Even today the term General Staff is used for this function at the highest levels of the Soviet Union. Indeed, officers at the General Staff level are an important component of the forces on the right that have made it difficult for Mikhail Gorbachev to run his country.

The troubling part came with the twentieth century. The causes for World War I were complicated, and even today, after much research, we cannot fully explain them. Often we sum them up in the catchphrase "Sarajevo," the Bosnian town where the assassination of a Habsburg archduke triggered the mobilization of Europe's armies. In any case, it is clear that militarism and stupidity on the part of the Reich army played a big role in starting and prolonging the war. German guilt—Hitler's militarism and cruelty—is even clearer in the case of World War II. Four and a half decades later, the officers of Germany's new army, the Bundeswehr, still proceed carefully and slowly, but with a measure of the old pride, through the shards of their nation's broken history.

Modesty has been the tactic postwar Germans have chosen to navigate this difficult path. The Allies, who had encouraged West Germany's rearmament, watched the Germans warily, afraid they might be reviving the monster they had only so recently felled. The Germans doing the rearming were perhaps even more reluctant. In 1955, the year the nation firmed up its plans to create the Bundeswehr, a poll in the young weekly magazine *Der Spiegel* provided a picture of the West German attitude. Some 30 percent of West Germans thought war was "probable or possible" in the next three years. A poll in the same magazine in the same year showed that, even in the face of this threat, arms were not popular: 77 percent of men and 76 percent of women preferred the sight of a man in civilian clothing to that of a man in uniform. This represented a massive reversal from the days of World War I, when a hit song celebrated the soldier as "the handsomest man in all the land." When the first German officers arrived at Allied headquarters to discuss membership in NATO, *Der Spiegel* reported, they came dressed in dark suits. There was "no heel clicking, no piercing looks, no clipped nods, no spirited strides, no harsh voices." To observers, the officers looked like "diplomats who had forgotten their umbrellas."

German soldiers and German politicians argue that this tiptoe strategy has worked. Lord Ismay, NATO's first secretary-general, described the North Atlantic Treaty Organization as a vehicle to keep "the Americans in, the Russians out, and the Germans down." Today, a German has Lord Ismay's job: a former West German Defense Minister, the confident, bald, Manfred Wörner. Asked about Lord Ismay's famous put-down, Wörner spreads out his arms regally on the back of a sofa and offers a smiling rebuttal. "In two respects, NATO has been successful. We have kept the Americans in, and we have kept the Russians out. This, of course, is not keeping [the Germans] down, but keeping them *in*."

To a degree, Wörner is right; Germans now hold the two most important positions at NATO, his own and that of the chair of the military committee. At NATO's headquarters in Brussels, though, Wörner mediates NATO's internal squabbles, and over the past decade, Germany and the "German question" have more and more often been the central issues. In the mid-1980s, when nuclear deterrence was still NATO's unquestioned goal and its focus, the tension centered on the deployment of new short-range missiles in Europe; the United States argued that the missiles were necessary and the Germans argued that Central Europe had weapons enough. After the arrival of Mikhail Gorbachev, and the subsequent agreement to remove medium-range nuclear missiles from Central Europe, the debate shifted to a more fundamental question: Did Europe need NATO at all? When East Germany opened up, an even more basic question came to the fore: Would West Germany have to choose between staying in NATO and German unity?

Back home in Germany, the ranks of those who back a less military nation are growing. The first sign of the recent shift came after Gorbachev and Reagan agreed to pull out the intermediate-range nuclear missiles. Civilians who only five years earlier tolerated Allied tanks plowing through their crops and Allied planes shrieking over their heads now began protesting so loudly that those tanks and airplanes began to appear less often. When, two years later, the prospect of

German unity emerged, the anti-military feeling grew. Even soldiers argued that, forty-five years after the war, it was time to cut back the military presence in the civilian life of West Germany. This time, too, Western opinion turned: West German soldiers who had counted on the United States as their strongest ally in the INF debate found themselves abandoned by an America preoccupied with reducing the military and cashing in on its "peace dividend." Politically, the West, including the West German government, rejected the idea of conditioning German reunification on German neutrality. When Saddam Hussein provoked a crisis in the Middle East, the U.S. turned to a uniting Germany for aid—and found the German response wanting. Wherever the wavering Germany comes to rest, though—inside the NATO alliance or outside it—it will, at least at first, be a less military Germany. This prospect provokes an odd feeling of disappointment among German officers. Through their own advocacy of "restraint," of defending Germany modestly and quietly, they've brought about their own redundancy.

The best place to witness this "restraint" method of leadership is in Blankenese, a waterside district on the edge of Hamburg best known for the pink *Krabben* served in its restaurants and the white linen sported by its inhabitants. Here stands the Federal Republic's officers staff college, the Führungsakademie, or Leadership Academy, and it is here that Axel von Claer works. The Führungsakademie's predecessors were structures like the Kriegsakademie, the War Academy, a proud and ascetic structure designed by the classicist architect Friedrich Schinkel on the Prussian capital's grandest avenue, Unter den Linden. "New-built and proudly / Stands the War Academy," went the nineteenth-century jingle. By contrast, the low red-brick wings of the

Führungsakademie with their footpaths and duck pond seem humble—like a secondary school or a sanatorium.

The story of these simple buildings is the story of the military history of modern Germany. The structure was built in 1937 and later enlarged; Hermann Göring, Hitler's showy *Reichsmarschall*, used the place as a base for his Luftwaffe. The British revenged themselves after the war by taking over the structure, which fell into the British zone of occupation. When Germany rearmed, the British ceded it to the Federal Republic's military—but not before ensuring that they would be remembered. Officers at the academy today report that, on one of their last nights in Blankenese, rowdy British soldiers decorated the crotches of white nude statues in one building with indelible blue paint. This souvenir survived the German love of *Sauberkeit* only six months—the time it took recruits to scrub the figures back to white.

In the postwar part of Germany that has been called the Federal Republic, the Führungsakademie has had an important place. If West Germany had waged a war, its generals and colonels would have orchestrated battles according to military principles learned here. But when Germans describe the academy, they mostly say what it is not. The academy is not a Generalstab—that mighty elite instrument of the German military that fought World War I and was abolished after the war. It is not a War School—this Germany's new military opted for the less aggressive designation of Leadership Academy. The Führungsakademie does *not*—at least not this year—provide education to all German officers—East German officers have received their schooling from the National People's Army, headquartered in East Berlin. The Führungsakademie is not in Bonn, so long the capital for the two-thirds of Germany on this side of the Elbe. The Führungsakademie does not train an army that controls the nuclear weapons on German soil—a nonnuclear Bundeswehr was from the first a condition for German rearmament. Even the symbols that represent the Führungsakademie work hard to suppress aggression. In the academy coat of arms, the Third Reich's erect eagle shrinks—the bird now tilts modestly and bends its wings. The motto in the eagle's claws bespeaks self-control: "Mens agitat molem," or, roughly, "Mind over matter." The only thing that seems unabashedly German about the Führungsakademie is the cuisine—the lunch served a guest one day consisted of *Schweinehaxe*, sauerkraut, potatoes, and beer.

On a warm September Thursday, the Führungsakademie puts on a typically modest demonstration. Some sixty officers in blue, blue, and gray (air force, navy, and army) line up on the hard, creaky wooden seats of the festive Moltke Hall, named after the hero of the Franco-Prussian War. They then move outside to the grass lawn to receive diplomas for completing some of the academy's advanced courses—courses with relatively bland, administrative titles like "Discussion Leadership," or abstract ones like "Security Policy and Armed Forces." The marching band plays the German national anthem, but the words that are supposed to run through the listeners' heads are the third verse to the Haydn music—the Nazi-tainted first verses of "Deutschland über Alles" were stricken by the Federal Republic. A graduate wins a prize for his research on a major power—but to find that major power, he had to look beyond his own country. His theme: "Possibility of Use of U.S. Forces Abroad." The officers, an elite group aged thirty-three to forty or so, have just completed what would have in the old days been the prerequisites for entering the prestigious Generalstab, membership in which meant automatic arrest by the Allies at the end of World War II. But there is no longer a General Staff in Germany, so they must content themselves with achieving "General Staff level."

Among the audience this Thursday morning stands an example of the sort of officer this education produces—Axel von Claer. Von Claer's job is hardly a warlike one—he plans courses for officers from foreign countries who are guests at the Führungsakademie. When von Claer dons his gray army uniform, he often does so with reluctance. "I just don't feel comfortable wearing it," he admits with a smile. But von Claer is also a proud soldier, in large part because of family tradition. His father served on the General Staff in World War II and later worked to build up the Bundeswehr. His great-great-uncle Eberhard, a two-star general, directed troops in the first year of World War I. A three-star general, his great-grandfather Otto is the bearded fellow in the office portrait.

To listen to Axel von Claer trace his family tree in a spare moment in the officers' *Kasino* is to hear of the change that's revolutionized military life in Germany. Serving in the military was first of all a matter of pride for that first general in the days of the Kaiser. Otto de Claer spent sixteen years as von Moltke's adjutant, a position which entailed more than its modern equivalent, aide-de-camp. Otto was, for example, responsible for the selection of the General Staff and accompanied his master in victories at Sedan and Paris. A second picture on Axel's wall shows Otto de Claer standing among glowing Germans on the right side of a table. On the left side, the defeated French look down. The picture is of the surrender at Sedan in 1870, and Axel's great-grandfather was nearby when the defeated Napoleon III handed victor Wilhelm his sword at Donchéry. At that point, this old family of country nobles—they trace back to Anglo-Norman origins—was known as de Claer, the "de" a reminder of the family's roots farther to the west. But in 1882 Otto de Claer and his brothers petitioned the Kaiser "that Your Majesty have the grace to permit that we be called . . . von Claer from now on." This request—typical of the straightforward patriotism in the newly formed Reich—was promptly granted in a royal *Kabinettsordre*, and from May 1882 on the family was known as von Claer.

The German Reich in those days was represented by another von Claer, Axel's great-uncle and namesake, Alexander. This von Claer served as the Reich's first military attaché in Peking and was the member of the diplomatic corps who supervised the protection of diplomats and their families during the bloody Boxer Rebellion at the end of the century (a German chargé d'affaires was killed in the rebellion). Later, from a posting in Seoul, von Claer reported to Berlin on the progress of the Russo-Japanese War (another observer reported from the other side in St. Petersburg). In those days, Germany was scrambling across the world, like Britain, hurrying to establish colonies in Africa and the Far East. Great-uncle Axel played his part in the reconnaissance; in the service of the Reich he once rode on horseback between Seoul and Peking, a distance of several thousand kilometers.

The next period of history was less felicitous for the German nation. Von Moltke's nephew, also a Count Helmuth von Moltke, was, as head of the Prussian General Staff, in large part responsible for the Schlieffen plan, the strategy committed to war on Germany's western front. Soon after the assassination at Sarajevo in the summer of 1914, Germany was pulled into war on the Habsburgs' side. The Chancellor and the Kaiser waffled and considered a limited war in the East, but were unable to halt the army's march on France through neutral Belgium. That move brought Britain, anxious to protect the Channel and outraged at the violation of neutrality, into what was to become the long and pointless World War I.

The Schlieffen plan and its consequence, World War I, gave the world clear evidence of the grand-scale misfortune the Generalstab system could lead to. When, in the summer of 1914, Kaiser Wilhelm realized what he was getting into, his government sent messages to Vienna to try to halt the escalation of hostilities. Historian Golo Mann describes the scene:

"Bethmann-Hollweg [of the government] sent restraining, even imploring, telegrams to Vienna. But they were neutralized by a very different kind of advice which the Prussian Chief of the General Staff, von Moltke, telegraphed to Austria: they must immediately place their whole army on a war footing. 'What a joke!' said Berchtold [the Foreign Minister]. 'Who's in charge in Berlin?' This was it. In Berlin many different authorities had long been issuing parallel or contradictory orders. But when war was in the offing, the war machine, perfected over decades, and its chief engineers, the generals, took over command." At the Führungsakademie, there is a Moltke Hall and a painting of von Moltke near the commandant's office, but both commemorate von Moltke Number One, the man who took Paris in 1871. "We don't talk about the other von Moltke," a colonel seated beside Lieutenant Colonel von Claer confides at a mess lunch of stew and fruit yogurt.

The von Claer tribe paid for their nation's militarism along with their countrymen. Beside the two painting reproductions on Axel's wall hangs an old black-and-white photo of toddler Axel, laughing with his great-great uncle Eberhard von Claer, a retired general. "The youngest and oldest members of the von Claer clan, divided by eighty-five years but united in joy," reads the handwritten note on the other side. For most of the family, though, such regeneration was impossible. Six von Claer soldiers fell in the First and Second World Wars, and Axel von Claer and a cousin are the only male members of their generation to carry on the line.

A few blocks away from the photo and von Claer's academy office lives human evidence of how close those war years remain. Today Carl-Gideon von Claer, Axel's father, lives a pensioner's life in a bungalow which his wife, a jewelry maker, also uses as a workshop. While the couple's black pet duck, Nefertiti, wanders about the backyard outside, this von Claer, clad in vest and tie, sits in the living-room chair and tells of a career that spanned from the Reichswehr of the Weimar period to Hitler's Wehrmacht to the Bundeswehr. When von Claer first became an officer in 1933, he joined the 16th Cavalry Regiment in Erfurt, which trained with sword and saber. By the time he retired, in 1964, von Claer was lecturing his own army's generals about "fraction of damage" and "possibility"—alien terms from the complicated new lingo of nuclear tactics and operations.

What made a German become a soldier in those days? Carl-Gideon's father was a Protestant vicar in a small town in the Rhineland, but many of the other von Claers had been soldiers. "I never wanted to be anything else," he says. With pride he recalls the popularity of his regiment. "It was a sporty affair, very exclusive." He also points out that of a hundred and fifty applicants in his year, only three were accepted. From his armchair, von Claer announces several times—as if repetition will convince—that from the beginning he felt himself a traditional soldier, not a Nazi.

When Carl-Gideon von Claer explains that time, his son Axel nods in agreement. Back at the academy, most of the

officers, particularly the older ones who were born during
the war or shortly after it, also try to explain the military's
role in World War II. In their explanation, one name shows
up more frequently than any other: Ludwig Beck. Werner
von Scheven, the commandant of the academy, tells the
Beck story. General Beck, chief of staff of the army, tried
to convince Reich leaders that Hitler's bellicose policy was
dangerous and would lead Germany to "the worst consequences"—the sort that had brought about the First World
War. When Beck's efforts went unheeded, he resigned. But
officers after him, including his successor, shared Beck's
views, and even planned their own putsch against Hitler. "In
this case, the officers were in the right and the government
was in the wrong," says the commandant, comparing the
situation with that of World War I. But foreign capitals—
principally London—rejected appeals for help from this circle of mutineers, and Chamberlain concentrated on reconciliation with Hitler. "There were soldiers and officers who
backed Hitler," sums up the commandant. "But there were
also those who did not."

Carl-Gideon von Claer notes that many members of the
aristocracy found themselves, like the members of the Beck
circle, at odds with the Nazis. They were repelled by Hitler's
elite SS, whose careerism and cruelty struck them as arriviste
and barbaric. The Nazis, for their part, found the nobles
snobbish, or worse, dangerously subversive. The latter suspicion was not unfounded: noble names, including a von
Moltke, plotted the second major effort to stop Hitler. A
count, Colonel Claus Schenk von Stauffenberg, in 1944 organized an attempt to blow up Hitler at the Führer's eastern
field headquarters, the Wolf's Lair. Count Stauffenberg
himself placed the bomb under the wooden meeting-room
table. The officers planned to take control of the Third Reich

after Hitler's death, and make peace with the enemy. But Hitler survived the explosion—the thick table protected him—and Stauffenberg and many others were executed. The count died uttering the words "Long live Holy Germany."

Carl-Gideon von Claer was a member of neither the Beck nor the Stauffenberg ring, but he can explain the problem the noble officer generally faced in Hitler's military. "We felt ourselves in a bind. We said to ourselves, no matter how the war goes, we will be in trouble. If we win the war, the SS will swallow us. If we lose the war, it will be the Allies doing the swallowing." Being a soldier under Hitler was "terrible," von Claer says, not like the happier days of the 100,000-man army of the Weimar Republic. The old man smiles when he speaks of his first regiment—next week, the remaining members will meet for a reunion in Hersfeld.

The fall of the von Claers at war's end and their rise after it are typical of many German families. Carl-Gideon von Claer made it to the rank of lieutenant colonel, and then landed in a British prisoner-of-war camp in Schleswig-Holstein. Axel himself was born on May 27, 1941, coincidentally a day that signaled bad news for the Reich: it was the day the Allies sank the *Bismarck*. Baby Axel and his mother left their home in Bad Freienwalde in flight from the Russians and settled in American-occupied Thuringia. When the Allies ceded Thuringia to the Russians soon after the end of the war, the von Claers fled again—Frau von Claer gave her golden clock to U.S. soldiers in exchange for the necessary gasoline. After the war, Carl-Gideon sought work, and found it only as a simple laborer in the kilns of a West German ceramics factory. But when Germany began to plan its rearmament less than ten years later, Carl-Gideon von Claer's second military career began. In Bonn, Adenauer had employed Theodor Blank, a fellow Catholic and Union leader, in a job rather euphemistically titled "Special Assistant to the Chancellor for Matters Related to the Increase of Allied Forces." The "Büro Blank," as it was known, was the embryo that grew into the West German Defense Ministry and Bundeswehr. It was here that Carl-Gideon von Claer went to work in the hope of correcting his own and Germany's errors in the past. "My friends in the Chancellor's office called me and said, 'Don't miss this. If you come and work with us, you will have a chance to build the new Europe.' "

So Carl-Gideon von Claer went—in civilian dress—to Bonn and began planning the Bundeswehr. He also played a role in Germany's fast-paced reconciliation with the United States. When, in the mid-1950s, the United States government decided it was time to cooperate with the new German government on matters of military training, it issued an invitation for one German officer to attend the command and general staff college at Fort Leavenworth, Kansas. That first German officer was von Claer, whose family was still so poor that they sailed to America in the cramped cabins of a freighter. Axel and his brother attended an American high school while their father took instruction in the arts of the weapon that decided World War II, the atom bomb. From between the yellowed pages of his old U.S. textbook, Carl-Gideon von Claer pulls a photo of himself from that period. There was, as yet, no Bundeswehr uniform, so the von Claer who stares from the photo is dressed in a U.S. uniform— albeit without insignia.

The *Amerikajahr* was one of excitement so great that it still resonates in the voices of the von Claer family today. Carl-Gideon von Claer kept a diary in which he described the wonders of the American supermarket, where shoppers

That von Claer's decision to go from the military to the press seemed such an unusual one shows how fragile the young democracy of West Germany still was in the early 1960s. The military, the representative of new national might, lived uneasily with the press, the representative of new domestic freedoms. The bitterest and most important of their clashes came around the time Carl-Gideon von Claer joined *Der Spiegel*. The magazine's publisher, a young man named Rudolf Augstein, printed a number of articles attacking the nation's young Defense Ministry, charging that it was preparing nuclear war in Germany. Augstein's particular target was the conservative Defense Minister, Franz-Josef Strauss, whose ambitions to attain the position of Chancellor he hoped to spoil. In the fall of 1962, *Der Spiegel* gave Germany an early version of Watergate when it printed reports from secret documents that allegedly involved a war scenario that included 10 to 15 million war dead—and the likelihood of German humiliation to boot. Strauss retaliated by searching *Der Spiegel*'s offices, ordering a military attaché to arrest an involved official in Spain, and putting Augstein in jail. In this confrontation of issues—press freedom versus national security—press freedom, and, it is fair to say, democracy, won. Augstein emerged from jail a hero and Bonn sent Strauss packing. He returned to Bavaria, and though, more than a decade later, he was to campaign unsuccessfully for the position of Chancellor, many argue that the "*Spiegel* affair" finished Strauss's chances of becoming the West German leader. Carl-Gideon von Claer, for his part, enjoyed a happier relationship with *Der Spiegel*. His reporting on military affairs for the magazine earned him a reputation: "Claer is fair," his old colleagues said. He stayed at the magazine twelve years—"until all my contacts had retired."

There's enough of the soldier remaining in the old man,

though, so that he has trouble with the peace-oriented nation that Germany is today. The afternoon of the visit he is angry about a case that recently passed through the German courts. A doctor who had called German soldiers "potential murderers" before an audience was tried in the courts for having offended the dignity of the soldier—and was acquitted on the grounds that every man has the right to voice his opinion. For the latter principle von Claer has plenty of sympathy: he was, after all, on the staff of *Der Spiegel* for so long. But in this case he sides with the military: "The army should protect its junior members. That didn't happen here."

Carl-Gideon von Claer and his old Bundeswehr colleagues worry mostly about the state of the German army today. They worry about what will happen to the Bundeswehr if the defense budget can't grow, and they worry what the army of a united Germany will be like. But often, and even in these exciting days, these worries about the future are connected with serious reflection about the past. They talk, for example, about the great military names who resisted Hitler. They mention Count Helmuth von Moltke, great-grandnephew of the famous field marshal after whom the Hamburg academy hall is named, and Count Albrecht Bernstorff, whose uncle had been ambassador to the United States. Often, their reflection is confined to a single date: July 20, 1944, the day when that clique of officers, led by Claus von Stauffenberg, tried to blow up the Führer at his Wolf's Lair. For their failed attempt, many officers and their collaborators died. For modern soldiers, "July 20" has become the code phrase to describe that other military, the one that resisted Hitler and felt itself his victim.

A more recent event often pops up in these same discussions, one that can be summarized in a single word: "Bitburg." "Bitburg" is the shorthand Germans use to refer to their struggle with themselves and with the world outside Germany over how to present or revise the history of the Third Reich. "Bitburg" itself happened in 1985, a heated discussion that was the result of a plan by President Reagan to pay an official visit to a cemetery in the West German town where, among others, graves of soldiers from the Waffen-SS were to be found. Germans wanted Reagan and other statesmen to show the world that now, so many years after the war, the time had come to honor Germany's war dead. Many observers, in particular a vociferous press, sought to prevent or criticize what they perceived as a tribute to a military group who were Hitler's most loyal servants. Reagan did visit the cemetery—with the din of international protest in his ears. In the months after the short visit to the cemetery, it came to be a symbol of German pride, a troublesome symbol of what the world might come to expect from an increasingly confident Germany.

Discussions about "July 20" and "Bitburg" also take place in the von Claer family. Responding to an outsider's query concerning how he feels about Bitburg, Carl-Gideon writes a few paragraphs in his clear, spiky Old World script:

> I don't see a problem. Among more than 2,000 Wehrmacht fallen lie some 40 soldiers of the Waffen-SS. Should one have prepared separate cemeteries for the Waffen-SS? This unrealistic idea is one which would not have occurred to even Hitler, or Himmler . . . These SS people were abused just as we all were, hundreds of thousands of soldiers who spent six years fighting for Hitler's insane goals.

Underneath his father's writing, in a neater, more modern hand, Axel von Claer has added a postscript that refers to the officers' rebellion against Hitler: ". . . and let themselves be misused until July 20, 1944."

The interesting thing about this discussion and about Bitburg is that they took place so many years after Germany's "trial" in the courts of Nuremberg. Oddly enough, as the number of years between the present and the twelve-year Third Reich grows, so does domestic and international sensitivity to the issue. What's changed of late is that Germans now resist international censure. Lately, their resistance has taken an explicitly political form: support for Franz Schönhuber, the Bavarian television personality who, in the early 1980s, published an autobiography with a positive picture of his tour as a noncommissioned officer in the Waffen-SS. The book cost him his job but gave him a political career. On the strength of support for his view—that young Germans like him enjoyed their service in the SS and thought they were doing the right thing—his political party, the far-right Republikaner, began breaking into local governments across the nation in 1989. Before the Republikaner, a similar backlash had direct political consequences in Austria. International criticism of Kurt Waldheim for covering up his military service so angered Austrians that they elected Waldheim their President.

The Germany where such things happen is the country where Carl-Gideon von Claer's sons, Helmut and Axel, have had to make their way. Helmut, his younger son, took a look at the family history and became a conscientious objector. Part of the decision stemmed from practical reasons. Helmut had just married and didn't want to take a year away from his schooling as a designer and photographer. But the decision, brother Axel reports, also had a political basis. Helmut later died of multiple sclerosis, but before his death he supported the revolutionary left-wing critics who shook quiescent Germany in the late 1960s and were known as the "Extra-Parliamentary Opposition."

For the other brother, the military became a career. It was not the old-style army he joined, but the new Bundeswehr, the Bundeswehr of a democratic Germany and the citizen soldier. It was an event in Europe that put him on the same track that his relatives had traveled—the repression of the Hungarian uprising in 1956. "I knew I'd be either a soldier or a doctor, and when that happened in Hungary—well, that was the push I needed." And so he entered the new army —the one his father had had a hand in training—and became the modern citizen soldier.

To play this difficult role, Axel von Claer draws much support from his old family tradition. By day he wears the green fatigue sweater of the army man—and also the green ring with his family seal of ostrich feather, crown, and mantraps. His wife, Susanne, a doctor, wears the same ring on her finger. At home he has a larger glass version of the family emblem hanging on the wall in the dining room. On the bookshelf also stands a copy of the Gotha, the directory of the German nobility. Von Claer's living room has a Biedermeier desk, and a giant armoire with the family seal on it looms in the smallish dining room.

The aggression of this proud past has translated itself into a benign wanderlust in Axel's life. As a young couple, Axel and his wife went through five used VW buses, camping their way across the Continent and in North Africa. "We got the idea in Paris," he says, "when we saw some Englishmen who had parked their bus right beneath the Eiffel tower. We thought that was neat." Their oldest daughter, Sitta, has a North African name, a tribute to five exciting weeks the von Claers spent visiting a friend for his wedding in Morocco. Their openness to the world—a feature rare in the Germans, who generally like to travel but don't like to play host—has yielded them numerous friends abroad. Susanne von Claer recently traveled through the Soviet Union to Siberia with a British friend. On the von Claer bookshelves lie piles of copies of *National Geographic*—a gift from an American friend who also supplies them with occasional shipments of American peanut butter and fruitcake.

Today the von Claers live in countryside to the southwest of Hamburg. They chose their suburb for professional reasons—it was where Susanne could find work as a doctor. But they are also aware that the area has a special meaning in Germany's past. Not fifteen minutes from their home, at the end of the subway line S21, is an important symbol for the German tradition that inspires Axel: Friedrichsruh, the estate Kaiser Wilhelm gave Otto von Bismarck to thank him for unifying Germany. Here, in a wood-and-brick house on the edge of the Bismarck estate, stands a museum lined with tributes Germans sent their first Chancellor by way of thanks for his services—silver and gold breastplates, Meissen vases, even an old iron cannon. For many Germans, Bismarck is a forgotten name. A poll published in *Der Spiegel* in the autumn of 1989 showed that only 24.7 percent of high schoolers knew the right answer to the question "Who founded the German Reich?" Twice as many students knew that "NATO" was the right answer to the more modern question "What's the name of the Western military alliance?" But though Bismarck may not stir all of West Germany's youth, he does continue to inspire some. Every year small crowds gather to celebrate his birthday and the founding of the Reich on the grounds of Friedrichsruh.

Although they aren't among that group, there is a family that, like the von Claers, lives in this neck of the woods and is heir to a special military tradition. Their name is Paulus, and like his friend Axel von Claer, Axel Paulus is also an Alexander called Axel. Axel Paulus himself is a tall, dark-browed man in an elegant double-breasted suit. He works as a consultant of the most modern variety—he trained in part at McKinsey & Company. But he, too, has an unusual past. His grandfather, who became Field Marshal Paulus, was the general who directed the ill-fated Sixth Army at Stalingrad. Besieged on the cold borders of the Volga, he surrendered in spite of Hitler's orders to fight to the last man. For that act his entire family was arrested by the SS and thrown into various camps. Axel himself serves as a reserve officer in the army; he says this helps him in his work. "In business, there's a lack of leadership, and when I arrive, I help them. I almost get the feeling the people need Prussian leadership."

The von Claers and Pauluses are a special group of officers of whom there is something of a concentration in Hamburg. They dine together and are family friends—both Axel von Claer and Axel Paulus have wives named Susanne. On a Friday evening they may be found eating together in a small restaurant near the von Claers' chalet-shaped home in suburban Hamburg.

Where this kind of pride served the earlier von Claers and the Pauluses on foreign battlefields, it serves the new generation on the domestic battlefield of peace-loving contemporary Germany. Axel's generation of soldiers has never known a war—and it is unlikely that Axel will see a war before the end of his military career. But his desk work at the Führungsakademie prepares him for another, if less onerous, test. Whereas Axel's great-grandfather marched into Paris, Axel must march into hostile classrooms. As a battalion commander, he headed a group of soldiers housed in a barracks in suburban Hamburg during the angry days of the missile debate in the early 1980s. Axel's battle was not fought with a short clash of weapons; it was a lengthy battle of words that lasted for days. When crowds of mothers and babies arrived one day to protest at his barracks gates, the weather was terribly cold. Von Claer and his colleagues defused the hostility by serving the protesters hot tea. More recently, Axel represented the military at a discussion on the Soviet Union and disarmament—before a catcalling audience of *Gymnasium* children and teachers. For him, the connection between military and politics is vital, and one which it is the soldier's duty to make. "There was one important point that had to be made," he recalls over a dinner with his wife and Axel Paulus. "That the INF decision [to deploy medium-range weapons if the Soviets didn't remove their counterparts] was a good one. You have to act strongly with the Russians, and that was what we did. So we got results, and it doesn't bother me that we did. I just told them that." The problem is that the INF vindication has been a short one—as soon as that battle was won, it began to seem irrelevant as Europe began to disarm.

Axel's wife, a dark-haired country doctor, also sees the situation as difficult. At supper she remembers the early school days of her older daughter, Sitta. At kindergarten, a child minder told the children that soldiers were "bad people." That sent the small girl home crying and asking whether her father "has to be a soldier." As a doctor, Mrs. von Claer herself has no trouble with confrontation by the patients of her country practice. "They need something from me, so they are not in a position to think in political terms." But at the dinner she argues with the two Axels, saying that her daughters suffer from being different. "We aren't like the other people, and they feel it, and there's hostility," she says—although this hostility is a nuanced one, buried among relatively good relations with the neighborhood. When Sitta, for example, was the only child to sign up for Latin lessons at her high school, she met with disapproval from other children's parents and even from teachers. "They perceive choosing Latin as an elite thing to do—which it is," says Mrs. von Claer. "And the children get punished in some form or other when they do an elite thing." The problem has little to do with Axel's profession. It has to do with class—in democracy-obsessed West Germany, educators of the past decades have fought to make German grammar school students and high school students feel equal, even when achieving that goal meant slowing down the more gifted children. In any case, Paulus argues with Axel's wife, saying he feels "nothing negative" when he is in the public world. But Mrs. von Claer reminds him that his sister feels differently. Years ago, when the two were medical residents, Paulus's sister introduced herself—and asked whether Susanne "minded" working with a member of the famous military family.

For Axel's branch of the von Claer family, this problem will one day come to an end. Von Claer has two daughters, and if they change their names at marriage, there will be no one carrying the burdensome noble name. West Germany's army is nearly all male, so no new von Claer will serve in the Bundeswehr in the 1990s or carry on the von Claer name in the officer corps. Says von Claer with appealing self-effacement, "Dynastically speaking, I am a zero."

The von Claers' problems may vanish, but the problems will remain for West Germany's army, the Bundeswehr. Ever since the days of Carl-Gideon von Claer, the army has tried to defend its role as arms bearer by making itself as non-military as possible. Today the academy maintains a faculty of professors, including social scientists from the left-leaning civilian world, to instruct its recruits. The Bundeswehr makes large efforts to "civilianize" its culture—at the Führungs-akademie, for example, officers pass through an unusually broad political education that might offer, say, courses on Gorbachev, on military strategy, on civil defense, and on map exercises of war games. In any case, though, the classrooms are moving away from the classic authoritarianism one would expect of the military—where a high-ranking officer lectured and more junior officers listened—to more demo-cratic seminars. Officers at the academy even criticize the Prussian image foreigners try to impose on them. "Prussian" itself seems almost to be a bad word at the Führungs-akademie, and when officers anticipate that they will be given that label, they launch into a preemptive attack. One colonel performed such a maneuver over lunch. "I once vis-ited an American unit stationed here on West German soil," he remarked pointedly. "I wasn't really expecting much of a meal, but what they produced was really good. So I sent for the cook—and he came, trembling, assuming I had some criticism. When I congratulated him, he fell silent he was so grateful. 'Sir,' he said, 'I've been in the U.S. forces many years, but you are the first one ever to pay me a compli-ment.' " That, said the colonel, is how "the Americans are: more Prussian than us."

This postwar shift in the soldier identity is not one that always goes over well abroad—particularly not in more bel-licose countries whose governments find merit in the old Prussian tradition. In the late summer of 1990, *The New York Times* reported that General Augusto Pinochet of Chile had livened up his remarks at a Rotary Club meeting by calling the Bundeswehr an army of "drug addicts, long hairs, gays and union members." The West German government was so miffed it took the time off from its reunification program to call the general's remarks "obscene."

When it comes to politics, the military are equally careful. As late as 1989, with arguments much more elaborate than those of their counterparts in America and Britain, the German soldiers defend nuclear deterrence. Most of them are conservatives, and like most conservative Germans, they back German reunification. But like politicians, they often choose to speak of it in terms of a "reunification of Europe," or in the context of the Common Market of 1992. The Führungsakademie hosted a group of officers from the academy's Soviet analogue, the Voroshilov Academy in Moscow, in the fall of 1989. Until German reunification, the academy had less to do with its East German colleagues across the border. Asked at a press conference on graduation day whether he was interested in meeting with East German officers in the spirit of *glasnost*, the General Inspector of the Bundeswehr, Dieter Wellershoff, rejected the idea with a bitter reference to East Germany's armed efforts to keep its population inside the border. "I don't know about you, but I have trouble dealing with people who fire on my countrymen."

Months later, the academy is a changed place; one that contemplates German reunification with wonder. Upon the suggestion of the mayor of Hamburg, who is cultivating a city partnership with Dresden, the academy is preparing to meet with its counterparts at the military college there. In January, a few months after the Wall goes down for East and West Germans, it also goes down for West German soldiers. Axel and family venture through the Brandenburg Gate for an excursion in East Berlin. For him, the event is a low-key one. "My wife asked me when I crossed, 'So what do you feel?' 'Nothing!' I replied."

Nevertheless, the von Claers, like so many German families and foreigners, collect their own souvenir chip of the Wall to take home with them. And the union of the East German army and the Bundeswehr Axel and all the others at the academy now perceive as "a matter of course." A few months later Axel is among a group of fifteen West German officers who spend a get-to-know-each-other weekend with fifteen East German officers in the countryside of (West German) Schleswig-Holstein. Later, he reports that the meeting was a difficult one. "Those poor devils," he says, speaking of the East German officers. "They were all [Communist] Party members, and have narrow lives—no future." As it turns out, many of them do have a future. Chancellor Helmut Kohl in the end agreed to a union of the Bundeswehr with the NVA, the East German army. As part of the deal, he has promised the Western army will absorb many Eastern soldiers, but not high-ranking officers. For soldiers like Axel, the change is exciting and confusing. On the one hand, the officers will have new territory to cover. On the other hand, they have to work with what were, until recently, their sworn enemies. In addition, some officers must retire—the new joint military is supposed to be slim. No matter how generous West Germany becomes at the union of the two Germanys, it will not be generous enough to build an army in which its officers work on the same team as ex-Communist officers of high rank. The typical modern German military man, ever careful, Axel is cautious about the idea of German unity. "German unity, of course, if it has to come. But only under a European umbrella." For the German military, he admits, now is a difficult time. "For so long—too long—we oriented ourselves to an enemy in the East. There is no longer an enemy there. Now what?"

The "what" soldiers like Axel face is for them a paradox: a post-reunification Germany that doesn't really want to be defended. At the officer graduation at the Führungsakademie in Blankenese, the graduates describe their difficulties with the new atmosphere. Klaus Bücklein, a thirty-five-year-old air force captain with dark hair, explains the difference this kind of education creates between him and his foreign colleagues. "Our education is much wider. For example, when I'm in a strange place, I'm interested in economic things, like currency exchange rates, whereas another soldier might have trouble even exchanging money." More specifically, he notes, the German education seeks to make "thinking citizen soldiers" of its officers, to avoid the blind obedience that led to the "only following orders" syndrome on display during the Nuremberg trials. He gives an example: "Once I asked an American what he would do if he was ordered to go to Beirut. He said if the President said he should go to Beirut he would go." Wouldn't a German officer follow an order? "Well, yes, the result is the same. But we would first discuss it. And our discussion—this is the result of World War II."

In Germany, though, even these philosopher-soldiers are not spared confrontation with the civilian population. Until recently, the air force recruits have escaped the general hostility leveled at things military by the German population. Flying was respected as a universal goal, an urge, that had nothing to do with politics or nationality. National tolerance of thunderous low-level flights dropped dramatically, however, after two air disasters upset the population in 1988. In Ramstein, in southern Germany, an air show turned into a tragedy when an Allied plane crashed into the crowd, killing 70 and wounding 300. Later in the year, a second plane crashed in a heavily populated area near Cologne. In the minds of West Germans, the events crystallized an important thought: "Now that war no longer seems likely here in Europe, we no longer need the military to defend us so energetically."

"Lots of my friends, pilots, feel as if they have been abandoned. That situation would be unimaginable for fliers in America," says Captain Bücklein. To be sure, notes the captain, the Germans are not the only targets of anti-military sentiment. Georg Pazderski, a newly minted army major, tells of being on military exercises with Americans in the countryside around Marburg an der Lahn. The American tanks destroyed a new road "and so angered the farmers that they went after the tanks with pitchforks!" Statistics collected by the federal government on the number of conscientious objectors refusing to join West Germany's draft army back up the major's words. One in every ten young West Germans opts for the conscientious objector status, a figure which is even higher than in the wild days of student protest in 1968, 1969, and 1970.

Captain Bücklein dates more fundamental change back to 1979 and the NATO two-track decision on the deployment of intermediate-range nuclear missiles. Right now, he says, there is no war, "and we can't prove that we have a purpose every day." The military, like all armies in the days of nuclear deterrence, sees its mission as protecting the peace, but "even if we were not present, there might still be peace," Captain Bücklein says, and opens his hands. "It hasn't been easier for us . . ." Henning Straus, a fellow graduate from the navy, compares German officers with foreign colleagues who have studied as guest students at the Führungsakademie. "The Scandinavian officers are the officers who are most like the Germans. But one thing is different—their relationship with their predecessors is smoother. Ours is an interrupted one."

These officers' future, and, to some extent, the future of

German society, rests on their ability to deal with that interruption. What kind of army will the new Germany have? To start, a diminished one—the concession it makes to the Soviet Union in exchange for unity. But even if a new, larger Germany declares itself "neutral," its size will, eventually, make that adjective pointless. How much less powerful will a rich united Germany be than the discordant Soviet Union? Will German soldiers defending that Germany be "good" soldiers of peace or belligerent ones? Axel von Claer likes to ponder such geopolitical problems, and he likes to think that they can probably be overcome. "Being a soldier is a good and interesting profession," he says, "and I am proud to be a member of that profession." From the hostile encounters with angry teachers and students, he retreats to the academy, to classes for visiting officers. Most days, he can be found there, hard at work in his green army-issue sweater and pants. From time to time, he gets up and paces a bit, past the two walls and the two sets of pictures, one set representing his ancestor and warrior Germany, one set representing his own peaceful life. The office is not a big one, but it is big enough to contain two worlds.

4

A Prince in Bavaria

BAVARIA IN GERMANY

There's something sad about the Prince Regent Theater on a weekday morning in fall. Outside the Munich theater, at the Nigerstrasse corner, a cluster of taxis wait—no passengers for now. Across from the theater, a neat Italian sautés *Austerpilze*, giant sweet mushrooms, but the white-clothed tables inside are still unoccupied. Richard Wagner reclines beside the theater, but he is only a stone composer, a bust looking over a quiet scene. Inside the theater are the silent offices of August Everding, Munich's *Intendant*, the director of Bavaria's state theaters. But no, says the secretary who picks up the phone in the white office, Professor Everding is not here. Very sorry. Professor Everding is doing a *Dutchman* at the Met; he's gone from Munich until before Christmas.

Bavaria gets lonely for kings. Today Munich is a self-important city with world-class traffic jams plugging its ring road and a Hermès boutique all its own, right by the Hotel Vier Jahreszeiten. The names Bavarians drop in other capitals are those of firms, like BMW and the telecommunications giant Siemens, not royal ones from Bavaria's old ruling clan, the Wittelsbachs. But Bavarians are still the same inward-turned people who buried their Ludwig II, their fairy-tale king, in the midst of tears and a thunderstorm.

They still have a habit of building up giants, hating them, and missing them when they are away—Ludwig II, Richard Wagner, even Adolf Hitler, and their postwar master, the neckless, knife-tongued Franz-Josef Strauss. The Prince Regent Theater itself has played a role in nearly every point of this drama, from Ludwig to Strauss. These days, the theater is the core—the *stage*—for a new controversy provoked by a new king. The controversy is over how to save the aging theater, and the king in question this time is a modern-day king, a king of public service to the arts. He is a smallish man with a wizardlike smile and wispy gray hair that flaps around his large bald spot the way Einstein's did. His name is August Everding.

The theater's home is the Prinzregentenstrasse, the fourth in a series of large avenues the Wittelsbach kings built to bring glory to their capital. Named after Luitpold, the steady regent who occupied the throne after Ludwig's death in 1886, this wide boulevard of museums and ministries has been traveled over the century by a variety of Bavarians— nobility, Nazis, *Bürger* out for a Sunday stroll. Gustav von Aschenbach, the wanderer in Thomas Mann's *Death in Venice*, first discovers his itch to travel when he steps out of his Prinzregentenstrasse apartment to take the air. Even today, even on a quiet morning, the Prinzregentenstrasse gives off a whiff of Bavarian independence—a visitor feels this is a real capital.

Partly this is because postwar Munich *has* seen itself as more than a state capital, as something more important for West Germany. What other West German city, Munichers long reasoned, could compete with Munich? Not suburban Rhineside Bonn, not blighted, political Berlin, not crowded, grimy Frankfurt, not out-of-the-way Hamburg. With more than 27,000 square miles of forest, cities, and mountains,

A Prince in Bavaria

Bavaria is a big state—West Germany's biggest, West Germany's Texas. Like their New World Texan cousins, Bavarians take pleasure in impressing visitors who call here, and, like Texans, they take pleasure in making themselves felt when they venture from home territory. International political events that rock other German states—Germany's unification a century ago, the Berlin Wall coming down, Czechoslovakia going free—seem to eddy around serene Bavaria. The *Freistaat Bayern* sees foreign policy in a different light: as an opportunity for Bavaria to make its mark in the world. One method the state has of making itself felt is through business. Along with neighboring Baden-Württemberg, Catholic Bavaria has generated an economic boom that puts to shame West Germany's Protestant rust-belt states in the north. Bavarians ridicule northern cities' problems of unemployment, and those who own their own homes boast about how much more expensive they are than houses in the depressed Ruhr region or that underemployed, left-wing port, Bremen.

Bavaria's most direct weapon, though, is politics. Strauss spent decades concocting mischief that rattled the teeth of officials and politicians in complacent Bonn. Bavarians like to remember the time nearly thirty years ago when their Franz-Josef, Strauss, was a big man in Bonn, and they like to reflect on a more recent moment, when Strauss piloted his own plane to visit Mikhail Gorbachev in Moscow. The visitor who strolls the Prinzregentenstrasse, walking past its four-meter-high Peace Angel and crossing the green Isar River to inspect the large Bavarian National Museum, can feel this big-scale Bavarian glamour.

The Prinze, as some Bavarians like to call it, is a handsome boxy structure with gold details that sits like a big Art Nouveau birthday present at the other end of the Prinzregentenstrasse. The theater was conceived in honor of two Bavarian giants—Ludwig and his muse, Richard Wagner—built under the auspices of another, Prince Regent Luitpold, and favored by yet another, Adolf Hitler, who stripped the structure of its *Jugendstil* doodads and converted it to a Nazi *Volkstheater*. The Prinze was the only big theater still standing in bombed-out Munich after the war, and the Americans used its stage to entertain their soldiers. Germans soon took it over again, and the Prinze stayed open until the building was condemned in 1963.

It took another giant, Franz-Josef Strauss, and a near-giant, Professor Everding, to launch a partial renovation of the Prinze in the early 1980s. Everding has said he prefers modest tributes, and to thank him for his efforts on behalf of the theater, the city produced one in the decoration of the ceiling of the Prinze's foyer. Among a clutch of painted characters, a Bacchus cavorts—a Bacchus with the unmistakable Everding grin. Specifically, restorers had done over the theater's auditorium and entrance and had even built a new stage over the orchestra pit adequate for theater, but not opera. The true stage, deep and cavernous, requires more money for its repair. These days Everding spends his time in Munich trying to raise funds from private sources and the state so the Prinze can once again do a *Meistersinger*.

What makes the Prinze a challenge—what makes Bavarians want to save it—is that it is not even a very important theater. Bavaria already has its Nationaltheater, a columned edifice modeled on the Odéon in Paris and containing 2,123 seats. Here Brünnhilde and Tristan agonize on a stage bigger than the Met's. Maximilian I, Bavaria's first king, built the Nationaltheater, and it was later rebuilt twice, once after it burned in an 1823 fire and again after bombs destroyed it in World War II. The state also has the old and the new

Residenztheater, known as the Cuvilliés and the Resi, respectively, which already do plenty to impress the tourists who opt for a bit of autumnal culture in between bouts at the beery Oktoberfest. For simple, quainter events they can turn to yet another state enterprise, the Gärtnerplatz Theater, which long ago had a bitter experience with private enterprise when it went bankrupt and had to be rescued by Ludwig II. Many members of the Bavarian Parliament—those who need money for more modest theaters in their constituencies back home in Regensburg or Ingolstadt—argue that further renovation of the Prinze is superfluous, that it would serve Bavaria better to distribute some funds in the provinces.

Those plainer people have another reason for resenting the Prinze: to them it seems nouveau riche. Lots of people were put off by the way the semi-renovation of the Prinze was presented, with a gala and guests in black tie or Dallas-style fuchsia silk—Munich *talmi*, they said when they saw it on television, *talmi* being a contemptuous word for something gold-plated. It is true that the motto that graces the Prinze's portico, "To German Art," is stamped in golden letters and that it takes a *Jugendstil* fan to appreciate the Prinze's frilly details, things like the golden shells that line the Prinze's walls just below its ceilings. When the Prinze comes up in conversation, these same critics point out something else: that the flat-ceilinged Prinze with its deep stage doesn't even have good acoustics. As far back as 1901, when the Prinze opened, a correspondent from the *Allgemeine Musik Zeitung* suggested that hanging curtains over the niches lining the walls within the theater—they sported statues of figures like Mozart and Goethe and, of course, Wagner—might improve things.

Now the *Retter des Prinze*, the "savior of the Prinze," as Munichers call Everding, wants to complete the job and fix up the theater's broken-down stage so the Prinze can do a *Meistersinger* the way it used to. Everding looks a bit royal, certainly a bit unusual: he walks fast, talks fast, and wears black pajamalike outfits that make him resemble the magical characters in the productions he orchestrates. As the *Generalintendant* of Bavaria's state theaters, he supervises the millions of marks of an empire that is, in its way, as mighty as many political empires: the empire of Bavarian culture. In a sense Everding is nothing exceptional; many cultural doyens of his rank are "characters," famous eccentrics. But he has the good fortune to work in Munich, a city that loves to make such figures into kings.

Munichers know that Everding isn't a native Bavarian, that he comes from Westphalian Bottrop and has worked for long periods in other cities. But they appreciate the fact that he belongs to the nation's magic circle of artistic talent, the limited list of names that circulates whenever a "serious" post in the world of German culture opens up. With their usual magnanimity they adopted him when he became their *Intendant*, their theater wizard.

Everding spends a lot of time abroad—one autumn, he directs in Warsaw, Tokyo, and New York. He excuses these absences with the guilty charm of a professional parent: "I may not be there often," he has told the Bavarian press, "but when I am there I am there more *intensely*." For their part, Munichers mostly accept this logic. They accept it for the same reasons they have accommodated other heroes: because they know Everding brings a bit of glory to Bavaria and, just as important, because Everding gives them something to talk about. Like Wagner and Ludwig and even Hitler, Everding conducts campaigns that keep Munich interesting, campaigns that cause squabbles in the *Landtag*, the Parliament, campaigns that he can discuss with reporters and that give publicity to Bavaria when he is in foreign lands. One such campaign is his program to develop a decent state ballet here; another is his school for directors with its hand-picked students. The biggest of these campaigns is the fight to save the Prince Regent Theater.

Restoring the Prinze to its full Wagnerian glory is a royal task. Ironically, it is Bavaria's "royal" mode—its noncapitalist mode—of operation that is turning out to be the biggest obstacle to the Prinze's resurrection. The state long ago replaced the monarchs here, but when it did it assumed the royal role as patron of the arts. Like Ernst von Possart, the first *Intendant* who supervised the Prinze, Professor Everding is finding that keeping the Prinze alive depends on that single source, on getting more money out of culture's venerable patron.

What Everding needs is $26 million more, about the same amount it took to complete the first half of the restoration, and less than half the sum the state spends on its Munich theaters every year. As Everding tells the reporters who visit him backstage on his overseas tours, he's trying hard to raise funds, in the modern style, from private contributors. On the surface, this wouldn't seem like an impossible task. Bavaria has big banks and big firms like Siemens. It even has a new kind of capitalist—for example, the elegant Count Matuschka, who goes around on crutches and who has surprised everyone in Munich society with his strenuous efforts to sell the ossified German business world on the idea of putting venture capital into Germany's unloved middle-sized businesses. Klaus Seidel, Everding's deputy, spends a lot of time on the phone with private patrons and the press, trying to drum up money; he even gives the number of his direct line to those who have helped or who he thinks can help more —for example, the Dresdner Bank. A citizens' initiative in

Munich—a private effort—has spent decades trying to raise funds for the Prinze, but the contributions it received were too few and in amounts too small, mostly gifts of DM 10 or DM 20. However, Gertrud Proebst, the daughter of the Prinze's architect, did leave DM 2.7 million ($1.7 million) for the restoration of the theater when she died, enough to get the recent "save the Prinze" campaign rolling.

Get Everding alone for a moment, though—say, in an opera-house back room—and he will take a nip from his Perrier bottle and confide that most of the necessary millions can probably only come from the state of Bavaria. That is why Everding lobbies the Bavarian *Landtag* when he gets home from his trips. When he's abroad, he likes to praise the tradition of private subsidy in other capitals—after doing his *Dutchman* at the Met, he published an article in a German paper at home with the headline "Why I Like to Work in New York So Much." Like everyone who's worked in Bavaria long enough, though, he knows that some things can be changed and some can't, and that one of the "can't"'s is the German system of arts subsidy. So he smiles and tells visitors that that system is *wunderbar*.

Bavaria is still a monarchy, Everding explains. In the old days, the Ludwigs subsidized culture and that was the way the people liked it. Now the state is the monarch and the state supports theaters—along with kindergartens and hospitals. Question him too aggressively and the lion goes on the offensive and tells you why Bavaria—Germany—is better. The Met can run through rehearsals in record time and still remain a world-class house, but the price for this American system is that the rest of the country, with the exception of Chicago's Lyric Opera and a few other places, is a desert *ohne Kultur*—without culture. It's fine for Britain to cut back its arts subsidy, if that's the way Britain wants it, but Germans are not barbarians and Bavaria needs a theater in Ingolstadt and one in Regensburg—the *Landtag* members are right. Even under conservative governments, Everding will tell you, German states would never think of pulling a Mrs. Thatcher.

The Prinze does, of course, have its allies, both within the government and outside it, and they're happy to report on the Prinze's progress. The new funds—mostly from a Parliament grant, partly from private contributions—paid for the restoration of the *Gartensaal*, a hall with vines painted on the ceiling, which is suited for guest lectures and the city's numerous champagne occasions, and a cleanup of the Prinze's Pompeii-style entrances and its big auditorium. The reconstruction also included the erection of a provisional stage over the old orchestra pit, a "Shakespeare stage," which was helpful in any case because those rocky acoustics sometimes failed actors during their monologues from the old stage. But the money didn't suffice to restore the true stage.

Munichers have a neat, rather geopolitical lexicon to describe the state of affairs at the Prinze. What was achieved so far is known as the *kleine Lösung*, the small solution, and the complete restoration they hope for is called the *grosse Lösung*, the big solution. These terms make history-minded outsiders think of the old debate over German unification. The rhetoricians at the Paulskirche in Frankfurt in 1848 spoke of the *kleindeutsch* unification, a unification without Austria, and dreamed of a *grossdeutsch* unification, one that included Austria. The German talk of "solutions" also inevitably brings to mind a less felicitous event in history: Hitler's *Endlösung*, his Final Solution, for the Jews. (This being Bavaria, no one mentions any of these analogies; most of such events are perceived here as having happened outside of

Bavaria, and what happened outside of Bavaria isn't really history.) The *kleine Lösung* has been enough to keep the Prinze operating—while the Resi, the main state theater, is being restored, the Prinze is hosting a few seasons' repertories.

Bavarians—like most other Germans—are so convinced that their system for preserving *Kultur* is the right one that they don't even mind the fact that most of the productions in those repertories offend or bore them. On a weekday morning a visitor can slip into the gold-and-white hall and watch the dress rehearsal of *Miss Sara Sampson*, a work about a young lady gone astray by Germany's first serious modern playwright, Gotthold Ephraim Lessing. When Lessing presented his play in 1755, written over six weeks in a Potsdam attic room on a wager, the audience cried over the fate of the poor girl Sara at the hands of Mellefont, her evil lover, and his girlfriend, "die Marwood." Almost immediately, *Miss Sara* entered German literary history as Germany's "first bourgeois tragedy," its first tragedy not about gods and mythical figures. It is as such that Bavarian fifteen-year-olds, at least the ones who attend university-tracked *Gymnasium*, study it today. In this production, a director imported from East Germany, Frank Castorf, converts *Sara* into what is meant to be a shocking show, complete with vomiting onstage and sex to the tune of the Beatles' "Why Don't We Do It in the Road." No matter how well done— and this production isn't—such extreme revision doesn't hearten Munichers, who find it, like a similar production in the same season of Schiller's *Die Räuber*, a pointless rape of the original work. "I went to the Prinze to see *Die Räuber*," one academic comments, "and as I expected, I was disappointed."

This *Miss Sara* also probably doesn't suit Everding either.

A Prince in Bavaria

During the same season *Miss Sara* is put on, he records his views on modern German theater in the weekly paper *Welt am Sonntag*. Everding describes a confused Chinese theater technician he encountered sitting next to him on an airplane. The Chinese tells how he'd just settled down with his wife to watch his beloved *Don Carlos* at Essen's new Aalto opera house when twenty men with erections walked onto the stage. Mr. Everding's point is that you don't have to be a prude or a philistine to wonder whether "those intellectual, untheatrical pedagogues" who dominate the Western theater world ought to "think things over a bit." In the same article, though, Everding declares that he still supports such productions in the name of artistic freedom, and Bavarians seem to agree with him: royalty must have its way, and in this case, the royalty is the German theater establishment.

As Munichers will tell you, the history of the Prinze is really the history of how Bavaria expresses its independence and glamorizes, willy-nilly, figures like Everding. While the rest of Germany was clamoring for revolution and reunification, Ludwig I, the grandfather of the king who loved Wagner, gave the town many of the major symbols that made it into a princely capital, building his museum for antiquities, the Glyptothek, the Nationaltheater, and the Monopteros, a small round temple in the English Garden around which Rastafarians in dreadlocks are fond of congregating today. When it came to ideas from abroad—ideas like revolution—the king was less enthusiastic. Faced with opposition set in motion by the anarchic Paris of the communes, he told the world, "My throne doesn't stand on barricades," and defended his monarchy. In the end Ludwig I abdicated; citizens sang the "Marseillaise" to him, but Bavaria still kept its distance from the changes sweeping Europe. A forerunner of the united nation, the first North German confederation was formed without Bavaria in the middle of the nineteenth century, and as Golo Mann notes in his history of Germany, Bavarians cast about wistfully for a way to forge their own future. "In the 60s, South Germans liked to point to the example of Switzerland, a small state occupying a respectable position in Europe. Could Württemberg and Bavaria not do the same?"

Bavaria loves powerful figures, but it is fickle in its love, as the kingdom's relationship with two figures from later in the century shows. Bavaria joined Prussia in the war against France and also for Germany's 1871 unification, but continued to show its fondness for independence. Ludwig II was one of the most romantic kings Europe has known, and spent much more time building his Disney castles at Neuschwanstein and Herrenchiemsee than thinking about foreign policy. Munich's treasury revolted against him and his excessive spending on his maestro, Wagner. But when Ludwig died with his doctor in a deep, weedy lake outside Munich, the Starnbergersee, the whole city plunged into mourning. A witness in 1885 described the scene: "A bunch of black clouds gathered over the quarter. The last car in the funeral procession had just gone, and the military accompaniment had left, when, before the frightened crowd, a mighty blaze of fire traveled down the street to the St. Michaeliskirche and a horrible roll of thunder followed . . . That was the heavenly finale to the earthly tragedy."

Toward Wagner, the Prinze's muse, the one whom Ludwig called his "beloved, holy one," Bavaria proved just as untrue. Summoned by Ludwig, Wagner came here—the composer needed the money—and got what with some kindness might be called a mixed reception. In one of the guidebooks that serves in the Prinze's current regeneration campaign, the author Dieter Borchmeyer recalls the recep-

tion Wagner met in the Bavarian capital in 1864—Munichers were even proud of their dislike of the revolutionary,
loud-toned composer. "No voice for Wagner in the big beer-
Athens," grumbled one commentator, complaining about
the philistine inhabitants of this monument-lined city. Ludwig nevertheless imagined a palace of a playhouse and joy-
fully wrote Wagner of his dream. "I have decided to have a
large stone theater built, so that the performance of the *Ring
of the Nibelungen* can be complete; this incomparable work
must have a worthy space for its performance." Ludwig hired
Gottfried Semper, the architect of Dresden's grand opera,
to set to work on the task, and budgeted five million Gulden.
But Wagner himself wasn't pleased with the grandeur of the
scheme. "How I hate this projected theater, yes, how childish
the king seems to me, that he insists so passionately on this
project; now I have Semper, am supposed to work with him,
talk about the nonsense project! I have no greater pain than
this one that stands before me!"

As it happened, the Semper theater never rose; after
procrastination on the part of Ludwig and some problems
raising the funds at the treasury, Semper handed the Wagner opera negotiations over to his lawyer and concentrated
on building another civic landmark that would give him
less trouble: the Ringstrasse in Vienna. The royal treasury
breathed a sigh of relief, and Wagner retreated to build
his own Bavarian utopia in a quieter spot farther north—
Bayreuth. As a musical mecca Bayreuth quickly became a
success—disciples congregated there to hear the maestro
stage his new works—and when Munichers perceived this
they decided they missed Wagner and wanted to build a
playhouse in his honor. Why should Franconia, the home
of Bayreuth, enjoy a glory that Munich was denied? Their
compromise offering was the Prinze.

Ludwig was dead, though, before the compromise was sealed, and the Prince Regent Theater was built in the name and the spirit of another monarch—his successor, Prince Regent Luitpold, a solid fellow who spoke Bayrisch to his servants, preferred hunting to politics, and safeguarded the throne for his deranged nephew Otto, Ludwig the dreamer's brother. The Prinzregentenstrasse was a grand boulevard, expanding to the east end of the city, undertaken by a private *Aktiengesellschaft* in the new spirit of free enterprise that characterized late-nineteenth-century German cities. At the end of the street builders planted a Peace Angel, four meters high and on a twenty-two-meter pillar for good measure, to commemorate the calm that prevailed under Luitpold's civil reign. The architect of the Prinze, Max Littmann, opted for an amphitheater formation in the auditorium which would be a people's theater where all tickets would sell for the same price and everyone in the audience could see the stage equally well. (Even the seating conformed to democratic principles: the Prinze, the same size as Bayreuth, had 1,028 seats, more than 300 fewer than Bayreuth. This was a gesture to the common man, who, it was presumed, lacked the capacity for suffering displayed by the Wagner pilgrims who tolerated the crowded, uncomfortable chairs of Bayreuth.) Wagner himself by then had already met his *Götterdämmerung*. But, from Bayreuth, his widow, Cosima, turned up her nose at the new Munich project. She disliked its commercial aspect and dismissed the whole affair as *schnöde Spekulation*—despicable speculation.

In typical fashion, Munichers defied the widow and deified her late spouse—Wagner—on their own terms. The building went up. In creating it, the citizens also did their best to deify the civil Luitpold, producing a statue of him as a Greek complete with toga to adorn the Prinze's opening in August 1901. (Leopold himself stayed away from the festive opening to mourn for Kaiser Friedrich's widow. He was, in any case, not much of an opera fan. German archivists report that words failed the regent when he tried to find a way to praise Bavarian chamber singers. In the end the only thing he could think to tell a singer was "You have a very loud voice.") The gala opening was nevertheless a grand one, with bits of greenery strategically placed to cover up the unfinished spots on the Prinzregentenstrasse. The premiere evening featured selections from Wagner's *Meistersinger*.

Dr. Seidel, Professor Everding's deputy and the man who does much of the groundwork in the Prinze campaign, has produced a handsome history of the Prinze, bound in maroon and available to would-be donors to the Prinze cause. He likes to talk also about the early years in the Prinze's history. Luitpold, the ruler who preferred potato soup to finer items on the court menu, was nevertheless no barbarian—he brought streetcars, electricity, and running water to Munich. His reign, 1886–1912, was a good time for art in Munich. It was the period when writers like Henrik Ibsen, Frank Wedekind, and Rainer Marie Rilke and painters like Paul Klee brought the city a cultural renaissance. "Munich shone," wrote Thomas Mann, who lived here. At the Prinze, Richard Strauss conducted his operas *Feuersnot* and *Salome*. In the back pages of the maroon-covered volume on the Prinze, Dr. Seidel even prints a recipe for another cultural product of the Prince Regent era: the Prince Regent torte, a cream-stuffed extravaganza of eight layers, one for each district of turn-of-the-century Bavaria.

As in other times, the Prinze in this period also served as the site of collision between several Bavarian idols. One of the pamphlets printed for the "Save the Prinze" publicity campaign tells how nobility came into conflict with Wagner's

Flying Dutchman. One evening, the opera was already scheduled, the performance sold out, when a princess died, the kind of event which generally meant a mandatory closing for a house with a royal sponsor like the Prinze. Ernst von Possart, the director, made every effort to postpone the burial and save the opera—in vain. He reportedly returned to the theater, dejected, and announced to the singers: "Oh, my dears! We have to refund the money for the *Dutchman.* The burial can't be postponed. The princess won't hold together that long." Another story describes how Ludwig III, the Prince Regent's son, dutifully showed up for a performance of *Parsifal.* After the first act, though, this royal deity turned to his entourage and attacked the other deity in question, Wagner. "Gentlemen, I thank you," he said, departing. "Ten horses couldn't drag me here again."

Dr. Seidel and the others also tell about the less happy days that followed, when World War I sent Bavaria into chaos. The Prinze closed for the duration, and when it opened again, it became Bavaria's only "Prinze": Kurt Eisner, a revolutionary, toppled the last Ludwig. For a few days in the chaotic period around the end of World War I, Bavaria was a *Räterepublik,* its own republic of councils, a small variant of the big new Soviet Union. The state soon reverted to a more modest form of government: in 1919 it became the *Freistaat Bayern,* the free state of Bavaria. The Weimar period was a good one for culture. During these years the Prinze hosted some important premieres: a first performance of Frank Wedekind's *Herakles,* another of Franz Werfel's *Paulus unter den Juden.* But it was not a good period economically: fewer people, in particular fewer foreigners, showed up at the Prinze's doors for performances. The *Bayerische Kurier,* a local paper, mourned the transformation: "How different it was, a few years ago . . . today the program

has changed because of the war." After arduous negotiations—the wild inflation rate made financial transactions
difficult—the private society that owned the Prinze was
forced to sell it to the state of Bavaria for a mere million
marks. The state had replaced royalty and private contributors as the patron to which art turned, but soon Munich
would produce another hero: Adolf Hitler.

When Dr. Seidel gets to the Third Reich in his lecture,
he does what most educated Germans do when they touch
on that subject—he speeds up his words and lowers his voice.
Germans don't mind talking about the Third Reich, but they
often prefer a particular set of themes, themes that play down
the dimensions of their nation's old love affair with the
Führer. Munichers, for example, will tell you about the
White Rose, a small student group who resisted the Nazis,
and its most famous members, the Scholl siblings, who paid
for their resistance with their lives after they were caught
distributing anti-Nazi fliers around the university. Or they
will point out that the subway stop in one of the nicest sec-
tions of artsy Schwabing is called *Münchner Freiheit*, Munich
Freedom, after the citizens who took a stand against the
Nazis at the very end of the war. When cornered on harder
issues—what happened in Dachau, a town outside Munich,
for example—they do, however, acknowledge reality and
describe the gruesome history of that site, the Third Reich's
first concentration camp. Dr. Seidel is no exception—he talks
about how Munich was the *Haupstadt der Bewegung*, the
capital of the movement, from which National Socialism
spread to other cities.

On this subject Dr. Seidel admits that the Prinzregentenstrasse and the Prinze played a particularly important role
for the Nazis; they liked the street's grandeur, and it became
one of their main and favored thoroughfares in the newly

Nazi Munich. Across from the Prinze, in a building where Munichers these days pay their traffic fines, Hitler once kept an apartment. Here he managed the rise and consolidation of the Nazi Party and here also, in the same building, his beloved niece, Geli Raubl, shot herself. (City records for 1923 list him neutrally as "Adolf Hitler, Schriftstell"—Adolf Hitler, writer.) Hitler nevertheless liked the apartment so much that he bought it in 1934, shortly after he became *der Führer*. The black cars of the Nazis sallied regularly down the Prinzregentenstrasse to Riem, where they held parties with complaisant women and bet on horses. A bit down the street from the Prinze, past Käfer, one of Munich's fanciest delis, is the Haus der Kunst, where the Nazis mounted their infamous show of "Degenerate Art," which condemned precisely the kind of Expressionist work that flowered in Munich during the early-twentieth-century renaissance.

As for the Prinze, Dr. Seidel's maroon volume records that it served Hitler the same way it served its other kings: faithfully. One of the first Nazi plays ever presented in the Prinze was a now forgotten work entitled *"All Against One—One for All."* The November 1933 performance was scheduled to commemorate an important event in Nazi history, Hitler's beer-hall putsch in the city's Bürgerbräukeller ten years earlier. Shortly thereafter, Strength Through Joy, Hitler's recreational and social works agency for the common man, took over the Prinze and renamed it the Theater of the People. (The advertisements were presented on attractive orange posters: "The Theater of the People Is *Your* Theater.") Hitler had the Prinze redecorated—red, gold, and white—to give it a more "harmonious" appearance, and removed the "degenerate" Art Nouveau decorations in the two foyers. The Führer liked the theater so much that he planned an extension of the structure, with space for storage and workshops.

But the coming of war interrupted the work—and soon brought an end to the Prinze's Nazi period. When the bombing ended, Munich was 45 percent destroyed, and the only theater left standing was the Prinze.

One of the best ways to get a feel for what the Prinze was like after the war is to spend an hour with Elisabeth Lindermeier at the Max II, a café favored by Munich theater people just down the street from the Hotel Vier Jahreszeiten. Today, Elisabeth Lindermeier is a friendly, energetic widow with rosy nail polish who writes her own culture column in a Munich daily. Back then, she was Elisabeth who sang to Prinze audiences in a pink dress when ration cards were still the rule in rubbly Munich. As a young girl she was bombed out three times with her parents and ended the war in Westerhausen, between air raids practicing Wagner and Mozart on the piano. Frau Lindermeier says that the time after 1945 really was the "zero hour" that the literary folk like to call it. It was a time of hope, particularly for young people. Older singers who had sung in Hitler's opera were unacceptable politically, so there was room at the top for young ones, like her. Another set of *personae non gratae* were the members of the Wagner clan, who had been so close to Hitler that the Wagner children called the Führer "Uncle Wolf." The postwar Prinze's repertoire did, however, include Wagner's music—notwithstanding the fact that SS guards had played Wagner to Jews as they marched them into gas chambers. Ask a Bavarian why Wagner wasn't banned, and—if he likes Wagner—he'll tell you that no unneurotic German will allow the Nazis to co-opt German culture.

Frau Lindermeier is a nice woman, and she looks particularly nice—excited, really—when she sits at a table by the window in the Max II and tells about her career at the Prinze. Things started simply, with instruction from her teacher,

Hans Hotter, and lots of practice at home. One day Elisabeth's teacher sent her to the Prinze's new director, Hans Knappertsbusch—just, as he put it, "so they can get to know you." Miss Lindermeier sang—among her selections were an aria from *Tannhäuser* (the requisite Wagner) and one from *Figaro*. Knappertsbusch engaged Miss Lindermeier— albeit with a warning that she shouldn't imagine that she would be singing "the first violin." The size of the job didn't matter. Miss Lindermeier was in heaven.

What kind of street was the Prinzregentenstrasse in the years Miss Lindermeier went to work there? An empty and hungry one in a Bavaria angry over what the war had brought it, wrote the Swedish journalist Stig Dagerman, who reported in Germany in the late 1940s. "There is nothing in the world more deserted and more desolate than a large empty artery in a bombed city on a cold morning. The sun throws its beams on the gold of the Peace Angel . . . The gardens of the old legations are strewn with pillars in ruins . . . A mud-covered jeep continues its descent . . . Here is the austere center of government where the state governor, Dr. Högner, spends a few hours every day playing with the idea of having Bavaria secede from the rest of the country, a project based on the theory that Prussia, having already brought Bavaria to disaster twice, should not be allowed to repeat the act a third time." Bavaria indeed turned out to be the only one of eleven West German *Länder* to vote against the Basic Law, the West German constitution, on the grounds that states should have more power than the document gave them. But the state did vote to recognize the law, and with that recognition reluctantly joined the Federal Republic.

What kind of house was the Prinze that Miss Lindermeier entered? A poor house, with so little heating the audience sat through performances in coats, hats, and gloves, taking the last off when the time came to applaud. A house where performances took place in the afternoon—the Allied curfew prevented evening events, and in any case in the evening the Americans used the Prinze for the earthlier purpose of entertaining their troops. A house that was immediately sold out because the demoralized Bavarians were just as hungry for music as they were for food. A house whose costume department was so poor actresses had to wear each other's shoes—"a highly unpleasant experience." Nevertheless, it was an environment in which Elisabeth and others bloomed. Her first big role was the tubercular Antonia in *Tales of Hoffmann*, for which she wore a pink dress and was less nervous than her teacher. Knappertsbusch's original warning notwithstanding, she was soon singing bigger roles. If you ask her today what her biggest triumph was, she smiles and reports that she got forty encores for *Madame Butterfly*.

Elisabeth Lindermeier wasn't the only young artist to rise in the world via the Prinze. Another was a young conductor from Switzerland named Georg Solti, who did such a good job, she thinks, "because he was conducting most of the works for the first time." Leonard Bernstein came from New York to play in those postwar years, one of the first signs of reconciliation with the people the Germans had tried to annihilate, the Jews (although in the literature announcing this event Germans still, inadvertently, do Bernstein some disservice—they Germanicize his first name to Leonhard). Economically, these were nevertheless hard times for the Prinze. Before the currency reform, salaries were tiny, although people like Elisabeth Lindermeier could augment theirs by singing for the Americans, who paid in "hard currency"—a carton of Camels or Lucky Strikes. That was worth a pound of butter or some ham. She was able to buy a used BMW-Cabrio, which she drove until a colleague wrapped it around a tree for her in the English Garden. The currency reform that built the nation hurt the theater, because it sent ticket prices so high many Munichers couldn't afford them. Nevertheless, as Frau Lindermeier recalls it, it was an exciting time. She lived as a boarder at number 18, Prinzregentenplatz, right across from the theater and right next door to Hitler's old apartment, so that if she wanted, she could look out her window at his old balcony and thumb her nose at his ghost.

Sadly for Frau Lindermeier and the other *Künstler* who love the Prinze, the rise of Munich that came with the *Wirtschaftswunder* also spelled the gradual decline of the theater. Lots of German businesses chose to locate here—Siemens, for example, moved many of its operations to safe Bavaria and away from risky Berlin. At first things looked good for the theater; it could even add a new foyer and restaurant, in high-1950s style, soon after the war. But the new money meant the city could rebuild the old Nationaltheater, and the state players moved back there, and the Prinze lost its special role as replacement for the bigger houses. It bid goodbye to the world with a New Year's Eve performance of *Hänsel und Gretel*—then the city condemned the building and closed the Prinze.

The *Bürger* who are trying to save the Prinze point out that even then, in the black days after the closing, they were already working to revive the theater. Klaus Schreyer, a professor at the film academy, wasn't involved then, but he spends a lunch at the Mövenpick restaurant in the radio station lovingly outlining the early efforts for the Prinze. A citizens' initiative materialized and launched into a campaign of operas and benefits; its membership included an illustrious roster of sponsors, among them Carl Orff. In the name of saving the Prinze the Bavarian state opera put on performances of sure moneymakers that appealed to Munichers' old-fashioned idea of who they were in the same way the Prinze did: *Der Rosenkavalier, The Marriage of Figaro, The Magic Flute.* The group also produced a special Prinze medallion—gold on one side, silver on the other—for Prinze contributors. Citizens from Munich, from all over Bavaria, and even from Austria—a princely house is a princely house—mailed in their contributions of DM 5 or DM 10 to show, as the text of one speechifier noted, that "the Prince Regent Theater still has its friends."

Part of the new energy came from a simple change: Munich was getting richer. Less showy Munichers get embarrassed when they explain: in the 1980s, Munich became a yuppie city. Bavaria's conservative government earned a solid reputation as dependable, and perks like weekends less than two hours from ski slopes increased in value as Germany turned into a middle-class country.

Foreigners, particularly Americans, came to the Oktoberfest, and the city recovered so well that it could build the subway and those big tentlike structures that housed the Olympic Games. Munichers lately have become a monied group: Dallmayr, the old elegant deli with the restaurant upstairs, still buzzes, but Munichers these days do more serious food shopping at the larger-scale Käfer, down the street from the Prinze. In a single year, Gerd Käfer reported to the compilers of a local tour book, the store bought 5,000 lobsters and six tons of smoked *Lachs* for customers.

This was glitz of a different quality than the glitz of Düsseldorf's Königsallee or the more low-key wealth of Hamburg. It was prouder, bigger, and more provincial. Society revolved around Franz-Josef Strauss, the Prime Minister, and around rich media people like the Burda brothers, who threw parties here and skied with Munich friends in

St. Moritz. German television even produced its own version of *Dallas* about Munich—called *Kir Royal* after the champagne-and-cassis drink Munichers like to down at their cocktail parties. Unlike *Dallas*, *Kir Royal* made fun of its subjects—one scene takes place under a white statue of the lady Bavaria, at a soirée where the Prime Minister, a thinly disguised Strauss, arrives in a helicopter whose motors are so loud that they drown out the words of the television reporter emceeing the event. But the popularity of the show— it returns to television in reruns—was due to its deeply Bavarian message: *Wir sind wer*—"We are somebody." To the rest of the German world it said, "Watch Bavaria."

It was in these years—the 1980s—that the Nationaltheater and the Residenztheater no longer seemed enough for what was becoming a world-class city. Civic initiative remained weak—for all its work, the citizens' group had raised only half a million marks for the Prinze. Soon, though, came the bequest for the theater from the architect's daughter, and then Everding stepped in. The new *Intendant* declared his priorities early in 1982 by moving his offices to the dark, unrestored Prinze. With benefits, speeches, and energy, he rallied the public around the Prinze cause—as part of the fund-raising efforts, one admiring newspaper reports, Everding auctioned off not only original scores of Richard Strauss and Carl Orff but also tenor Luciano Pavarotti's shirt. Restoration experts scratched off layers of paint to find the original blue and yellow of Ludwig Mössel's interior. In a storm of galas and speeches that raised DM 4 million, Everding presented his new Prinze—and immediately tumbled into a typically Bavarian controversy. Everding and his sidekick, Dr. Seidel, presented the theater as the Prinze—a name only some Munichers remembered their parents using for the structure. In the theater's Sleeping Beauty years, another

Prinze had risen in the city: the ice-skating rink by the opera house. As usual, Munichers were reluctant to see their loyalties tampered with and so launched what the local *Abendzeitung* called "avalanchelike protests" against the revived theater's name. Also as usual, the controversy soon calmed —it was, in fact, the expression of citizens' pleasure that they once again had a Prinze to discuss over their *Kaffee*. Propelling "Prince" Everding's efforts was the support of a more established, political prince, Governor Franz-Josef Strauss. Strauss and Strauss's men, for their part, did their work in the *Landtag*, the Bavarian Parliament, a structure located at the end of one of Munich's other grand avenues, the Maximilianstrasse. When the Prinze reopened in 1988, Strauss, the biggest Bavarian lion, was present to dedicate the new hall with Everding.

That it took Everding-cum-Strauss to bring the Prinze to life again tells a lot about the political life of Bavaria. More than any leader in any other German state, Strauss reigned in Bavaria—Bavaria was his kingdom. He set the conservative standard here, and brought it to Bonn, where he caused trouble for his party's bigger brother, the Christian Democratic Union. In 1979 voters roundly turned down Strauss in favor of the more statesmanly northerner Helmut Schmidt. Some voters even felt so strongly they said they'd rather leave Germany than live in a country where the Bavarian lion was Chancellor.

Munich, traditionally a more liberal city than the snow-capped towns around it, didn't exactly love Strauss either. His spluttering, anti-Communist lingo, his opportunism, and his heavy-handedness made many citizens feel he wasn't *salonfähig*—fit for polite society. They rejected him just as the city rejected Wagner a century ago—although for entirely different reasons. To them, Strauss was a fat philistine, a nepotist who helped his son's career in television, an enemy of culture who blocked the candidacy of a famous left-leaning professor when he came up for a chair at Munich University. To a large degree, these criticisms neglected legitimate strengths. Strauss may have appeared coarse, but he was far from unintelligent, confusing aides-de-camp and opponents with his knowledge of aerodynamics until the year he died. He brought Bavaria political power and big business. And he was not a Nazi, which is what the students drinking *Radler*, a mixture of beer and lemonade, in the English Garden liked to call him. The majority of Bavarians loved Strauss, and when he alighted in towns like Straubing for a winter campaign rally, they stomped their moon boots and cheered his every phrase.

Like a true king, the lion left no strong successor when he died in 1988. Politically, at least, Strauss left lots of playing room for a new would-be hero, Franz Schönhuber, the far-right politician who has made a specialty of representing the gripes of "orphaned" groups like the exiled Germans or the *Aussiedler*. Like Adolf Hitler, Schönhuber first turned political in Munich. Hitler's Munich was a chaotic, desperately poor city, packed with vigilantes and putsch makers. Schönhuber's Munich was rich and complacent and dominated by a solid figure of power, Strauss. Yet both of them found their first supporters in the city's beer halls. In the Löwenbräu beer hall students and professors gather to hear their leader in what is called—without any selfconsciousness—the Dachau room. Schönhuber stands for limiting the number of foreigners entering Germany, for German unification, and for pride in the German past. The first part of his platform is not much different from that of his French analogue, Jean-Marie Le Pen. He also says he is not a Nazi, and that his fledgling group really is not even very right-wing. At the moment, what he says doesn't matter too much—his party is only a small one, and its candidate lost the campaign for mayor of Munich. Indeed, shortly thereafter—at midyear 1990—the party started to flounder and ousted him from his position as their leader. Regardless of their names, though, such figures appeal to some Bavarians for old reasons: they represent no-nonsense authority, and simple populism.

It is the absence of a strong king now that is stalling the completion of the rescue of the Prinze. Everyone in Munich knows that the *kleine Lösung*, the small solution, however much hoopla it caused when it was completed, was not quite satisfactory. For now the Prinze can only be a *Sprechbühne*, a stage for plays, and its old orchestra pit hides under the boards of the provisional stage. Just as in the immediate postwar years, the Prinze is busy—as then, it is serving as a replacement for the Nationaltheater, this time for a second renovation. But as it did then, too, it faces a deadline. When the Residenztheater is restored, in another two years, the Prinze again will become redundant. Without pressure from Strauss, *Landtag* leaders aren't interested in making the Prinze a priority.

Professor Everding and others have swallowed their disappointment by opting for realpolitik and creating a third option, the *schlichte Lösung*, or plain solution. The advantage of this program is that it costs only DM 15 million, and so seems realizable, given the size of the donations and what the reluctant *Landtag* is prepared to offer. With a *schlichte Lösung*, the Prinze can again play Wagner.

Whether the Prinze gets a *schlichte Lösung* or a *grosse Lösung* depends this time on whether Everding can develop into a strong enough leader or get a stronger leader behind him. For now, the *Intendant* runs around Munich, his black garments flapping, raising money and telling company boards about the Prinze. Everding is working on the *schlichte Lösung*, but he still hopes for the big solution and he thinks he may get it after the next elections. He continues to jet about and put in appearances on international television, but much of his time remains devoted to the Prinze. Participants on a national talk show devote an evening to discussing the likelihood that Berlin will replace other cities—meaning, for example, Munich—as the new Germany's cultural capital. Everding, a naturalized Bavarian but a loyal one, points out that Munich was a cultural venue before the division of Germany. "And why shouldn't it remain one?"

In the meantime, this fall the Prinze is hosting *At the Goal*, a work by Thomas Bernhard—Bavarians call him "that wild Austrian"—as well as Pirandello's *Six Characters in Search of an Author*, and, sometime soon, Shakespeare's *As You Like It*. As the autumn morning passes, actors arrive through the back door on the Nigerstrasse, a stagehand starts the rehearsal with a clap of his hands, and the sun actually begins to shine outside on the Prinzregentenstrasse. Now no one in the hallway, no one lugging scenery backstage, seems worried. The actors and the stagehands know the truth—even if that truth is a kitschy one, an Old World one. The truth is that no one is sure where the king will come from, when he will come, or who he'll be. But the Prinze—Bavaria— needs him. So, of course, he will come.

5

Barbara's Work

NORTH SEA

DENMARK

BALTIC SEA

Hamburg

●Berlin

EAST

GERMANY

POLAND

●Düsseldorf

●Leipzig

●Bonn

●Weimar

WEST

GERMANY

CZECHOSLOVAKIA

FRANCE

●Stuttgart

●Munich

AUSTRIA

THE TWO GERMANYS

The item in the newspaper runs only nineteen lines, shorter than the masthead next to it.

"With his wife and two children, the master goldsmith Erich L. succeeded in escaping through Hungary . . . Herr L. wants to work again . . . He is looking for tools and machinery that could help him rebuild his life. Of course, the family is lacking everything else as well. Every donation to them is helpful."

A simple first name signs off at the end of the article: "Barbara."

Barbara helps refugees, but she isn't the big welfare office with the grimy elevators over the shopping center in Hamburgerstrasse. Nor is Barbara the Red Cross, which serves tea to arrivals from Poland or the Soviet Union after they trundle off the buses at the camps in Friedland or Giessen. Barbara *is* a charity—and one devoted to a more central group that preoccupies this nation: East Germans trying to fit into Western society. Before the Wall came down, Barbara concentrated on refugees. After November 1989, she *still* concentrated on refugees. For even with that political change, thousands of East Germans continued to wash about Germany, wanderers confused after the disjunction caused by the end of Communism. Like many other organizations in institutionalized Germany, Barbara provides "DDRler" who've risked the step to the richer Germany with concrete items: bananas, blankets, deutsche marks.

For four decades Barbara has also supplied the arriving Germans with a more intangible piece of equipment. Ask the refugees—those who came in 1953 when the guard wasn't looking and they made it to the Bahnhof Zoo in Berlin, those who came in 1989, swimming the Danube and traversing other lands, or walking through Berlin's Brandenburg Gate—Barbara answers German dreams.

Who is Barbara? Most Hamburgers know her from her spot in the upmarket weekly *Die Zeit*. There, for thirty years, she has been presenting cases like that of Erich L. and asking for donations under the logo "Barbara Requests." Some Hamburgers know that Barbara's real name is "Refugee Start Help" and that Barbara is really a group of elegant ladies—*feine Damen*—who work out of an office around the corner from the spires and copper roof of Hamburg's Rathaus. A few even know that there really is a Barbara: Barbara Oster, the daughter of the hero Hans Oster, the general who, in 1938 and 1939, worked with Ludwig Beck to try and stop Hitler from launching his war. It was Barbara Oster who first started taking apples and flowers to the Wandsbek Barracks back in the 1950s, when West Germans weren't much better off than the refugees they visited. She and some other ladies—Jeannette Hesse, the Countess Dönhoff—got together and consulted their husbands and decided on a mission: "to help where the state cannot." Instead of spending half the donation funds on bureaucracy and organization, they would build a lean structure that focused on getting the refugees "started."

It isn't in her charter, but Barbara's charm is really that she does something more. She *recognizes* the refugees, as artists, as workers, as Germans. There's something conspirational about the ladies who work in the top-floor office at the manual typewriters—something that would make a good backdrop for a spy novel. Theirs is a conspiracy to pluck the shards of the old broken Reich from the ground, dust them off, and give them new life. When a musician arrived from the East without his precious flute, the ladies found a secondhand silver one so he could practice his profession in the West. When a pensioner fresh from East Germany mentioned he'd always wanted to tour the world, the ladies got him a passenger's spot on a freighter. It is Barbara who has always made the arrivals feel that they not only are beginning a new life but are coming home.

Barbara Oster herself doesn't spend much time at Refugee Start Help anymore. She married a refugee—the other ladies smile and say it was "our best start"—and is now Frau von Krauss who has a new grandchild in Düsseldorf and lives at Tafelberg. But in the year after the Berlin Wall's collapse, Barbara is facing the most exciting chapter of her life. These days the thousands of East Germans arriving are providing West German goodwill with a historic test. For decades, West Germans begged the regime in East Berlin to lift travel restrictions. As years of barbed wire and the Wall passed, and the mediocre, petty Walter Ulbricht gave way to the equally cloth-eared Erich Honecker, these requests took on a biblical, hopeless note: "Let my people go." Then the West Germans got their wish. In 1989, 348,854 East Germans moved to the Federal Republic—many with no more than a change of clothing and a few tacky East German marks rolled in their denim pockets. After November 9, 1989, more of them came, seeking jobs in West Germany's sophisticated industries. During receiving hours on a Monday a dozen of them are already lined up at Barbara's doorstep.

To the drivers of the blunt-nosed East German Trabis looking for parking spaces around that doorstep, even the sight of it is confusing. Laeiszhof, Laeisz Court, is a broad-shouldered old shipping office, an elegant sign of this city's tradition of water commerce. The blue-and-white interiors present a luxurious contrast to the more utilitarian social welfare offices these arrivals are encountering this week— not to mention the contrast with worn official structures of East Berlin. In East Germany, private charity outside the Church was virtually nonexistent, and the couples entering here hesitate before they step into the wooden elevator that brings them five stories up to Barbara. In the clean narrow stairway before Barbara's doors, suspicion dominates con-versation. The refugees have been directed here—state social workers sometimes send them along—but they sense right away that they are encountering a bureaucracy of a different nature. What is this building, actually, and why would some-one want to "help"? "Help," back home, came only in ex-change for something—information that could aid the MfS, the hated Ministry for State Security, or maybe the Com-munist Party. One gentleman does note with a smile that the building's street address inspired hope—it is Trost-brücke 1, Consolation Bridge 1.

Inside the door, recognition begins. To be sure, Barbara's reception area sports a bank of typists—ladies in cardigans pecking at typewriters. Nevertheless, the place feels like something East Germans *are* familiar with: the private home. They file past a roof garden and into the glass-walled office of Barbara's business director, Marina Wolff-Bühring. A bowl of Ritter chocolates stands on one corner shelf, the worktable is square and simple. "How can I help you?" asks Frau Wolff-Bühring—again, the "help" word. Welcome to Hamburg society.

Private matters are usually what East Germans take up with Barbara. Jürgen and Roswitha from Mecklenburg bring one such problem this Monday afternoon. Back home in Schwerin, Jürgen played the electric double bass in a pop orchestra for twenty-six years. But Roswitha had problems with her kidneys—problems which East Germany's insufficient health-care system couldn't handle. In 1984 they first applied to leave the country, and ever since Jürgen could only work half time. Now that they've finally made it over —without much clothing and without Jürgen's instrument —the West German state is helping Roswitha. But the city forms and applications have no line on them that fixes a problem like "missing double bass." Jürgen gets confidential and tells Barbara the truth—there's no way he could have brought his instrument, because taking it would have got his boss and friend, the orchestra director, in trouble. Barbara understands: a matter of honor. Frau Wolff-Bühring asks a couple of questions—how much does a used double bass made in America go for?—and informs Jürgen that "maybe" he can be helped. The couple leaves and Frau Wolff-Bühring gathers papers together and smiles. She is certain Barbara can get Jürgen the instrument. And she does.

Barbara may be different from other refugee help organizations—different from other German organizations, different from organizations abroad, different from the UN High Commissioner on Refugees. But Barbara's charges are also different from all other refugees. After Jürgen and Roswitha, and after Frau Wolff-Bühring has taken a break to do some paperwork, comes Kerstin with her daughter Ulrike. Kerstin doesn't look like a refugee. She has red cheeks and a black sweater and looks like one of the artsy girls to be found in the neat in-house restaurant at Hamburg's opera. Although she got to Hamburg just this month, Kerstin has already found her way into the theater scene—afternoons, after making the rounds of the welfare offices, she pulls the strings on the dragon puppet in a little marionette playhouse in a black-painted boat right on the Alster.

Kerstin is also what the Western world would call a middle-class girl—even if she does come from East Germany, a nation long devoted to classless society. She grew up in Zingst, a town on a peninsula not far from Rostock, where she grew up among interesting people who talked about books and figures like Fassbinder, the filmmaker. Like girls from Blankenese, Hamburg's choicest suburb, she went to boarding school, where she fell in love with an exotic foreigner—this being East Germany, he was a Libyan. Ulrike's father was another man, but Kerstin and he didn't get along, and when she got tired of living in East Berlin, where there was no *Perspektive* for her work as a seamstress or in advertising, Kerstin even considered marrying a "Wessie" —a West Berlin man who might help her get an exit visa— but, she recalls, it didn't seem a decent thing to do, to marry for political reasons. So when things opened up in Hungary, she took a train to Budapest, and a taxi to the West German embassy, and the next thing she knew, she and Ulrike were in West Germany. Kerstin is such a sociable person—and so is Uli with her too long blond hair—that they made friends at nearly every stop in their East-to-West sojourn. As soon as Kerstin arrived in Budapest, she chatted up another refugee in the train station; here in Hamburg she and Uli have charmed a theater director, Gilbert; in one of the camps on the way Uli played with a child who swam with its parents across the Danube—"and," explains Uli, "only swallowed a bit of water."

To Barbara, Kerstin presents a problem that's familiar in every Germany—bureaucracy. In the camp in Bavaria, Kerstin relates in a rush of words, she found work right away. A local couple offered her an apartment and a salary if she'd sew in their leather factory. But the apartment never materialized, and the couple were "cheap," and when Kerstin took a sick day to visit her sister, who'd made her way to Hamburg with *her* child, the couple fired her and charged her for the apartment—even though Kerstin had never lived in it. Kerstin got something out of the whole adventure—weeks in the country, a purse she has with her this afternoon that she made out of leather remnants from the factory. But now she wants to stay in Hamburg.

The problem is that as a "refugee" she is registered in Bavaria, and she needs Barbara's help to fix it. For Barbara, this isn't a problem—she calls in a fellow from the local office of the Christian Democratic Union, the conservative party, who blinks and shifts in his chair because Kerstin is so cute and honest-looking. Kerstin and Uli and the CDU had already met in Barbara's corridor, and Barbara takes this in. Barbara isn't political, but she knows when to pull strings, and Frau Wolff-Bühring looks over her glasses when she says "the good CDU will surely make an effort with the papers and find Kerstin an apartment. And if there's no apartment to be found," she says, and the CDU man shifts again, "maybe Kerstin can even stay for a bit with the CDU."

The same day Barbara gets to work on Kerstin she also takes on Utz, a twenty-five-year-old with a blond ponytail. Even before Utz has been interviewed, he has made friends with one of the ladies at the typewriters in the reception area. The room where he has his interview, small and with a square table, looks like a suitable site for an evening of bridge. It actually once served as that—the lady of the Laeisz family used it to entertain in after she was bombed out of her apartment in the war and before better times came and the family let Barbara use it. Utz is like Kerstin. He doesn't seem like a refugee, and the problems that happened to him seem as if they could just as well have happened to a West German. Utz wants to study literature. He tried to do that in East Germany, but because he didn't like the Volksarmee and got out of it as quickly as he could, "the Party didn't like me, I guess," and he was put in a food-technology course. No matter how often he tried to change courses, his application was rejected. In the newspaper he points out a picture of "the lady who is responsible"—then Education Minister Margot Honecker, the wife of the man who led East Germany until recently.

West Germany doesn't have "the party obstacle," but it has another one, and that is what is depressing Utz. For the past twenty years West Germany's overloaded university system has churned out humanities graduates, so many that the taxi drivers in Munich or in Frankfurt are often really specialists in Brecht. All the social workers Utz has seen have told him to do something practical—but Utz wants to study literature, maybe some more English, so he can read Jack Kerouac (whose name he pronounces "KA-ru-AH," perhaps because he reads it as he reads Russian). Barbara's help here is mainly spiritual—Frau Wolff-Bühring makes herself Utz's ally in the war against demography. "If that's what you want to study, then you study it," she tells him, and starts advising him on how he can brush up his English with a stay in Britain as a *jeune garçon au pair*.

As Barbara sees it, the difference between West Germans and East Germans like Utz and Kerstin is minimal. She has developed a way to remedy a difference that does count: economics. Refugee Start Help is a classic charity, a charity in the Anglo-American sense, or in the Swiss sense, as Jeannette Hesse, who is a Swiss Burckhardt, sees it. The ladies who run the organization are Barbara, but they are also housewives, in many cases responsible for dauntingly comfy Hamburg households. As the years passed "and we saw how inefficient all the contributions were," Barbara stopped focusing only on stacking used clothes and teapots and launched a new venture: Barbara's store. Barbara's store works like any other store in Hamburg, except for one difference: the people who shop there don't have to pay any money.

What appalls the ladies from Refugee Start Help is that the refugees have little sense of cash. They take the "welcome money" from the federal government, or their welfare check, and they spend it all—in one spree!—downtown at Karstadt. So Barbara decided to do the shopping for them and opened a special "refugee" storeroom in Laeiszhof. Here, on Thursdays, refugees come and select pillows and china, even Villeroy and Boch, from the stock that Barbara has carefully assembled with contributed funds. "It's much cheaper for them that way," says a lady bundled in a coat as she unloads dishes—on her face is satisfaction, the satisfaction of twenty years of household thrift put again to good use. What she doesn't add is that the things in the store are nice and that no one leaves the place with an empty feeling: Barbara received nuts and raisins in quantity as gifts for the arrivals, and, being Barbara, she wrapped them up in individual packets, presented with a bit of gold ribbon. Each refugee who leaves the storeroom gets a packet to take with him— and if he doesn't have a car, Barbara packs him and his new "stuff" into her VW or her Volvo and gives him a ride home.

For others filing through here this Monday afternoon, Barbara's magic consists mainly of encouragement. East Germans who flee the ossified bureaucracy of their regime often find when they arrive in places like Hamburg rules and regulations that, at first glance, look just as impenetrable. Their Trabis can't take West German gasoline, and if they leave them parked in the wrong place too long, the city tows them away. "Honored Ladies and Gentlemen," begins a handout that's pressed into the hands of arrivals at their resettlement centers around the city—and then it orders the confused arrival to visit six offices "in the following order and no other."

Frau Wolff-Bühring worries aloud that she hasn't devoted enough attention to today's batch of guests. In at least one way, though, Barbara is better equipped than ever to handle an onslaught—she has the cash. West Germany today is a fancy country, and it's getting fancier. Every year more Germans read *Die Zeit*, and they see the Thursday notices, and they know the tradition, and this year they handed Barbara DM 10 million. They provided the same amount in goods, and the total is more than twenty times the money the organization had at its disposal in 1982, the year when WRON, the Polish military police, was shutting down Solidarity.

The main reason Barbara is ready to help, though, is that West Germans have always been ready to help East Germans. Back in the early 1950s, when Barbara Oster and the other ladies started talking, Germans from Königsberg to Breslau were arriving by the thousands, and the numbers were just as daunting as they are today. The Reich was gone, nothing left of it but the old *Reichsbahn*, but Hamburg was still a bombed-out town just starting to rebuild, full of widows and unemployed veterans who were discovering they couldn't find a way to fit in. The problems of the Germans arriving from the East were the same problems the West Germans were still confronting: how to start life again, where to make a home, where to get cigarettes.

In some ways, of course, the ladies who formed Barbara were different. As Jeannette Hesse can tell you, they didn't like the Red Cross very much; it seemed to her that half the donations to such groups were swallowed up by the organizations' bureaucracy. Jeannette and her friends were better at *saving*, and when they heard about what Barbara Oster was doing in the Wandsbek Barracks, "we put our heads together and thought of another way." They were people who somehow still had some money, sometimes—Jeannette's husband, George, for example, from his import-export business.

This year Jeannette is turning eighty, but she still has a lot of energy, and she is still happy to tell how Barbara was formed: first the wives got together, but they brought their husbands to the second meeting. "One of the husbands agreed to pay the postage costs. Another person promised to take care of all our printing. And everyone put some money in a pot so that we could pay Barbara Oster to manage the affair."

Even Jeannette Hesse admits that Hamburg is probably the only German city where this kind of charity—private charity in the Anglo-American style, charity in the Swiss style—could flourish. This is a trading city—sturdy brick warehouses dominate its center, not gilded castles, and there's something un-German about the way Hamburg shows off its business. Business is somebody here—somebody who takes care of the city and creates charities to help its citizens. Jeannette is an architect, and she acknowledges the nature of this relationship. "Form follows function" holds here just the way it does in Chicago—that is, the warehouses along the waterfront *look* like warehouses. Just look at Fritz Höger's Chile Haus, a lovely brick building that looks like a ship and is in all the architecture books—and would be even more famous if Fritz Höger hadn't also gotten too close to the Nazis.

There's a cliché about Hamburg's spiritual proximity to England, that when it rains in London the Hamburger snaps open his umbrella, and people like Jeannette Hesse will tell you that the cliché is true. Hamburgers like to think they are more English than they are like, say, those burping Bavarians. Today, much of the fine brick downtown nestled near the Alster, the Elbe, and the sea has gentrified itself into shopping arcades, but this is still a maritime city. The warehouses along the water still hold tons of cinnamon and sugar, ships from the Soviet Union and Hong Kong still line the big port, and even the snappier dressers still favor the sailor look. Jeannette is wearing a pale blue cardigan—it's said one can wear anything in Hamburg, as long as it is blue. Understatement plays an important part in the character of Hamburg's wealthier citizens, citizens like Jeannette. Whereas in Munich wealth makes its presence known in Rolex and gold lamé, in Hamburg even the fanciest couple still arrive in Burberry.

Jeannette's calling card reads "geb. Burckhardt"—née Burckhardt—a reference to the fact that she is a descendant of the historian who, more or less, sent Germans into their mad, passionate affair with Italy. Her Elbe-view apartment bespeaks elegance—a painting by Léger hangs on the wall, along with works by her old teacher, the architect Le Corbusier, and a hundred-year-old Bonsai tree grows like a luxuriant oversized broccoli on her balcony. But the apartment is sparsely furnished, with chrome Le Corbusier-style chairs she herself designed and a few select antique pieces. The front door doesn't even have a plaque with the family name, just a set of initials for her husband's name, "GH."

Jeannette Hesse is mainly retired now—she even stopped writing her architecture criticism when she noticed "the language changed so that it wasn't the language I was using." But she still has that strong Hamburg sense of civic responsibility, and she can talk for half an hour into a tape recorder about Barbara's first famous cases and why Barbara was doing a different kind of work. For example, the refugee who made the trip around the world. "He was a captain, more than sixty-five years old, and we thought of putting him in an old people's home—he certainly didn't fit in at the barracks [where some refugees were housed]. But he objected. 'I didn't come here as a refugee to get stuck in an old people's home,' he said. 'I want to see the world.' " With the help of a husband, Barbara was able to provide such a trip, and he traveled as a passenger on a freighter. Jeannette thinks that was a good ending for the man's life. "When he returned, he always spoke of his 'world voyage,' and he later died peacefully."

One of the nicest memories Frau Hesse has is of the way she herself got involved in going to the refugees and helping them. Barbara Oster was a woman with a strong will, and soon she had all the ladies going to the Wandsbek Barracks. One of Jeannette's assignments was a certain Countess Wedel from Pomerania, whose husband had been shot and who was now staying there, destitute, with her two children. Jeannette recalls that this countess was sweeping the ground, and when Jeannette approached her she turned away—she said no, it was God's will that she landed here, she was sure it was God's will. But Jeannette got her to sit on the barracks bed. She said, "Gräfin, I want to help you," and in the end, through George, her husband, they were able to get things for her, to arrange an apartment for her in an old people's home. The point, though, Jeannette says, is what the Gräfin remembers of this encounter. Thirty-seven years later, just recently, the two ladies met again. " 'Do you remember what we did for you then?' I asked. And do you know what she remembered? She remembered that we had given her a silver teapot. Because that was the one thing that acknowledged who she was."

The ladies who work at Barbara's don't like to have it pointed out, but one reason they have so much sympathy for the old Eastern nobility who lost their lands is that a lot of them are nobility, too, or came from the East and left things behind there themselves. In 1988 Barbara produced a small report of her activities—printing costs funded by special donation, to be sure—in which Marina Wolff-Bühring exhorted members and donors to remember their focus: "We must give the Germans who come from the GDR our spiritual, as well as our practical, support." Of the ten ladies listed as members of Barbara's board, four of them are "vons": Etta Freifrau von Werthern, Jutta von Berenberg-Consbruch, Marie-Luise von Ilsemann, and Leonore Freifrau von Gleichenstein. One of the most important people in the formation of Barbara has been Marion Dönhoff, the countess, who got Barbara the spot in *Die Zeit* near the letters section in the first place and made sure she was able to keep it all these years.

A visit to the Pressehaus in Hamburg provides a glimpse into Gräfin Dönhoff's kingdom. As publisher—*Herausgeberin*—Marion Dönhoff rules the lettered, refined world of West Germany's most thoughtful magazine along with the man who in the 1970s was the nation's most elegant Chancellor, Helmut Schmidt. Today Marion is eighty and energetic, a real newspaperwoman who would rather talk circulation and printing plants than history with visitors in her office. When she's in this mode, there's something in-

ternational about her—she's a German version of the Washington *Post*'s Kay Graham. But she is a Kay Graham with a
special past. *Die Zeit* celebrates her dedication with a headline reading "Prussian, in the Best Sense," an odd German
phrase of praise meaning she has an elegant, ordered sense
of leadership but none of the qualities of the bad Prussia
that produced bossy authoritarians and followed Hitler.

The carpeted halls of *Die Zeit* are the countess's second
kingdom—the first is lost in the East. In her memoirs,
Countess Dönhoff recounts how she left the family home,
the castle of Friedrichstein bei Löwenhagen in East Prussia.
She left on horseback in the cold winds of January 1945 with
her old Spanish crucifix in her saddlebag. That terrible
experience—terrible for "die Dönhoff," terrible for her
family—did have some good results. It inspired the countess
to record her family's centuries in East Prussia in a modest,
moving elegy called *Names No One Mentions Anymore* which
Germans of all backgrounds can pick up at the bookstore
when they get curious about that part of Germany's past.
Her own expulsion also inspired the countess to work for
Barbara—and for all other refugees. This fall, 1989, she's
worried about all the East Germans and where overcrowded
Hamburg with its wobbly tax base can put them, but she's
just as concerned with what Margaret Thatcher is doing
about the Vietnamese boat people.

Having a "von" before your name was, however, never a
requirement for gaining recognition or help from Barbara.
Lots of people in Hamburg—or in other parts of the Federal
Republic—can tell you that the 1988 report is not just talk,
Barbara really wanted to give "spiritual help," and, more
importantly, she looked for some "spiritual" quality in her
refugees. These are people like Werner and Marthe, aged
seventy-one and sixty-five, people who send in marks and a

letter of thankful memory to Barbara at Trostbrücke now, and who live out near the Christuskirche in Eimsbüttel. Marthe was standing with one of her children in her arms in one of the camps when—she still remembers it today— a lady came up to her and asked the crucial sentence: *"Hat Ihr Mann schon Arbeit?"* "Does your husband already have work?"

This Barbara and Marthe talked a bit, and then Werner met the lady, and the next thing they knew he was earning DM 225 a month as a gas station attendant. This was 1953, but even then, Werner says, "you had the feeling they were picking their people, at least a little bit." Barbara was looking for special people, he explains, not drifters, but people with initiative. There were other people staying in the barracks —for example, poor people who couldn't afford an apartment—but Barbara wasn't as interested in helping them. She wanted to help Werner, who left his home just outside Berlin because "you couldn't say what you thought"—then it was even worse, because it was the Russians whom you got in trouble with if you got in trouble. "Stalinism was still the thing then," says Werner when he explains it, and Werner knew about the Russians, he'd been their prisoner to the east in Sagan and had escaped. Everyone forgives Barbara, though, for being a little bit selective, "because she was interested in helping people from the DDR."

What happened to Werner and Marthe after their time in the barracks also became Barbara's concern. Today Werner and Marthe live well, they serve coffee on rose-patterned china, but when they crossed over from Bernau and arrived in Hamburg at Whitsun, they were poor, so poor Marthe couldn't afford the bananas in the fruit and vegetable shop across from the barracks. She would make bread soup—her son Klaus still remembers that he liked it—and Barbara ladies would come by with a little flour, or sugar, to help them make it to the end of the month. When Werner and Marthe got their first apartment, Barbara gave them some beds, and it was with Barbara's help that at Christmas in 1953 Marthe could bake her first "Western" cake. Barbara herself wasn't particularly rich in those days, and after a minute's reflection—after all, it's been thirty-five years—Werner and Marthe laugh and recall that their Barbara drove an Isetta, one of those little three-wheeled numbers that meant its owner had some money at a time Germans didn't yet know they were having the Economic Miracle.

Werner and Marthe tell you that a funny thing happens to Barbara alumni—they become new Barbaras. Werner and Marthe are old now. Werner's war wounds, from a grenade, still ache. They don't travel very much. But they give charity to new arrivals. And their son Klaus—who was so young he can't remember that Barbara arrived in an Isetta —goes back to East Germany to see relatives. Klaus is a somewhat sad figure. He works in a meat-packing plant on the awful early-morning shift and still lives with his parents, but something heroic shows up in his face when he starts to talk about how badly his aunt and cousins have had it back home and what it's been like when he has gone over for a visit. Marthe can talk about it, too, about how when she went back "it was worse than we remembered it," how there was meat in the stores, but only *Schweinebauch*—fatty pork belly—and who wants to eat *Schweinebauch* all the time?

Klaus tells a typical anecdote about the crazy economic life in disintegrating East Germany. His cousin needed a lawn mower, but there were none to be had, and then he heard a rumor that on the other side of Germany they were for sale, so he drove there and bought two and traded one when he got back home. Who can live in such a country? Werner and Marthe and Klaus aren't particularly political people; they say they vote for the conservatives "mainly because they talk less than the Social Democrats." But they feel, and they want to make sure people know, that the right thing for Germany is German reunification. Germany needs to stop being nervous and become a nation again, says Werner. "No Pole would say, 'Poland is lost'—what Germans have been saying all these years about their country —only Germans hide their light under a bushel," says Werner. They're proud to be Germans and being helped by Barbara in the past and helping her now is part of showing that.

These days it's easy to think and talk about "the German question"; reunification is a fact. But Werner and Marthe point out that for years it wasn't an in subject, it was "a dead topic," and West Germans talked instead about being Europeans, or what America was doing to Daniel Ortega and Nicaragua. Those were years in which Barbara proved her hardheadedness—a perusal of a second little booklet Barbara has produced to review her first thirty years' work shows that. The years Barbara helped Werner and Marthe, 1953 and 1954, were easier years because people were moving and the Russians were frightening and it was the beginning of the Cold War. But Barbara stayed alive even in years after that—years when the Wall and the watchtowers along the German–German borders kept so many people from crossing over that her existence seemed nearly irrelevant. The pamphlet provides a record:

"In 1954, 28 members were already active . . . They gave, among other things, coal and vitamin-rich food for children . . . A musician got a set of tails, another a bassoon . . .

"In 1955, 150,000 refugees came from the Soviet zone . . .

Frau Elly Haniel founded a branch office in the Rhineland. She visited the camps and helped to get individual families out of there . . ."

Some ladylike impatience with bureaucracy is evident in some of the entries: "In 1957, 264,500 residents came from the Soviet-occupied zone into the Federal Republic. Refugee Start Help 'started' 563 of them. There were a few who otherwise would have stayed, doing nothing in the camps." Here Barbara makes clear her displeasure at the Federal Republic's narrow definitions of who was trainable and who not: "They didn't fit into any program, because they didn't have any training yet, or were 'too old'—45!"

The pamphlet is matter-of-fact when it reports history: "In 1961 the Wall was built. 210,000 Soviet-zone refugees came West, among them 48,000 so-called illegal cross-overs . . ."

Then came the harder years, when Barbara fought on even though the battle seemed to be over. The year 1962 was particularly tough: the ladies of Refugee Start Help saw their own town, Hamburg, flooded. "In 1962 'only' 21,000 more refugees came. In the wake of the Hamburg flood catastrophe, Refugee Start Help mounted a large clothing and furniture drive. 411 young people got a bridging gift . . .

"1963, after two years of the Wall, we founded our Berlin office on the 'front.'

"In 1964 we wrote a report—yes, refugees are still coming. 1,020 of them got their start with the help of DM 141,578 in cash."

And Barbara changed with the times. Early on, she'd made it her goal to help East Germans—and East Germans alone. But the Czechs' failed revolution in 1968, their barren Prague spring, moved West Germans—in Barbara's case so much so that she changed her mind: "1968 was the occasion of the Czech crisis, and we changed our bylaws so that we could take people from other Eastern-bloc states. We received DM 100,000 each from two publishers, for journalists and other intellectuals from Czechoslovakia. We helped 413 German refugees at the start." Even in the driest years, Barbara stayed tough. "In 1972 we promised to continue to help as long as refugees come from the East! Among others, we 'started' two families of doctors, a stage designer, and a graphic artist with wife and twins." In 1976 Barbara " 'started' a marionettist, who still performs in Hamburg today."

"In 1977 we 'started' a pair of doctors who swam out of the GDR pushing their small son in a rubber dinghy before them . . .

"In 1978 we paid to equip a female jockey with silks, saddle, and bridle."

These days things are different—and so is Hamburg. In one year, Hamburg, a city that is already short 30,000 apartments, is taking in 20,000 or so new Germans from East Germany and farther east, so many that they have to house them on two boats named the *Marko Polo* and *Casa Marina* in Oevelgönne harbor, so many that Schnelsen, a place until recently inhabited mostly by sheep, now features a mobile-home park full of "DDRler." People are panicking a bit. When the numbers really get big one month, the *Hamburger Morgenpost*, a tabloid that people like Werner, Marthe, and even the ladies at the Trostbrücke read, reacts to the prospect of a million new refugees in West Germany with the headline: "Germany Can't Endure That." But even people like Marthe and Werner recognize the paradox in the sentence: "Germany" can't "endure" the arrival of its own people? Barbara's office at the Trostbrücke certainly is overloaded, rarely have so many refugees been seen riding up and down in the wooden elevator, but of course Barbara will handle it, and so will Germany.

One way to see how Germans are handling it—the way Barbara sees it—is to visit Schnelsen, the mobile-home camp near Ikea, the furniture supermarket, on land that used to be a sheep field. On a weekday morning rows of white mobile homes, less dirty than they could be, stand numbered in the mud, but the East Germans themselves aren't easy to find. Most of them are in town, dealing with paperwork. The first thing a visitor notices is that even in these provisional circumstances, the arrivals have set up households. Because it is raining, the tenants have rigged up linoleum awnings at the sides of their mobile homes so that their first West German vehicles, their bicycles, won't rust. In the offices a social worker in a red sweatshirt smokes Stuyvesants and receives visitors who arrive to drop off baby clothes "for the poor Germans." The problem here, explains the social worker, who is tired of folding used clothing, is that this system is unjust. "Everybody," he says, likes the East Germans. "Everything will be fine for them." But the other refugees, the *Aussiedler* from Poland and Russia, are getting pushed aside by their more German fellows. He points out that a hierarchy has already established itself in the camp: a hierarchy in which the East Germans are on the top. Below them are the refugees from Poland, who are officially Germans, with German blood, but whom everyone in Schnelsen, where people are in a hurry, call Poles. Some 377,000 ethnic Germans—if you include the other ethnic Germans arriving from Romania and from the Soviet Union—have come to West Germany this year, so the *Aussiedler* are a big group to discriminate against. Nevertheless, they face discrimination. The "Poles" leave the bathrooms in a mess, the East

Germans say, and the social worker grimaces in recognition—it's true that "German" Germans are more orderly, cleaner. The Poles make a mess of the clothing piles, say the Germans, and they are right there, too. The social worker has sympathy for the "Poles"—after all, he points out, they come from a more "messed-up" economy. But if somebody is going to make it right away at Schnelsen, it is going to be the East Germans.

The social worker is interrupted when a man in a leather jacket arrives offering two spare rooms in his apartment. The man came over from Leipzig himself years ago, and he makes up a small "room available" sign to put on the Schnelsen bulletin board. But the man says he actually wants to rent a room only to someone from Leipzig, and he rejects a blond fellow who comes from the northern part of Germany. Best of all would be a girl, says the man, and "no Poles"— she has to be a German.

Such scenarios chagrin the social worker, who spent many years helping homeless and political-asylum candidates from places like Ethiopia before he got this new assignment. "An East German who wants a job gets one, and he gets an apartment, too," he says. Even an *Aussiedler* may succeed. But with an unemployment rate of more than 11 percent, what will happen to the 3,000 homeless in Hamburg and Third World political refugees like Tamils? The social worker waves his burning Stuyvesant in the air—several refugees waiting to talk to him watch it—and says that all the housing the government is building for the new arrivals still may not prevent "certain people" from making political life ugly in Hamburg. By "certain people" he means the new anti-foreigner right-wing party, the Republikaner, who did well in the polls earlier this year, even before refugees flooded cities short of funds like Frankfurt, Hamburg, and

Berlin. Hamburg already has its share of social unrest; for years the city has been forced to confront a group of squatters who have created a small anarchy zone along a segment of waterside Hafenstrasse. The social worker thinks things will get worse. He thinks that even if the Western half of Germany decides that too many refugees are arriving and tightens the regulations, even if refugees stop coming and stay in their Eastern homes, the number who have already arrived will continue to cause problems.

Predictably, the West German government did change its policy. Before May 1990—six months after the Wall came down—East Germans in West Germany enjoyed all the social benefits of their West German equivalents. After that month, the West German government narrowed the perks and encouraged East Germans to return home. People like the social worker argue that this change reflects a deep-seated indifference to German brethren—an indifference that shows how weak German national feeling truly is.

What many other Hamburgers would tell the social worker, though, is that they think he is wrong. They would reply that it was fine for Germany to spend all those years helping foreigners like political-asylum candidates; it was something postwar Germans had to do to show the world they were different from the Nazis. But now that the East Germans are arriving again, it is Germany's greatest obligation to focus on blood brothers. Germany is also a nation, a nation just like any other, they would say, and it has to help its own people. To outsiders this may sometimes sound Nazi—"*ein Volk, ein Reich*"—but the Hamburgers say that the Schnelsen mobile homes are too full for them to worry constantly about history. To see their logic, the logic of good-will, at work, all you have to do is spend time with Kerstin.

Many of the good things that happen to Kerstin happen

because she is a German and someone people like to help. Gilbert, the man who runs the Europas Marionettentheater, the small playhouse on the Alster, liked Kerstin right away and hired her to hand out tickets and publicize his play about a child dragon during the Christmas season on the Jung- fernstieg. He also lent her his apartment—he lives with his girlfriend, for now, anyway—and lets her daughter stay there even though she might damage some of his artwork. Kerstin soon finds work as a trainee at Karstadt, the department store, not far from her new apartment, but in a way, she writes in a letter to a new friend she's made in Hamburg, all this help is overwhelming. "It is very good in the begin- ning. People have taken care of us, sometimes too much so, so that it took all my energy sometimes to be taken care of so much. It sometimes is hard for me not to seem un- grateful."

Kerstin knows that there are areas where other people can't help—for example, with her problems with Ulrike. Working in the marionette theater is fun, but, she admits, "it is very bad for Ulrike," and she is glad that Ulrike is now going *ordentlich*—in an orderly fashion—to school. All the changes, the camps, the nights in strange beds, were so bad that the young mother began to worry about the child. Ulrike told her, Kerstin writes, " 'I'd rather not be alive.' That gave me something to think about."

Neither can Barbara and the state and Helmut Kohl with his ten-point plan for German unity help in the private affairs of Utz, the young man who wants to be a university student. Already, in his first weeks in the camp, Utz has a chance to visit the university. A lady volunteer is driving him to the campus and will go over the course book with him. He sits in an Italian restaurant, orders cappuccino, and goes over his résumé in English so he can send it out and get his au pair job.

But even though the borders are opening up all over—Utz can't believe what he reads in the paper—they are not opening up fast enough for what has already happened in the life of Utz. It sounds trite, he says, but it is too late—too late for his father, a professor who has "obeyed the system" ever since he got in trouble decades ago for trying to revise the university curriculum. Utz has a sad letter from his father at home in Berlin, but he is even more worried about his girlfriend, a teacher whom he left behind "because she was ambivalent about leaving." What's disturbing Utz today—the day he is planning his courses at the university—is the news that she's in Potsdam Hospital having an abortion, and it's his child. "It's the wrong time to have a child," is what Utz's girlfriend told him, and he can't even phone her. It's impossible to get a connection from a phone booth on the street at Schnelsen to Potsdam Hospital. Utz shakes the newspaper—time is changing everything—but even though he isn't a right-to-lifer, he still can't stop talking about his girlfriend and the baby. "A child," he says, a blond boy fingering a course book in an Italian restaurant. "Isn't every time the wrong time to have a child?"

Barbara knows there are things she can't fix, which is why she calls herself Refugee Start Help and uses the verb "start" to refer to what she does for her refugees. Frau Wolff-Bühring says there have been cases when families have come back, say, after a few months, and Barbara has said all right, this is a second "start." But after a year or two, all the ladies at Trostbrücke agree, you can't come back to Barbara, you are on your own, that is part of the test. "Sink or swim," Werner and Marthe remark when they see a visitor out their door; they know it's a truism but that's still what they say. They think most will swim.

On a Thursday afternoon Barbara's "store" is open, and Kerstin's sister, Silke, comes with her boyfriend to select some things. The lady shows her some lamps—does she want one with a yellow shade or one with a blue shade?—and Silke savors the choice a bit before opting for blue. The main point, Barbara knows, is that a German is a German, and not everyone may like it, and even the Germans themselves may stop it, but for now, Germans are coming together. Silke collects her bundle and gets ready to depart. The rest is detail.

6

The Empire Abroad

The question is whether our republican democracy has so developed and established itself that another form of state is no longer possible. The answer cannot be affirmative, but rather—and not only for Germany—must be negative . . .

At all times and in almost all lands, nobility was responsible for leadership . . .

—From *Kleine Geschichte des deutschen Adels*,
  (*Brief History of the German Nobility*),
  a primer by Robert Steimel published in
  West Germany in 1959

NORTH SEA

DENMARK

BALTIC SEA

EAST
GERMANY

●Berlin

POLAND

●Bonn

WEST

GERMANY

●Castle
Schwarzenberg

●Prague

CZECHOSLOVAKIA

FRANCE

Castle
Worlik ●
●Mikulov

Danube   River

Danube   River

AUSTRIA   Vienna●

A NOBLEMAN'S CENTRAL EUROPE

services the Schwarzenbergs received the palace in Vienna. The city celebrated the line's achievements with Schwarzenbergplatz, a landmark circled on maps by disoriented tourists. Before World War II, the Schwarzenberg realm stretched farther east—Schwarzenbergs served the Habsburg Kaisers by ruling a good chunk of Bohemia.

"Karri," as Prince Schwarzenberg is known to his friends in Vienna, Germany, London, and Prague, is one in a long chain of nobles who stud the modern Germanys like unexpected pearl doodads on a workaday jacket. Who are the German aristocracy? Like their counterparts in France and Britain, they are, above all, a set of clans who have inherited old traditions that would seem to make only a fair fit in a Europe preoccupied with Japanese competition, making Europe a better marketplace, and organizing loans for struggling Eastern Europeans. In Germany, they face additional burdens. Since the war, they've lived under two governments—the Federal Republic of West Germany and East Germany's Democratic Republic—whose highest priorities did not include catering to institutions like the old nobility who were part of the Reich. East Germany officially referred to itself as "the Worker and Peasant State," and Germans on both sides of the border often associated the tradition of blue blood with Hitler and his emphasis on the "master race." A 1959 primer on nobility—the kind of booklet parents with "vons" before their names give to their offspring —contains analogies that itself inevitably remind one of the Führer's eugenecist lexicon. "In the ant world, as in the world of bees, the individual is born to be a queen, a worker, or a drone, and it can't develop up, or down, into another class." Even more damning, in view of German history, is the author's first definition: "Let's make it clear, in the case of the Germans the *Volk* consisted only of free men, for unfree men legally, and in the beginning also biologically, did not belong to the *Volk*."

For the nobility of Germany, though, *all* of the twentieth century meant decline. After the Kaiser abdicated in 1918, and after the West German Federal Republic was established in 1949, these heirs got to keep their names and their properties—when they could afford them. A good number of these nobles, like some of their British or French counterparts, spend their days working to maintain prominence via feverish activity on the social circuit—prominence earned by their forebears through political activities. Their great-grandparents led battles; they lead the commentary in weekly gossip columns. In Germany, the most publicized of such figures of late has been the aging Johannes von Thurn und Taxis. His family is known for founding the Continent's first successful international postal service. Today Johannes is mostly known for his presence at parties in Munich and the spiky punk hairdos of his younger wife, "die Gloria."

Some aristocrats have found work more appropriate to their families' old traditions of leadership. One of them is Otto von Habsburg, the heir to the Holy Roman Empire, the man who could have been king of Austria and Hungary if Archduke Franz Ferdinand hadn't gone to Sarajevo in 1914, or, perhaps, if later that year Germany's officers hadn't devised the Schlieffen plan and invaded France. The republic of Austria hasn't wanted the Habsburgs to be politically active in Vienna, for fear that Otto's return would set off a wave of monarchist sentiments. So he has settled in Bavaria and exercises his imperial-scale talents out of what is becoming Europe's new imperial headquarters: the European Parliament in Strasbourg. Now the changes in Eastern Europe are providing a new role for these old names—in particular, for those who even before the changes fought for more freedom for its citizens. Otto Habsburg returns to Hungary to crowds that hope he will run for President; Prince Karl returns to Czechoslovakia, and becomes an adviser to the nation's new President, Václav Havel. They have no plans to reclaim their old empires. But with quiet political visits and public speeches, they are emerging as an odd force that is shaping the new Central Europe.

To witness the impatient Prince Karl's weekend trajectory into chaotic, revolutionary Czechoslovakia is to see the important role the Old World plays in the new one that Eastern countries like this one are beginning to build. The winter of 1989–90 was a special one for Czechoslovakia—Civic Forum, the broad citizens' resistance, took power, the Communists broke and the nation launched a shift to democratic plurality. Outsiders and euphoric, nervous Czechs sometimes refer to the events of the early months as the "velvet revolution," velvet because, except for a bloody police putdown of demonstrators one November afternoon, the change proceeded without violence. The Czechs soon began to wonder, though, which way their nation will go.

Several weeks later, at the Mikulov border station where Prince Karl waits for his passengers to complete visa applications, post-adolescent guards stand silent and confused behind their glass windows. A digital clock hanging on the wall reads 00:00, as if, this week, even setting a timepiece involved too many political questions. The four zeros, in one way at least, are appropriate: this really is "zero hour" for the new Czechoslovakia. When the prince's VW pulls up at the second border stop, the customs official at first thinks the mustachioed man behind the wheel represents just another routine crossing. As soon as he flips open Prince Karl's passport, though, his eyes widen and he respectfully invites the driver to get out of his car. Prince Karl's car is loaded with documents that, until weeks ago, would have been cause for detention. Now, the guard just blinks when the prince replies that he has books for the nation's leading dissident and future President, Václav Havel. For the next twenty minutes, the guard and his colleagues do hold up the prince and his entourage. But they do so less to interrogate him than to seek his counsel on the nation's economic situation.

Just over an hour later, Prince Karl reaches grimy, gold-rimmed Prague for a personal homecoming. The prince pulls at the steering wheel in excitement as he drives past the city's train station. "Forty years ago, nearly to the day, I left this town from that station," he mutters, as much to himself as to his companions. "I am so glad to be here again now." At the front desk of the swanky riverside Intercontinental Hotel, clerks greet the prince by name. The hotel is full—sorry, no rooms now—a Zairean with a suitcase is told. But for Prince Karl, four rooms materialize instantly. One clerk smilingly hands the prince a bit of cloth with the Czech national colors—blue, red, and white—to attach to his lapel. "For you, *Knizhe*," he says. "For you, Prince."

Prince Karl was born here, and here he was baptized with the Czech form of his name, Karel Jan. With his parents he lived here in town and at the family castle, Worlik, until the Communists closed their grip on the nation in 1948. He's returned to Czechoslovakia a few times recently, but it is only now, when the Communists are leaving, that he can hope he may find a place again in his old country. After checking in, he proudly strolls streets dotted with opposition posters reading *Stavka*—strike—his blue duffel coat flapping. Accompanied by Viennese friends and several reporters, Prince Karl marches along pointing out the sights of his hometown. To his right, the Jewish cemetery, where graves are packed so tightly they look like bundles of autumn leaves.

On his left, a bit later, comes a church—he ducks in for a moment alone to think about the days when he served there as an altar boy. The prince is in a hurry, but for a few seconds he makes one more stop. "That was our house," he says, pointing to a run-down lime-colored mansion on an old street. "Later"—he grins to himself—"maybe we can go to my place"—by which he means stopping at the old family castle, now a museum, miles outside Prague, in countryside Worlik.

This homecoming is important to the prince, but it also means a lot to Czechs. As socialist icons fall here, citizens look back in time for older icons to replace them. The Schwarzenberg name—to which Czechs often give their own quaint pronunciation of "Schwanzenberg," or "tail mountain"—is among the mightiest of these icons. The southern Bohemian holdings of Karl's ancestors before World War I are listed in history books. A Schwarzenberg once possessed: "7 *fidei commissum* estates totaling 315,000 acres, 4 freehold estates comprising 45,000 acres, and 12 castles, 95 dairies, 12 breweries, 2 sugar refineries, 22 sawmills, and several graphite mines. Presiding over 73 parishes with 87 churches, he employed 5,000 peasant families and several hundred clerks."

Even those Czechs who reject the Schwarzenbergs' historical and territorial claims to authority respect the current Prince Karl for another reason. For years the prince has chaired the International Helsinki Federation, the umbrella organization for the national human-rights groups that sprang up in 1977 to serve as watchdogs and monitor Eastern-bloc violations of the human-rights principles proclaimed in the Helsinki Final Act. Prince Karl has concentrated on helping dissidents in Czechoslovakia. He renovated rooms in his family castle at Scheinfeld, West

Germany, so they could serve as a documentation center for Czech literature, and he supported the founding of a small publishing house devoted to producing exile copies of Czech samizdat. Among authors the prince has backed, for example, has been Václav Havel, the playwright-turned-President.

The prince's destination this afternoon is a dilapidated art gallery that is the stronghold of the new central political power in Czechoslovakia, Civic Forum. Students in sweaters stand guard at a passage to the building's rubbish-lined courtyard. Even though, on this afternoon, the Communist regime still rules Czechoslovakia, "guards" like this are necessary, for the media crush on figures like Havel has already begun. Prince Karl is an old friend, though, and he and his companions are allowed to pass. The morning is cold, but the prince leaves his friends outside to stamp their feet on the steps while they wait. Inside, he must advise the sandy-haired, modest Havel on how to pull off a revolution.

The Karl conducting urgent political business here is a bit different from the noble dilettante he likes to present to a visitor in Vienna. After his departure from Czechoslovakia into exile, the prince spent a youth typical of European nobles. For a while, he stayed with his maternal grandmother, a von Fürstenberg. When he was older he studied forestry (a utilitarian enough discipline for someone whose family still retains lands in Germany and Austria) and law (one of his most illustrious forebears, Johann von Schwarzenberg, was a renowned legal expert, translator of Cicero, and friend of Martin Luther). Like most of the modern Europeans who've inherited castles, Prince Karl needed a source of funds to maintain his Vienna edifice. His solution was to turn the Palais into a hotel that quietly and classily markets the Schwarzenberg name. The Palais Schwarzenberg, first built three hundred years ago and subsequently improved upon by the Fischer von Erlachs, father and son Johann Bernhard and Josef Emanuel, is a fancy structure with baroque halls, and it advertises in small pamphlets of the kind designed for the discriminating market. (A discriminating market but an accessible one—reservations for the Palais Schwarzenberg are available on a toll-free number.) The guests who pull up at the castle doors and tread the red carpet decorated with the Schwarzenberg "S" pay 3,500 Austrian schillings, $290, for the privilege of a night here. Rent for a half day's possession of one drafty wing—gold leaf, Rubens's "Remus and Romulus," cupola, and all—is 20,000 schillings, or $1,600, meals not included. Slouched in a red V-neck sweater in a chair in his hotel's bar, the prince puffs on a pipe, only getting up to buss acquaintances on the cheek when they stop by. He "complains" to a visitor about the work the Helsinki Federation has required of him. "If you're as lazy as I am, it's very hard."

This act—and an act is what it is—belies a long family tradition. When Prince Schwarzenberg travels through the Eastern bloc on behalf of Helsinki, he is following an international Schwarzenberg tradition. The Schwarzenbergs first became an important name in Franconia, where Karl's ancestor the legal expert lived. But then they traveled east to the Habsburg empire, a phenomenon which Prince Karl explains this way: "In America, in the nineteenth century, people said, 'Go west, young man.' In Europe, in their time, the motto was different. It was 'Go east.' " Schwarzenbergs settled in Bohemia and Austria and became prominent servants of their empire. The Kaiser built the monument on Schwarzenbergplatz to honor Karl von Schwarzenberg, the soldier who routed Napoleon.

It was Felix zu Schwarzenberg, another family member,

though, who played a role in putting down rebels in Vienna in the 1840s: the "red" Viennese wanted a revolution like the rest of Europe; Felix and other nobles wanted to restore order to the empire. This they did—with Schwarzenberg in the lead. As Prime Minister, Schwarzenberg did more than pull strings—in effect, for certain periods, he ruled. The historian Golo Mann describes the situation in 1848: "As the feeble-minded emperor no longer fitted into the new order, Schwarzenberg got rid of him in December, replacing him with his nephew . . ."

Banging his pipe on the coffee table in his hotel bar, Prince Karl tells of where the Iron Prince, as Felix was known, had an even greater effect, an effect that went beyond squelching a few left-wingers in Austria: he prevented the unification of Germany. At the Frankfurt Paulskirche in 1848, representatives of the German states were meeting to form a German nation. Many of those present, the Prussians among them, wanted to unify the various German states and principalities and make Germany one country. It is a measure of the size of the dreams being dreamed at the Paulskirche that this option was known as the *kleindeutsch* solution, the small German solution. Others dreamed even bigger than the Prussians: their goal was the *grossdeutsch* solution, Germany and Austria together in a single Reich. As Karl—and the history books—tell it, Felix was an advocate of the latter solution. He wanted "a Central European empire, a German league under Austrian hegemony," with, to be sure, Vienna as capital. It was an unrealistic goal—who could imagine an empire that included Zagreb, Cracow, Venice, and Frankfurt? Many argue that the Iron Prince's advocacy of it was merely tactical, that he fought for it without believing in it merely to block the smaller, more attainable project of a unified Germany. In this sense—and even Karl will admit it—Felix zu Schwarzenberg managed to hold up German unity for twenty-five years. When unity finally came, it was war that brought it—the Prussian victory over the French in 1871. As Golo Mann sums up of Felix: "On March 4, 1849, he dismissed the Austrian Diet and decreed the constitution of a centralized unitary state. A stroke of the pen did away with the historic rights of the Magyars, Croats, Italians, and also the Germans. Hencefore the multi-lingual colossus was to be one state, like France."

There's an irony here for Karl von Schwarzenberg, and it's one that he shares with many of the other old names now working to build Eastern Europe. The very cultures his ancestors frequently made it their goal to subordinate, he himself is seeking to help. Prince Karl's explanation of this phenomenon starts with the beginning of the twentieth century—"the beginning of our decline," as he puts it. With the land reform of the new Czech republic after World War I, two-thirds of the Schwarzenbergs' Bohemian properties was taken away. The rest of it was confiscated a few decades later—Prince Karl knows the date precisely, August 17, 1940—by Hitler's Gestapo. As for the family's relations with the latter: "They didn't like us and we didn't like them." Prince Karl's uncle Heinrich was held for a time in Buchenwald. The Nazis didn't quite know what to do with the Palais Schwarzenberg in Vienna. As for the Burg in Schwarzenberg, "there we had bad luck," the ironic Prince Karl says with a grin. The Nazis converted the structure into a *Gauschule*, a district school, for adult political indoctrination where Germans studied such things as Hitler's crazed eugenics program. The way Karl sums up: "When the Americans came in 1945, they saw the swastika flags waving and thought Schwarzenberg [the castle in Germany] was a nasty Nazi nest. So they let it be plundered." The Schwarzenbergs eventually got their castle back—minus all the furniture. As for the Palais in Vienna, two bombs targeted for Vienna's south station had hit it and twenty artillery shells had torn up its park. That damage, as Prince Karl recounts it, turned out to be convenient: the hole from the bombs was where he added a set of new rooms for hotel guests.

What is life in Vienna like these days for a family like the Schwarzenbergs? In part, a life like that of an old noble family in any Western European city. The prince and his wife, Teresa, have been married for many years. He has a sister who lives in New York and a brother in Switzerland. Karl and his wife have moved into a suite of apartments in one wing of the castle—it's on the left as you drive up. The Schwarzenberg family got their Austrian property back after the war, and to this day Prince Karl supervises a forest of spruce and larch in Styria whose annual yield comes to something like 58,000 cubic meters of lumber. But the lord of these lands has a frivolous side, like most of his generation. For his fiftieth birthday party, Wolf Biermann, a legendary songster and East German exile beloved of the German-speaking generation that came of age in the 1960s, reportedly entertained his guests. Viennese acquaintances describe the prince as a man who is rarely alone. When he travels to Prague for this weekend, he brings special guests, a woman who works in the theater and used to be a dancer and a man who is also plugged into the Czech dissident network. "We're something like his court jesters," says the girl in a spare moment in a Czech café-bar waiting for "Karri."

Even with the consolation of "court jesters," though, it's not hard to see that Prince Karl's life is one of resounding irony. Just outside the Vienna Palais, for example—more or less at the prince's front door—stands the Schwarzenberg-platz, where the Karl who vanquished Napoleon sits astride a horse, immortalized in bronze. The large square contains a second tribute to the imperial world from which the Schwarzenbergs come: the city's *Hochstrahlbrunnen*, a nineteenth-century jet-spray fountain. A third monument, on the same square, honors the event that brought humiliation to the noble clan: the tall Red Army monument, built to commemorate the Soviet march into Vienna—and, implicitly, the Soviet occupation of Central Europe that lost the Schwarzenbergs their Czech home. The Viennese, who share much of the sense of loss felt by their erstwhile rulers, have a joke about the statue and the fountain near it. They say the city turns the fountain spray so high it blocks the view of the Red Army statue—and so, for a moment at least, enables onlookers to forget the memory of the Soviets' ten-year postwar occupation here.

Perhaps it was the experience of these injustices that put Prince Karl on the side of those whom his ancestors sometimes oppressed—the side of Central Europe's smaller, sometimes downtrodden ethnic groups. Fluent in Czech from childhood, driven from Prague by Communism, Prince Karl began to work for the oppressed Czechs. His publishing house in Scheinfeld is small, but it had done important work. During the dark years of underground life and prison, dissidents writing in Czech such as Havel received support from the prince and his committees. The documentation center is a museum dedicated to the exile cause. A pamphlet modestly catalogues its exhibits: "complete series of editions of books by Czech exile publishing houses; book production from the exile of the years 1948–68; periodicals of the Czech exile (mostly complete)." Prince Schwarzenberg is not the only financial backer of the project, but his formal name, Karl Johannes zu Schwarzenberg, is listed among the founding members. Czechs associated with the center—Václav

Havel is an honorary member—regard Schwarzenberg as a hero. Says Vilem Precan, the émigré curator of the Schein-feld center: "Simply put, he is a Czech patriot."

What role can a hero like this one have in Eastern Europe? On Saturday afternoon, after closeting himself with Havel, Schwarzenberg and his "court jesters" race to the Magic Lantern, a Prague theater that has served as headquarters for the new, powerful citizens' front, Civic Forum. On the streets, Czechs are busy with their mournful, history-minded expression of their new independence. Posters and hand-written signs announcing strikes hang in shop windows along Wenceslas Platz, the city's long central square; the words *Obçanske Forum*, Civic Forum, hang on doors. The air is cold, but it is the pollution, not the temperature, that makes it catch in pedestrians' throats. Walking through Prague be-hind the speedy Schwarzenberg, one gets the feeling this is an organized revolution, a revolution with an international spirit; Czechs have their own pressing affairs to worry about, but some of them have taken time to think about the op-pressed abroad: a small poster announces a demonstration scheduled for two o'clock the next day to express sympathy for the Chinese students living in the shadow of their post-Tiananmen Square regime. This first week in December, the Communist government has not yet fallen, but television is already free; a TV set in a window near the Magic Lantern plays footage of the violent November demonstration where police encircled and beat citizens, and a crowd on the street stands transfixed, watching the blue and black shadows on the screen above their head.

Inside the Magic Lantern, Civic Forum is celebrating. The ostensible purpose of the evening is to thank the theater for providing a home for the new movement in the past weeks; but the euphoric faces here reflect the greater celebration of freedom almost seized. Schwarzenberg sits in the first row of the hall, his black head visible from any part of the theater. On the stage, a Czech singer in jeans and sneakers leads the crowd in singing a Czech version of "We Shall Overcome" —America's civil rights movement is an important precedent for this group. Corks from bottles of foaming red wine, poor man's champagne, pop toward the ceiling, and people embrace one another. Many of them also embrace an exuberant Schwarzenberg, who soon departs—to spend the evening drinking with Havel.

Sunday morning at the Intercontinental Hotel: a rueful, hound-eyed Prince Karl appears at the breakfast buffet. He had wanted to go to church, he explains to the others at the round table, but the evening with Havel "went on a bit too long." This is an intellectuals' revolution, and today Schwarzenberg will attend a meeting that reflects his particular intellectual contribution to it: the Writers' Union is meeting at yet another theater, the Realistic Theater. At the theater, the coat-check line is full of prominent faces in the twenty-year history of the Czech resistance. Pavel Landovsky, an actor who played in the film of Milan Kundera's *The Unbearable Lightness of Being*, is nearly swallowed by a crowd of eager foreign journalists. What do these changes mean? For Schwarzenberg, the moment is special, because during the dark years he was an important source of support for many of the writers and thinkers in this hall. Sitting in the back corner on the far right—in the last seat in the hall—Václav Havel tries in vain to go unnoticed. One of the first items of business is an unpleasant one. A Civic Forum supporter reads a new blacklist, names of writers so compromised by the old regime that they may not participate in the new intellectual leadership. Another item of business is more cheerful. A writer gets up and lauds Schwarzenberg's help.

In the hall, writers drink fruit juice and negotiate. Many of them are wearing small buttons, produced in Hungary, proclaiming what at this point still seems a wildly dreamy goal: "Havel for President." In the hall, Schwarzenberg, wearing a shirt with a "KS" monogram sewn onto it, stands among writers offering concrete help: he makes a note as one would-be printer for the new free press gives him an order for some basic supplies—like paper. "Write the Truth," reads a sign, a reminder of the difficulty even the most idealistic authors will have in adjusting to the new, freer world of literature. A reporter from the French-language service of the BBC thrusts a tape-recorder mike at Schwarzenberg and asks him whether he has any political ambitions in Prague. Will he move here? "I'll help where I'm needed," says Schwarzenberg, smiling beneath his mustache.

That the rebels here take so well to Schwarzenberg has to do with more than his publishing house, or his Helsinki work, or even his noble name. Their affection derives in no small part from the fact that the Schwarzenbergs have passed a peculiar test, a test to which all Central European nobles have been subjected: their record under the Nazis. In Czechoslovakia, in Austria, in Germany, and in Hungary, even those born after the war know that there were nobles who collaborated with the Third Reich and gave it strength. The participation of noble names in the construction of the Third Reich was serious enough to put a taint on the whole class after the war. Hitler came from Braunau, near Linz, but it is the footage of Nazis marching through the Prussian Brandenburg Gate that people remember, so clearly that even the primer on nobility acknowledges it: "And now to Prussia!" it expostulates ruefully. "A name that one couldn't say after 1945 without provoking a flood of vituperations."

But it was also the German nobility—figures like Colonel Claus Schenk von Stauffenberg—who organized the attempt to blow up Hitler that so inspires the officers at the Hamburg academy.

Schwarzenbergs weren't leaders in this famous July plot. They had declared their opposition to the Third Reich even earlier. People from this part of the world know that despite its German roots Prince Karl's family disapproved of the Nazi annexation of the Czech Sudetenland, that they sided with the Czechs on this matter. They know that the prince's uncle Heinrich spent time in Buchenwald. Like the Austrians who restored Schwarzenberg territories in Austria after the war, they feel special respect for the Schwarzenbergs because they were *anti-fa*—anti-fascist, opposed to Hitler.

But the specific Czech affection for the Schwarzenberg name also has to do with dates that are beyond recent memory, beyond the 1968 Soviet invasion here, beyond the year 1938, when Hitler annexed the Sudetenland. When Czechs look at Prince Karl, they see a modern man—a "Wessie," a man with money, a man whose luggage is labeled with green American Express tags that have his unusual name— Prince Schwarzenberg—printed on them. But they also see someone from history. Their national memory stretches back to earlier landmarks—to 1914, the year World War I erupted, the year the old empire that ruled this place fell. It stretches as far back as Jan Hus, the fourteenth-century theologian who fought the Catholic Church before Luther and represented Bohemian particularism. It is no accident that the statue of Jan Hus in Prague's Old Town Square serves as one of the gathering points for supporters of Civic Forum. Measured against the exacting standards of this long memory, the name Schwarzenberg fares well.

The clean Schwarzenberg record frees Czechs to indulge

in old feelings about royalty, even feudal feelings. The Bohemia of the Schwarzenbergs, even in the early twentieth century, had something of the medieval. Karl's forebears were the lords, and the peasants and the dairymen were their subjects. On his last morning in Prague, Monday, Schwarzenberg prepares a Christmas package to drop off at the house of a friend. Before the prince checks out of the hotel, a young Czech writer in a blue wool sweater seeks him out at the Intercontinental breakfast buffet. Petr Placak is here because he is a writer. He has a mimeographed copy of his novel, called *Medorek*, to deliver to Havel's publishing house. But there is another reason for his presence here. "I am in the opposition, of course," he explains, staring at the letters OF, for *Obçanske Forum*, surrounded by a heart drawn on a piece of paper lying on the breakfast table. "But I do not believe in democracy." For people like him, Prince Karl represents the old ordered world, the world of Catholicism, of Thomas Aquinas. "I'm here because I am a monarchist," he says with a glance at Prince Karl, who is filling his plate at the buffet. "Now is the time for the return of old things."

Far across the continental map, on the other side of Germany, there's another venue where old nobility like Prince Karl is beginning to take a leading role: the European Parliament in Strasbourg. There are, of course, German nobles in the Bundestag—the most prominent of these is the articulate, arrogant head of West Germany's liberal party, Otto Count Lambsdorff—he is a member of the Baltic nobility. But out-of-the-way Strasbourg served nobles with a yen to continue their families' old international traditions. During the 1960s, 1970s, and 1980s, when most of the public viewed them mainly as interesting dinosaurs, Germans with noble names were elected to the European Community legislative body. In those quiet days, that arcane place—it seemed, at the time, a mere weak appendage to the relatively weak Common Market—seemed appropriate for relics of monarchy. Two of the most prominent noble names represented in the Parliament these days are Franz Ludwig Schenk, Count von Stauffenberg and son of the resistance colonel executed by the Nazis, and Otto Habsburg. Within the Parliament, they quietly fought for the rights of peoples from Eastern lands—Stauffenberg for the German minorities to the east of the Germanys, Otto Habsburg in particular for his family's old subjects the Hungarians. With the changes in Eastern Europe and the strengthening of the European Parliament, though, their silent constituencies and they themselves have, suddenly, become "important." Inside the hall, Otto campaigns for tightening Hungarian links to the European Community. In Otto's case, these political activities have become so important that they now reach beyond Strasbourg. Long an outsider to Hungary and Austria, he recently began returning to Hungary—to be greeted as a long-lost king. In the autumn of 1989 Habsburg traveled to Tolna in Hungary, where he delivered a lecture on Hungarian history to a packed auditorium bedecked with flowers. "We are capable of great things," he told an enthusiastic audience. In Strasbourg, the dapper octogenarian Habsburg spends breaks in the red-carpeted corridor outside Parliament's main hall being interviewed by foreign journalists, who come from as far as Hokkaido, Japan. Now that the Germanys are unifying, can the Habsburg heir imagine a union of Germany and Austria, with Vienna as capital? "No, not yet."

For the *Hochadel* and lesser *Briefadel* from Germany, this change brings a new sense of responsibility. Cynics in

Germany—and there are plenty of them—note, with accuracy, that the Eastern European political and cultural vacuums left by socialism vindicate the old, neglected nobility. Now that the Communist idols are falling, one observer notes, "every fellow with a 'von' before his name is coming out of the woodwork." But the change also helps to give Germany a new definition, and an opportunity for the country to come to terms with its old roots. Families like the Schwarzenbergs, or the von Kleists from parts of East Germany, or the Bismarcks who had lands around Berlin, are wakening from what seems a long sleep now that the status of those lands is suddenly changing. There's even a move afoot to reclaim old properties. The West German *Frankfurter Allgemeine Zeitung*, for example, reports that aristocrats are popping up at their old doorsteps to take stock of what remains of their former homes and properties. West German property owners of all classes, not just nobles, are busy making jaunts to the East to research inventory lists they will later present when they take legal action to reclaim their property. Often, though, actual restoration is not what old nobles are seeking. Many of them are from the generation born into the Federal Republic and have never known possession of those lands. However, they are grateful for the new appreciation of their families' history. Even for those nobles who have no lost lands in the East to rediscover, there is a new pride and a new sense of responsibility. Thus in 1990, year one of the new governments of the East, some of the frivolity that characterized the German nobility in the 1980s begins to abate and a new seriousness takes it place. Prince Johannes Thurn und Taxis and his wife, Gloria, for example, start the year with the presentation of a special exhibit on six hundred years of Thurn und Taxis economic achievement; the exhibit focuses not on the family's social accomplishments but on its contribution to modern postal systems and the improvement of communications in Europe.

Prince Karl von Schwarzenberg, for his part, is not seeking the return of his dairies or his fiefdoms. He wants instead, as he says, to "help" Czechoslovakia. Soon after this December, with Havel miraculously in place as President, his role crystallizes. Schwarzenberg is named to a special presidium—a kind of presidential advisory service—that will counsel Havel. He is eventually accorded noble quarters again: this time, counselor's rooms in the presidential castle of Prague's hill. Havel eventually even makes him chief of staff. After his exciting weekend with Havel in revolutionary Prague, he gets into his car and heads home to Vienna. At Mikulov, it is as if the border between Czechoslovakia and Austria is already breaking down. There is no line of cars waiting, and the automatic mechanism that lifts the striped barrier pole is out of order, so that the Czech customs guard must lift the pole for the prince by hand. From his car window, the prince espies a friend in a Fiat with Czech license plates passing the other way. The two converse for a bit from their vehicles, and even as the other driver starts moving toward Czechoslovakia, Schwarzenberg cranes his neck and continues talking after him. "Whew," he sighs, exhausted but a little regretful, when he finally gives up and moves his own car into Austria. Vienna may be where Schwarzenberg lives just now, but more and more, Prague is becoming home again.

7

A Jewish Place

NORTH SEA

DENMARK

BALTIC SEA

East
Prussia

Hamburg
(19,794)

Berlin
(172,672)

G E R M A N Y

POLAND

Cologne
(16,093)

Leipzig
(12,594)

Breslau
(23,240)

Silesia

Frankfurt
(29,385)

Nuremberg
(8,603)

C Z E C H O S L O V A K I A

FRANCE

Bavaria

Munich
(10,068)

AUSTRIA

SWITZERLAND

○ JEWISH POPULATION
IN GERMAN CITIES
BEFORE THE WAR

Like most downtown residents of most cities in the world, the people who live in Berlin's Bleibtreustrasse feel squeezed. Bleibtreustrasse was fashionable in the days of student revolt here twenty years ago, when young people gathered in its bars and cafés to plot German revolution, and it is fashionable—too fashionable, residents say—in the more gentrified, crowded city that is Berlin today. Students dressed in black from the nearby Technical University spoon Tirami su on street corners. The heavy doors of the big shouldered *Gründerzeit* buildings swing open and closed as Berliners conduct a day's business. Tourists turning off from the Kurfürstendamm hog the few spare parking places in front of apartment buildings. High rents mean boutiques vending bespangled Milan fashion are replacing the butchers and shoemakers who used to serve the neighborhood.

These days, the Bleibtreustrasse squeeze is provoking a peculiar neighborhood battle. Space is so scarce in this district of the city, Charlottenburg, that three grammar schools packed side by side near the corner of Bleibtreustrasse and Mommsenstrasse must share a concrete playground hardly big enough for one school. When the city announced plans to expand one of the schools, neighborhood parents revolted. Meetings led to petitions, and tempers ran high. "They want to encroach on the only playground that exists in this neighborhood. Should they be able to do that?" asks a mother of a boy who attends the neighboring school. "I say no."

The mother's argument might make sense—if the school that wanted to expand were not a Jewish one, and if the country it wanted to expand in were not Germany. Forty-five years after the war ended, West Germans and their government still lower their voices when they talk about "Jewish questions." The parents of West Berlin's Bleibtreustrasse did march—and the Jewish School will nevertheless be adding classrooms on the school grounds. Eventually, the city has promised, the school will move away from the Bleibtreustrasse. Until then, this neighborhood conflict bubbles on, one of a series of disputes involving Jews in different spots across Germany.

What are Jews doing in Germany anyway? Blunter Germans ask the question, but most often it comes from Jewish observers, outsiders looking in on Germany. What Jew, when he can live in Switzerland, Britain, the United States, or Israel, chooses as a home the land that nearly succeeded in exterminating his people? There is a synagogue a few blocks away from the Jewish School, on the Pestalozzistrasse. But it is one of only seven such religious meeting places remaining in Berlin, a city that boasted nearly two hundred synagogues and prayerhouses before the Nazis first took terror public with Kristallnacht. Some 175,000 Jews lived in Berlin before the war. Today the Jewish community of West Berlin counts some 5,000 Jews. Many fewer live in East Berlin. Some Jews are here because of a family connection— through a mixture of accident and planning, they find themselves back in the family's old home city.

The majority of Berlin Jews, though, are new to the city. They are from the Soviet Union, a deposit from the great

>184<

wave of Jews that has poured from the Soviet Union in the past twenty years. No matter how long they have been in Berlin, though, Jews here confront a difficult task. They must face the constant reminders of that abnormal crime, the Holocaust, as they try to live a "normal" life in modern Germany. For the Germans of the city, the task is also difficult. Germans may choose either to forget or to remember the Holocaust, but in most cases they like to do it on their own terms. The Jews and the problems they cause intrude dangerously on a subject most citizens would prefer to relegate to the safe category of memory. With German reunification before them, most Germans, in any case, are changing their focus from the past to the future. The united Germany they are building frightens Jews. No matter how many assurances they receive, a new big Germany, a Germany like the Reich, threatens this community.

To spend some time at the Jewish School in the Bleibtreustrasse is to inspect the odd arrangement Germans and Jews have created for their life together in postwar Germany. The Jewish School is housed in a nineteenth-century-red-brick building that faces the sidewalk. Arriving for the first day of school one September morning, parents and children find that steel gates and a guardhouse block the main entrance. Fifty years after Kristallnacht, Jews in Charlottenburg still need police protection—not from rightist thugs this time but from terrorists taking revenge on Israel in Europe's streets.

Pass through the gates, though, and the feeling of danger disappears. Above all, this Jewish institution looks like a normal German school. Just like parents anywhere, the parents of the new first-graders snap photos and take videos of their offspring. Just like six-year-olds starting school all across Germany this week, the Jewish children carry a long

tube of paper full of school supplies—a cornucopia of equipment for their new lives. Germans take all stages of education
seriously—they even have a special name for the first day of
grammar school, *Einschulung*—schooling-in.

The Jewish School is no exception. Children and parents
gather in the auditorium of the Uhlandschule next door—
their own building has no auditorium—for official greet-
ings from the school director and their new teachers. Older
children from the "grandpa" class, the fourth grade, sing
a song about the school bus to welcome the new students.
The only source of tension this morning seems to be the
refreshments—the school has a little reception planned for
the parents afterward, but when the ceremony starts, the
local bakery still hasn't delivered a fruit tart ordered for the
party. By the time the two new classes have wandered off in
two uneven lines behind their new teachers, though, the
tension is gone—the tart has arrived.

The reception takes place in the kosher dining room of
the Jewish School itself. Eight-year-olds clad in bright Esprit
colors play Ping-Pong with teachers in shaky high heels.
Inside the red-brick building, most of the signs are in German: "Girls' Toilet," "Director's Office." Red Riding Hood
and figures from other German fairy tales decorate the bal-
ustrades on the staircases. At first glance the only sign of a
difference is a series of wobbly Stars of David painted in
tempera hanging across the first-floor hall: the artwork of
one of the Jewish School's younger pupils.

Enter the classrooms, though, and the feeling comes: this
is a special place. Before the war there were pockets of Reform Jews who studied the Bible in German—some of them
were in Berlin. But the main language of Central Europe's
shuls was Yiddish. In the Jewish School on the Bleibtreustrasse, German is king. Hebrew retains the status of "pri-

mary foreign language," and Yiddish, the old ghetto language, is nearly absent. Toni, the religion teacher, hands out photocopied pages from Genesis to her pupils. "*Das Glück der ersten Menschen in Garten Eden dauerte nicht lange*," reads a child slowly for the rest of the class. "The happiness of the first people in the Garden of Eden didn't last long." The children gather the pages into small folders—page by page, they are making their own "Bible." Why doesn't Toni use a German textbook? Surely, the land where Luther, the great leveler, first opened the Holy Book for the common man produces children's Bibles in German. No, comes the answer, the Jewish School couldn't find the "right" primer—and so constructs its own. At lunchtime, teachers surrender control to child minders, most of whom are from Israel.

The atmosphere in the kosher lunchroom is indeed a bit like the children's section of a kibbutz—noisy, casual, friendly. "*Baruch atah adonai*," chant the children. "Praised be Thou, O Lord." Then they are served spaghetti on red-and-white-checked tablecloths. A girl spills a glass of milk and goes to the kitchen to get a rag to mop it up. A lost black yarmulke, the Jewish skullcap, lies on one of the steps of the school's stairs—a ritual symbol dropped in haste by some boy gone out to play.

The difficulties only show up later—for example, in class 4B. 4B, along with 4A, was the pioneer class at the Jewish School—these children were the first first-graders when the school was opened four years ago. The list of the names of the students in class 4B bespeaks confidence, seventeen Jewish names given to children who are growing up in Germany: Jaron, Jonathan, Ron, Nathan, Andreas, Benjamin, Samson, Vadim, and Zachi; Nurit, Catherine, Raksalana, Ruth, Dorit, Natalie, Avital, and Rinat. The nine-year-olds a visitor meets when he enters the class on the fourth floor also seem confident. They even show off a bit by providing the guest with a textbook and a pen.

Meet them one by one, though, and the fragility emerges. Raksalana is a flirt, and tells the guest right away that she likes to be called Lana. "Raksalana seems to me an awful name," she says. She was born in Berlin, but her mother, she says, is from Russia and Israel. Lana takes ballet and piano lessons, but her mother works nearly all the time. A mini-adult in a pink jumpsuit, she shows off her eyelashes and talks with junior sophistication about her family's financial situation: "Things are a bit tight at our house." Her father lives in America, and Lana doesn't think her mother will marry again soon. "My mother always wonders who will marry first, me or her, and she says it will be me."

Natalie and Peter, twins, are also in 4B. Natalie counts off a bewildering collection of half- and step-siblings and then explains that her father has a new wife. Is her father a German? "No, he's not a German, he's a normal human being!" she says—with a Berlin accent. Natalie describes herself as a "half-Jew." Peter is a bit stingier with information, but does mention that he has grandparents in both Poland and Berlin. Does he have a passport? "Of course," he answers. What nationality? "No idea."

Ruth is taller and darker than the other girls—both her parents come from Riga, in Latvia. She lives with her grandmother, who works in a slot-machine casino, and gets to put on "a tiny bit of makeup" when she visits her grandma at work. Sensing the question mark in the visitor's mind concerning this kind of employment, Ruth gets protective: "Only good people work there." Ruth's mother lives in America and has a new baby: the baby's name, Ruth informs wistfully and precisely, is Melissa Ann. Ruth has a German passport. "But I'd rather have an American one."

Ask about the German school across the playground and all the children reply with the same story—about a *Krach*, a fight, that took place last spring between children from the Jewish School and the kids attending the school across the yard. Children from the other school "attacked us," one girl explains, and giggles. "They said 'shit Jews' and we said 'shit Christians' right back." Predictably, the accounts of this event vary a bit. Another child, interviewed separately, reports that the other children said "fuck Jews." A third child says no words were exchanged at all. A fourth child, more careful, puts the interschool quarrel in perspective. "We have fights with the ones from the other school, sure. But we have just as many fights with other classes right here within the Jewish School."

Such precocious wisdom is the product of practice. Micha Barkol, the school director until the summer of 1989, says the children have been interviewed so many times by reporters from the curious German press, radio, and TV that they are "media professionals." In a sense, too, the children come from families that are "professionally Jewish"—many of their parents work for the Jewish community, or feel the link strongly. Benjamin, one of the most cheerful of the bunch, is up-front about his political connections: "My father knows Mr. Galinski [the leader of the Jewish community] very well." Their schoolyard fight with the children from next door is an unpleasant story, but in the context of, say, hostility between Muslim and Christian children in Britain, or Flemish and Francophone children in Belgium, it can hardly be classed as large-scale hostility.

The most striking thing about the children from 4B is not that they are Germans, or Jews, or Russians. It is that they are lonely. The girls fingered a visitor's wedding ring and tried it on their fourth fingers; the boys are distant at first but reluctant to leave when an interview ends. Of the eighteen children in the class at the end of the last school year, only four lived with both their parents in a traditional family. The rest live with a single parent, or with a grandparent, or in a new family. In part, this sad record has nothing to do with religion. The Jewish School belongs to a special class of school in Germany, the "All-Day School," which offers a combination of school and day care; children can be delivered at six or seven in the morning and don't have to be picked up until the late afternoon. This format is, naturally enough, attractive to divided families, or confused ones, or professional parents. In addition to being a special school with "special" benefits like religion lessons, Hebrew lessons, and kosher lunch, the Jewish School also is, it is fair to say, a bit of a social dumping ground.

That Jewish parents at the Jewish School so often fall into this category is, however, no coincidence. The Soviet families who arrive in Berlin often enter what other Berliners consider shady businesses: gambling, trading in smuggled icons or smuggled beluga. At the school and from parents, visitors hear stories of the tight links in the Soviet émigré community—how families who met in the resettlement camp in Austria years ago still phone each other when they have goods to fence. One child's father recently returned from a period of absence—in prison. Marriages made in the leap of departure from the Soviet Union often don't survive, just as they often don't survive the three-way tug for Jews exerted by Israel, America, and Germany.

This displacement creates a gap between the Jewish children and average German children that is "enormous," according to Sabine Meinhardt, the homeroom teacher for 4B.

"They're sweet children," she says, and she isn't merely being sentimental—fewer Frisbees fly and fewer children shriek in the Jewish play area than in the play area of the "German" school next door. "But they can't concentrate." The children of the Soviet families, she says, are in a "stress situation." "On the one hand, a lot is demanded of them. It is the typical immigrant story. They have to produce." On the other hand, she says, they are often "spoiled." She recalls inviting the children to a breakfast at which she served the children five kinds of *Brötchen* rolls made from white flour. "That wasn't enough for them, and it made me not want to have them over again. They said, 'Where's the caviar?' "

The Jews who teach at the school have the same kind of families as their pupils. The religion instructor, Toni, and her daughter form a typical Jewish School family—no father. Toni describes her plans to give religion lessons to a few children from the minuscule Jewish community of East Berlin. She thinks that will be more exciting than giving lessons in more mundane West Berlin and that the children might show up regularly. The project has an additional attraction, she admits embarrassedly, "because at the moment I have a boyfriend over there." German Jewry, in any event, is so emaciated that even when there was a surplus of teachers, the school had to fall back on non-Jewish teachers, like Sabine Meinhardt of 4B. The German teachers say they like the school—Frau Meinhardt recently had a chance to leave, but chose not to. But some also complain that they can't criticize the school directors, who come from Israel. If they did complain, they might face charges of anti-Semitism.

A typically mobile family—albeit an atypically unified one—is the family of Nurit, a girl in 4B. Her father, Michal Bodemann, was born in Germany, grew up in Italy, went to university in America, and teaches in Canada. Her mother,

1

1

Robin Ostow, is an American who has worked in Canada. Over Argentinian beef and fresh green soup at the Bodemanns', the family explains where they belong. The answer comes slowly, but eventually is clear: Nurit and her sisters sing the Canadian national anthem. Michal's brother is more of a true Berliner—he practices medicine here. Both social scientists, the Bodemann parents earlier did fieldwork in Sardinia, and when they returned there recently, Robin said, "it was such a relief to be away from Jews and Germans!" The Bodemanns are both on research projects that will keep them here for at least a year. They enjoy being in Berlin— but do so with the protection of their profession and their North American background. They employ a social-science vocabulary in their criticism of the school—they are afraid the school director might be too "authoritarian." Michal Bodemann has made it his mission to fight the authoritarian forces within the Jewish community.

Part of the "displaced" feeling among the children, though, comes from the school itself. "Last year, they told us the school would be expanded," says Susanne, a teacher. "But then it wasn't. Now they again say they will expand, but who knows if they will." When the school opened four years ago, the teacher surplus in Berlin made it easy to find instructors for this special school. Now, though, that surplus has suddenly disappeared. Teachers at the Jewish School say they plan to stay, but that for them staying is "a sacrifice." At the *Einschulung*, the first-day ceremony, Heinz Galinski, the leader of the Jewish community, promised that the school would find a new home, probably outside of crowded Charlottenburg. But many of the parents of class 4B have already decided that their children will leave. Frau Meinhardt regrets this. "The pity is, those leaving are the best students."

Some of the Jewish School's problems are problems that

afflict the entire Jewish community in Berlin. Two blocks down from the Jewish School in the Fasanenstrasse stands the Jewish Community Center, a modern structure diagonally across the street from the Kempinski, one of Berlin's most elegant hotels. Like the Jewish School, the Jewish Community Center is a bit of a fortress—on an average weekday policemen patrol its steps. Unlike the Jewish School, though, the Jewish Community Center seems joyless on the inside. Suspicious men with Russian accents at the reception desk stop visitors to ask where they are going, even though the center has both a library and a kosher restaurant which are open to the public. A broken bust of Moses Mendelssohn, the leading secular Jewish philosopher, stands noseless at the center of the front hall. The library is made of friendly blond wood, but the librarians themselves ignore visitors and carry on loud and lengthy conversations with each other about personal affairs—like how to get tickets to the Philharmonic. An officer of the community is happy to meet with a visitor for an informational discussion on the history of Germany's Jewish community. But even this innocuous exchange can take place only on condition that the director's office "is not informed that I met with you, please."

Such grimness is in part forgivable, for it is the grimness of determined mourning. Once, a large domed house of prayer, the Fasanenstrasse synagogue, stood on this site and seated more than 1,700 people. Now all that's left is a single arch, around which architects confected a new structure thirty years ago. Some of the books in the library testify to the rich Jewish contribution to German culture—to the Hannah Arendts and Moses Mendelssohns—others record the systematic German destruction of those people.

Partly, too, the defenses are against the postwar onslaught: the surly staff seem to be telling the casual visitor, "We are official, we have a right to be here." As hard as they may try to resist it, visitors to the Jewish Community Center who have also been to the other side of town find themselves making a cruel comparison. The Jewish Community Center has something of the bossiness of the aging totalitarian regime that until recently controlled East Germany. One reason for this is that Germany's Jewish community is also a gerontocracy; some Jews say it even has its own version of Erich Honecker, the East German leader who collapsed with his regime.

Like Honecker, this community's leader, Heinz Galinski, has been in power for decades. Like Honecker, Galinski was formed by years of incarceration under the Nazis. Only a year's difference in age separates the two men. The seventy-six-year-old Galinski is a mandarin-faced figure with a large, unlined forehead. A survivor of concentration camps like rocky Mauthausen, he returned to Berlin after the war in search of living relatives and found that none were left. It is thanks in large part to Galinski that Berlin has this center and a Jewish adult education program, and it is thanks to Galinski that the Jewish School exists. Galinski maintains excellent relations with his nation's government—he calls on the Chancellor, or the opposition, whenever he wants to, and is almost always warmly received. And like the wobbly, graying leaders on the other side of the Iron Curtain, Galinski has a pack of loyal followers—in particular, older members of the community, who had the same hardening experiences, and the Soviet émigrés, whom he has provided with jobs, social help, and general support.

Of course, it is unfair to compare the two men. Erich Honecker oppressed his people. Heinz Galinski merely fails to inspire his. And for many members of the Jewish community in today's softer times, this iron survivor of the Ho-

locaust is not the right leader. At a spring meeting of the
Jewish community, the tension is palpable. Members of the
Jewish community—men in suits, women with upholstered
shoulders and Rolexes—sit in an upstairs hall waiting for
Galinski. When he comes in, a delicate man in a gray suit
and red tie, people fall silent. The first item of business is
an issue on which everyone present can agree: that the rise
of a new right-wing party in Berlin, the Republikaner, is
alarming. "We are a people with a good memory," says
Galinski, and heads around the room bob in accord.

In a recent city election, the radical-right party polled
enough votes to make it into Parliament—and enough to
bring down the city government and give a chance to rule
to the city's left-leaning Social Democrats and a far-left
group called the Alternative List. Galinski calls for the pub-
lication of conversations with concentration camp survivors
—maybe that will remind the German people of the evils of
right-wing radicalism. A rabbi in a corner covers his eyes
with his fingers. It is hard to tell whether this gesture reflects
simple fatigue or a great and sad weariness in the face of
the new threat.

However, when Galinski says that thanks are due to the
departing mayor, a conservative, people start grumbling:
many in the room are glad that Berlin now has a left-leaning
coalition. The discussion gets rougher. A younger man gets
up and complains that architectural plans for a new Jewish
project were presented to the community as a fait accompli,
"without our participation." There are complaints that Galinski is using his office to campaign for reelection to the
Jewish community leadership. Galinski snaps back, an old
man attacked: "I admit my mistakes, unlike you." At a campaign rally just before the May election, the Jewish community's small opposition, the Democratic List, presents its

platform and its criticism of the Galinski regime. "Too little to do with Israel," complains one opposition candidate to the board. Artur Süsskind, a real estate developer who looks a bit like Paul Newman with a curly mustache, complains about the school: "The education of my children is being neglected." A young girl stands up and complains that the community doesn't do much for her: "I'm unemployed. Why isn't there any Jewish employment office?" A blue-and-white leaflet for the opposition even makes a pitch that's aimed against the heavy Central European fare offered in the Jewish Community Center restaurant. "How would you like . . . to have a restaurant . . . in which 'bagel' and 'lox' are not strange words? Why not a deli à la New York?"

Less humorous complaints are leveled against what is seen as Galinski's political opportunism. When the new Social Democratic mayor was elected, one speaker reports, "the telefax of congratulations from Galinski arrived before the others, even that of Erich Honecker." Someone else blurts: "This community center is an expensive mortuary. It is conceived as representation facing outward [to impress Germans], not as something for the Jewish people." Late in the meeting, someone gets to the heart of the matter: The Jewish community doesn't want Galinski to be its entire identity. He portrays himself as if he were indispensable, so that it seems "as if we would all have to emigrate tomorrow if he were no longer chairman." Another man's comment: "A stricter form of dictatorship exists nowhere."

Galinski wins the Berlin Jewish community's May elections, but the community's small opposition group gains additional seats. Over the summer, news of a new intra-Jewish squabble makes the rounds. Parents of a child from the Jewish day-care center neglected to collect him one afternoon when the center closed for the day. A teacher took the child home with her, and was reprimanded for it—mainly for insurance reasons, for under German law such an action entails a risk. The appropriate—and frighteningly cold—alternative is to hand the child over to a state foster home for the night. The latter course was backed by the ever-correct Jewish community, and in particular by Galinski. The problem that caused the whole affair was a typical Jewish Berlin problem. The child's parents live apart, and had got their signals crossed on who was to pick up the child. Nevertheless, the father, who later retrieved the child, criticized the community leader bitterly. "I'm not going to let a Galinski throw my child in the dirt."

Galinski himself does little to mitigate such hostility. To be sure, the seventy-six-year-old has his good moments. At the school's first-day ceremony, he stoops forward a bit to tell a row of seated six-year-olds about his own first day of school some seventy years ago: "I didn't sleep the whole night before, I was so nervous." During an interview at his Fasanenstrasse desk, he speaks convincingly of the political difficulties of defending Jews and foreigners in Germany. His forehead shines like a beacon as he worries about the rise of the Republikaner and argues that it is far more serious than the rise of other new far-right movements, like the National Front of Jean-Marie Le Pen in France. "It is more serious here because Germany has a different history than France." Later, on another occasion, it will be Galinski who raises the issue of Jewish worries about a united Germany. He publicly attacks Chancellor Helmut Kohl for failing to include a statement of regret about the past in the draft treaty of German reunification. For this, most Jews—inside and outside Germany—are grateful.

Galinski's pursed lips and his impassive gaze also give a second, unpleasant impression—the impression of arrogance. He receives even sympathetic visitors coldly, and gets angry as soon as the questions seem to be getting difficult. Asked about the justification for state subsidies to the Jewish School, Galinski turns cranky. "Our system is entirely different from America's. In Germany, we have no separation of church and state." To the question of why Jews want to live in Germany at all, Galinski provides a compelling answer: "There were 540,000 Jews here [in Germany] before the war. We have to continue that community." The problem is that he barks out his answer with an anger that is inaccessible to postwar generations.

Such a hard line has already done much to estrange many Berliners—Jews who have turned their backs on the Jewish community. But no matter how much the Galinskis of Germany may infuriate younger Jews and Germans, they represent something important to them: a last link to the old, lost community of German Jews. However much the survivors suffered in the war, the ones who are here still chose to live here because, if only by default, Germany is their home. Most of them may spend their days uneasily, even defeatedly, but as long as they live in Germany they are still spending them as Germans.

One of the most appealing examples of this sort in Berlin is Inge Deutschkron, an energetic lady whose description of her underground life in Berlin can be found in a bookstore on the Kurfürstendamm, just around the corner from the Jewish School. Inge, a teenager, survived the Nazis because she had a counterfeit ID card and a lot of luck; after the war, she abandoned Germany for England and a new life away from dark memories. Later, however, she returned to Germany with this astounding analysis: "England is a cold land, and after that experience, I needed warmth, not foreigners." Since then she has worked in Bonn as a correspondent for an Israeli paper and lived in Israel for many years. Now she is spending time again in Germany. "Though there are a lot of things here I don't like, I still am a German."

Figures like Frau Deutschkron are important because they are rare in Germany. Jews who survived the war, who speak German and read books and remember the old Social Democratic movement, do exist; but they exist mostly on New York's Riverside Drive, or in London, or in Tel Aviv, and not in Germany. Jews who live here and like to recall the vast wealth of that old culture take consolation in people like Frau Deutschkron. She is the living proof that what they remember really did exist. But as important as Inge is to Jews here, she is more important to average Berliners. Frau Deutschkron is invited to a community *Kaffee und Kuchen* meeting, and the attendees—old and young—applaud when she agrees to tell her tale. Snappily dressed in a black-and-white suit, the small, red-haired woman finds herself surrounded with attentive listeners.

The audience looks down when she tells of the difficulties the Nuremberg laws imposed on Jewish families. Wearing a yellow star meant the teenage Inge and her boyfriend couldn't meet anywhere—not in parks, not at the swimming pool, both places where signs hung reading *"Juden Unerwünscht."* They laugh with Frau Deutschkron when she tells how her mother made it through Berlin's final war days giving private tutoring—unwitting SS fathers hired her to drill their backward children.

When Frau Deutschkron finally falls silent, the room is full of emotion. The older Germans want to speak the most. A shaky old man tries to explain to Frau Deutschkron: "We didn't even know what a concentration camp was." An older lady tries arguing with her: "You yourself admitted you didn't know what a concentration camp was." A young woman gets angry: "I want one old person here, just once, to admit that he knew what was going on." (In some senses, they are all admitting it—by turning up at an event where a survivor is the advertised guest.) And all the Germans, even the bitterest younger ones, leave the hall remembering Frau Deutschkron's words: "During the war, we suffered because of Berliners, but we also survived because we had a lot of help from Berliners."

The best evidence of the Berliners' commitment to Frau Deutschkron can be found at Grips, the city's children's theater. For months the theater has been showing a version of Frau Deutschkron's memoirs, *I Wore the Yellow Star*. The work's dramatic title is *From Today On, Your Name Is Sara*, a reference to the Nazi regulation that every Jewish woman take that name. *Sara* is a lively play, but many Berliners are worried they will never get to see it. It is so popular that tickets are as scarce as those to hear a concert conducted by maestro Herbert von Karajan were before his death. Frau Deutschkron herself is amazed at the work's success. In her small Berlin apartment, decorated with a few choice pieces of Biedermeier furniture, she recalls: "I went by there one morning and saw a long line of people. I asked a child, 'What are you waiting for?' He said, 'We're waiting to see *Sara!*'"

Berlin isn't the only city that provides Germany with such figures. Frankfurt is the home of Marcel Reich-Ranicki, an older Jew with a scratchy voice and a birdlike eye who reigns as one of Germany's leading literary critics. Reich-Ranicki is a German Jew in the "old style"—he was deported to Warsaw and only survived the war by going underground with his bride in Warsaw. After the war, Reich-Ranicki rejected Germany. He changed his childhood surname—Reich—to the more Polish-sounding Ranicki to escape affiliation with Germany. He also went to work for the Communist regime. But eventually, in the 1960s, he, too, came back to Germany—and took the name Reich-Ranicki, a sort of official sign of the reconciliation of his German and non-German self. Reich-Ranicki's sharp, elegant pen shortly elevated him to regal status in West Germany's powerful, hierarchical literary establishment. From his post as literary editor at the respected *Frankfurter Allgemeine Zeitung*, Reich-Ranicki for decades made and unmade young German authors. Some of them hate him—*"der Literaturpapst,"* the literature pope, is what they call him—but most admire him. Why did he come back? Like Deutschkron, he sees himself as a Jew, and like her, he also sees himself as a German. "I am in Germany because the language in which I work is German," he told me in an interview years ago in his Frankfurt apartment. "Not even Adolf Hitler," he said, "could come between me and the German language."

Today, Germans can often be heard, publicly and privately, regretting what the massive loss of most Jews like Reich-Ranicki meant for German culture. Holger Börner, the governor of the state of Hesse, made a typical statement when his state concluded an agreement with the Jewish communities in 1986. "Our state became poorer through the destruction of the Jewry." Germany's intelligentsia express their sympathy by giving their children Jewish names: Sara and even Joshua are popular baby names. The same mother who complains that the expansion of the Jewish School will hurt her son has named that son Benjamin.

In the late 1960s, 1970s, and 1980s, a vast body of literature dedicated to portraying Jews and their relations with Germany sprang up in Germany. Ninety-nine percent of it described Jews sympathetically and attacked Germans, an impressive ratio given that these books were written in German, for Germans. Foreigners encountering this phenom-

enon often wonder whether America or Britain would work
so hard to document its own guilt if it had been the country
that created the Holocaust. Much of the protest of the generation that grew up in the 1960s, the unruly generation,
was founded in children's deep anger at their parents'
crimes. Peter Sichrovsky, a Jew born after the war, provides
some of the most compelling documentation of young Germans' feelings in a collection of discussions entitled *Born
Guilty: Children from Nazi Families*. Most of the subjects he
interviews express anger or confusion over their parents' acts;
few justify them. Even those who do, as Sichrovsky records,
still feel compelled to think about the past.

For non-Jews, selfishness plays a part in this study of the
Holocaust. In mourning the Jews, Germans focus on their
own loss as much as on the loss suffered by the Jews. One
such elegy so offended Jews and many Germans that it
caused a major political scandal in Germany: a speech by
Philipp Jenninger, president of the Bundestag, on the anniversary of Kristallnacht. In his speech Jenninger spoke
of the "fascination" that National Socialism had had for
Germans, and he described the escapist attraction of anti-
Semitism. The Jewish community, as well as many non-Jews,
took offense. The international press described Jenninger's
speech as Nazi. Jenninger, the general feeling was, had chosen to talk about the murderer at the funeral for his victim.
For his approach—not really an incorrect one, but one that
Germans felt was inappropriate—Jenninger paid what might
seem an unduly heavy price: he lost his post and the support
of his patron, Chancellor Helmut Kohl. "A Jew should have
been speaking there," says Michel Friedmann, a Frankfurt
Jew, when he analyzes the strange case. A Christian German
had a similar opinion: "Germany needed a concentration
camp survivor to talk on that day."

A Jewish Place

However much Germans value "survivors," one thing is
clear to them: these are symbols they won't have for long.
The greatest concentration of them in Berlin can be found
at the Jewish old people's home on the Dernburgstrasse, a
quiet street on Charlottenburg's algae-lined Lietzensee.
When the Jewish community holds elections, it makes the
old people's home a balloting place—a way of ensuring that
even octogenarians get some voice in community affairs. But
this constituency is dwindling. West Berlin's "young Jews"
are mostly Soviets, here from Baku or Georgia or Moscow
on the visas the Soviet Union has been issuing for the past
two decades. They often don't know much German, and
their Soviet education so deprived them of education in Jewish tradition that they often know less about Judaism than
the average educated Germans.

One of the best places to experience Berlin's new Jews,
the Russians, is at the annual community Seder. Passover is
a gay but serious affair, involving a considerable amount of
ritual. Over several hours, with many interruptions for
prayer, the Jewish family retells the story of the Jewish ex-
odus from Egypt. A slightly wobbly Heinz Galinski presides
over this ceremony, and though he and the Seder leader
stick faithfully to the text, most of it is lost on the hallful of
guests—probably because they themselves are preoccupied
with the trouble and work involved in their own recent ex-
odus. Parents and children, some of whom attend the Jewish
School, chatter right through the account of the plagues visited on Pharaoh and the story of how God gave Jews bread
in the desert—a tower of Babel at a Jewish holiday gathering.
Patience plays an important role in Seder: sweet red wine is
poured early, but ritual requires that guests refrain from
drinking it until later in the ceremony. A family from Riga
ignores this rule and starts downing glasses right and left—

a Seder faux pas. No new wine arrives. A small crisis looms. On the surface it seems this "Russian" problem stems from sheer rudeness, but it soon becomes clear the problem is sheer ignorance—and an impressive indifference to authority. An embarrassed mother sitting to the right of a more experienced Jew explains: "Maybe my husband should do what you do, because we don't know what to do." The husband in question, though, displays no interest in religion lessons. Here in the West, he seems to be saying as he enjoys himself, people are free!

An older lady from Soviet Russia at the Seder gives a first clue as to why 3,000 Russian Jews would choose to live in the former capital of a land that was doubly their enemy— their enemy as Jews and their enemy as Russians. "I looked around in New York," she says, "but I have a son in Germany. I like it better here because it's a bit more like home. It is tamer than America." As the world's richest social welfare state, West Germany has an impressive financial net ready for foreign arrivals and candidates for political asylum, a class into which the Russian Jews have heretofore fallen. From the start the families here enjoy rent subsidies, free schooling, unemployment money—albeit at the cost of facing the considerable challenge of fitting into demanding, overeducated West German society. The Jewish community also provides a helpful crutch for these arrivals and has become an organizational center for Jews. In the Jewish Community Center, a visitor is as likely to hear the *"Privyet"* and *"Zdrazvitye"* of Russian in the hallway as he is likely to hear *"Shalom"* or *"Guten Tag."* Vadim, the newest member of class 4B, provides an example of the practical implications of such problems. He comes so recently out of the Soviet Union that, his teacher reports, he is accustomed only to the

Cyrillic alphabet. "In the first days of fourth grade, he didn't know—yet—how to spell his name."

Such disconcerting scenes are part of a transposition that is taking place throughout West Germany—one that comes on the heels of a greater one that followed the end of the war. To be sure, a few German Jews—like Frau Deutschkron or Marcel Reich-Ranicki—made their way "home" to West Germany. But many of the Jews who landed in big cities like Berlin came from the East, from the Soviet Union or from Poland. The pale remainder of Central Europe's Jewry, they spent months or years in resettlement camps in Berlin and throughout Germany, and many of them, too exhausted or too old, chose to stay. Less educated and less assimilated than Germany's Jewish community, they were a group that historically had faced the disdain of more worldly Europeans—including and in particular Germany's assimilated Jews. Before the Third Reich proved the irrelevance of their snobbism, German Jews often made it their business to point out the differences between themselves and their bearded, exotic neighbors. One of the most elegant drawer of such distinctions between his kind and the "Ostjuden" was the satirist and poet Heinrich Heine. Heine, of Jewish background himself, sums up his encounter with Polish Jews in his 1823 account "On Poland": "The external appearance of the Polish Jew is terrible. A shudder runs down my spine when I remember my first experience (just beyond Meseritz, it was) of a Polish village inhabited mainly by Jews . . . I saw the pigsty-like hovels which they inhabit and in which they jabber, pray, haggle, and are miserable." Heine goes on to write of the Polish Jew with "his filthy fur, his populated beard, his smell of garlic . . ." but also turns against his own more assimilated confreres in Germany: "I value the Polish

Jew much higher than many a German Jew who wears his hat in the latest Simón Bolívar fashion and his his head filled with quotations from Jean Paul."

In the case of postwar Germany, these Jews scarcely had the resources or the energy to set in motion the kind of Jewish cultural life that bloomed here until the late 1930s. It's important, too, to remember that the Jews who settled in Germany were camp survivors—generally tougher and less elevated than the more delicate souls who perished in the work gangs or in the gas ovens. These Jews were part of the hard-core black market in cigarettes and dollars that flourished in Germany in the lean postwar years.

Marcel Reich-Ranicki, the literary critic, lives in Frankfurt, but, he reports, most of the Jews in the Frankfurt community are not Jews like him. "Most of them never learned to speak German properly," he says, noting that they speak in the "singsongy" fashion that betrays their Yiddish and Slavic antecedents. The result is a Jewish community in Frankfurt that, like the one in Berlin or Munich, can find little in common with the lost Jews whom it is replacing. "I'll give you an example," Reich-Ranicki says. "The Jewish community here has cultural events—meetings with speakers. The meetings are packed, we always draw a big audience. But eighty percent of the audience isn't Jews. It is Germans who are interested in Jewish culture, or in culture. The Jews who live in Frankfurt, though, are not interested." Back in the 1940s, 1950s, and 1960s, these few Jews stayed in part because Germans made it worthwhile to them—through compensation money and through help.

There is, of course, an answer to this: the new Soviets provide the Jews with a future. Zachi, Vadim, and Ruth will all grow up to be Jews in Germany, and perhaps will be able to maintain the failing community that has power in Ger-

Jews are in Germany because West Germany has offered them a world-class financial packet of social welfare services—in a sense, the local and federal governments have "bought" themselves a Jewish future. The funds at its disposal are at the heart of the problems facing West Germany's Jewish community today. As a regular part of their tax bill, West Germans contribute to the church—a modern-day tithe that is an important support for West Germany's big Protestant church, but also for smaller groups like the Jewish community. More than three decades ago, the government, in addition, launched the massive program of *Wiedergutmachung*—compensation, or, literally, making good again —for survivors of the Holocaust and their families. These moneys subsidize, for example, the Jewish community's gloomy cafeteria; other funds pay for the Jewish School. All this provided a temptation, and eventually the Jewish community was tempted. In 1987 Werner Nachmann, a leader of the Jewish community, died. He was buried with much ceremony and speechifying—a typical announcement in the newspaper eulogized him, listing the awards he had received from the West German government and German communities for his service to the nation. "The deceased leaves behind a gap, a gap that can hardly be closed," read the announcement. Shortly thereafter, investigation of his finances yielded evidence that Nachmann had indeed left a gap: of DM 30 million in federal funds earmarked for compensation payments to Holocaust survivors. The item received mainly subdued coverage in the West German press, which is usually eager to pounce on a scandal—the press protected the Jewish community. Such protection, however, is not forgotten. It comes dearer and dearer in a Germany whose press and television began looking on Israel with a hostile eye in the early 1970s, and has been almost entirely critical since the war in Lebanon in 1982 and the bloody progress of the *intifada* more recently.

In a way, the West German Jews face a more difficult task than their East German counterparts. East Berlin has a large Jewish heritage. When the Wall went up, the Jewish cemetery at Weissensee, one of Europe's largest with 115,000 graves, fell behind it. But the Jewish community there is a small one, old and tired. And the Jews who do live in the GDR have for the most part turned away from their roots. In a book on East German Jews, Robin Ostow, the mother of Nurit in 4B, records the reasons German Jews gave for their return to Germany. They came back, they said, because they were socialists. For them, being a socialist in effect "erases," or puts in second place, the problems of being a Jew in Germany.

One such East German can be found in the Bodemanns' kitchen: Vincent von Wroblensky, who teaches philosophy at the East Berlin Academy of Sciences. He comes from a family with a long socialist tradition—as early as 1905, his grandmother attended the socialist congress in Amsterdam. His mother lived in France during the war, and for a while Vincent and his brother stayed in a Jewish orphans' home in Berlin. In Robin Ostow's book, he recalls: "It is to be noted that Golda Meir was the director of the orphanage . . . Of course, Golda Meir wanted to include us in her [plans for emigration to what was then Palestine]. But my mother, who regarded our stay in Toulouse as temporary and who planned a move to Paris, was insistent. She told Golda Meir, 'I am not a Zionist, I am a Communist, and I don't want to emigrate to Palestine, because it is not my home.' " Instead, the Wroblenskys returned to Berlin. The case of another East Berlin Jew was more explicit: "I am a Marxist and a Communist and as such do not have religious ties." The most famous of the people advancing this attitude is doubtless Gregor Gysi, a friendly-looking divorced lawyer in his early forties. The bespectacled intellectual Mr. Gysi looks more like a professor from New York University, and before the fall of Erich Honecker he defended East German dissidents in court and occasionally advised his country's small Jewish community on property matters. When Erich Honecker fell and the Wall cracked, this East German Jew agreed to take on the role of one of history's bigger scapegoats: he became the head of East Germany's tired and already failing Communist Party.

For West Berlin Jews, the priorities are less clear. As long as they choose to practice their religion, and as long as they choose to do it with subsidies from the state, they will have to do so in the long shadow of the war and the Holocaust. When the war ended, the community began a long migration to what became the new state of Israel, a migration which created a tight link with that country. Throughout the 1970s and in particular since the war in Lebanon began in 1982, that connection has brought them increasing problems. For Germans, the Israeli aggressions have come to be seen as untenable—in the eyes of some Germans, the *intifada* deaths of Palestinians at the hands of Jews are comparable to the deaths of Jews at the hands of Germans during World War II. In 1983, German television aired a dramatic version of the trial of Adolf Eichmann with a live audience. The show was interrupted when a woman in the audience stood up and screamed: "Beirut is the same. Television should report the war crimes that are happening today"—not the ones that occurred in World War II. The actor playing Eichmann was so appalled that he left the stage. "Excuse me, but I can't go on," he said. The producer tried to record the audience's disquiet, but finally decided to turn the camera off.

A Jewish Place

Both older and younger Jews now have an even bigger worry: German nationalism. Even before the Wall came down, new evidence of growing German confidence, and even racism, began surfacing in Germany. Examples of this could even be found in the backlash over Mr. Jenninger's ill-fated address to the Bundestag on the anniversary of Kristallnacht. Jewish anger, and government anger, over this speech in turn provoked bitterness among German conservatives, who resent the power of the international Jewish community. Although Heinz Galinski's voice was only one of many raised against Mr. Jenninger, in many eyes he was responsible for Mr. Jenninger's ousting. At a meeting of young conservatives in Braunschweig, an organizer told a table of lunch guests that originally Mr. Jenninger had been invited to speak—"then Mr. Galinski prevented it."

Even before the protesters in East German Leipzig started chanting "Germany, One Fatherland," Jews had already found something to worry about in Berlin: the rise of the Republikaner, the new right-wing party. They have reason to be worried. The party's first leader, Franz Schönhuber, used the community's errors to launch an attack on them. In public, over and over again, Schönhuber called the Jews "a fifth occupying force"—after the Allies—in Germany. The Republikaner have been around for a few years, but it was only in the Berlin of the Jewish School that they first broke into Parliament, in a city election in January 1989. The far-right party got 7.5 percent of the vote here, and then proceeded to win seats in other cities and in the European Parliament in the June elections.

The Republikaner's popularity faded a bit the following year, and they do not pose an immediate danger to a small group on the edge of society like Germany's Jews. The Republikaner are first and foremost a sign of discontent within

Germany's ruling conservative party, and as such are a natural electoral phenomenon. Years of being in power turned the Christian Democrats into a party of the center and this alienated some of their extremist supporters. On the left the same phenomenon brought down the Social Democratic Party when it was in power in the 1970s—in the end, the Social Democrats' demise was in large part due to the Greens. Franz Schönhuber claimed he was "no anti-Semite." On public occasions he took care to mention that his first wife was a Jew, a fact which earns him points in Germany but which rings hollow in foreign ears—we hear old Nazis saying, "Some of my best friends were Jews." But there was a large gap between him and his more straightforward constituency—a gap that eventually brought about his ouster. Jews recognize that most of the Germans who vote for parties like the Republikaner back an anti-foreigner policy strong enough to make Jews more than uncomfortable.

That a party like the Republikaner is doing well in a time of economic prosperity is a sign that extremism has disquieting strength in Germany. Historically, far-right and far-left parties were born of economic hardship—the Nazis grew out of the hyperinflation of the 1920s and first came to power in the wake of the depression in the early 1930s. The Republikaner question pulls Jews both ways. In Frankfurt, for example, Michel Friedmann, a member of the Jewish community, is also active in support of the Christian Democratic Party, the conservatives. In order to strike back at the Republikaner and secure the right-wing vote in a city election in the spring, the CDU adopted a strategy that involved attacking "people like" Daniel Cohn-Bendit, an important figure in the left-wing since the revolutionary days of 1968. The result was anger on the part of Germany's Jewish community, who felt the attack on Cohn-Bendit was using anti-

Semitism to win votes. Mr. Friedmann came in for criticism from his own fellow Jews.

The "joyous autumn" that brought Erich Honecker's fall, dismantling of the Wall, and the prospect of a greater Germany also brought the most direct threat to German Jews. In Germany today, there is no large, frightening anti-Semitic group like Pamyat, the nationalist movement in the Soviet Union. But there is a new confidence in Germany and that disturbs Jews. They worry about the reports of neo-Nazi gangs showing up at the weekly demonstrations in Leipzig. They worry when they hear that Republikaner are trying to build a list of followers in Dresden and Rostock. Mainly, though, they worry that the "new Germany" won't work so hard on its special relationship with Germany's few Jews. In the weeks after reunification, the Kohl government does something to fortify this fear. It slows the processing of applications to immigrate from Soviet Jews who want to come to Germany.

In boom-town Berlin, where investors pack the hotels and East Germans fill the stores and buy up all the bananas, the threat appears at its most direct. Property values continue to rise, angering old West Berliners who never expected the influx of foreign spenders and East Germans. With tolerance for "strangers" like Poles at a low in the city, Jews wonder whether local anger will next turn on them. At the Jewish School, parents wonder whether they will still receive their subsidies and still be able to afford their apartments in a Germany too busy spending on reunification to pay much attention to subsidies for "old" groups like the Jews.

Such problems are likely to sharpen the school playground fight. "We have all kinds of minorities in Berlin now," says the mother of a boy who attends the neighboring school. "In Berlin, the problem is the settlers from Poland and the Soviet

Union, not just the Jews." The city, too, is asking itself philosophical questions about the subsidies for such a school. Mascha Kleinschmidt, a city official, explained the difficulties this way: "We have a Jewish School. Okay. But now there's a big campaign in Kreuzberg [a neighborhood with many foreigners] to open a Muslim School. There we have more problems—for example, over whether the state should subsidize a school that treats girls the way Islam does. So we ask ourselves philosophical questions about 'this kind of school.' "

In the meantime the Jewish School's academic year moves on—from Rosh Hashanah, the Jewish New Year, to Yom Kippur, the day of atonement. On a September morning the director's office was planning Succoth, the Jewish harvest festival, and hoped to invite the children from the school next door to visit. "I don't know if I'll stay here forever," says Sabine Meinhardt, collecting photocopies from class 4B during a break. "But as long as I do, for me being here is something exceptional."

One example of what she means is provided by ten-year-old Benjamin, a student in 4B. Benjamin was born in Berlin and has dark hair. He wants to be a public defender when he grows up. And unlike most of the other children in the class, he has a smiling, straightforward answer to the question of why he goes to the Jewish School. "Well, that's clear," he says matter-of-factly, and adjusts his Japanese watch. "It's because I am a Jew." If those uneasy cohabitants, Jews and Germans, share a point of view on anything, it is in their commitment to symbols like Benjamin. Both groups cling to their Benjamins, because the Benjamins are the exception to a truth both groups fear. The truth is this: there may be Jews who live in Germany, but there are no more German Jews.

8

One Family's Berlin

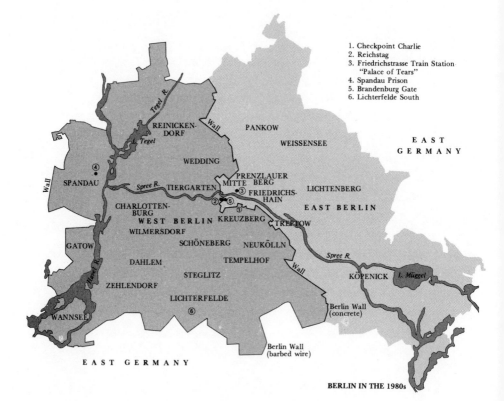

1. Checkpoint Charlie
2. Reichstag
3. Friedrichstrasse Train Station "Palace of Tears"
4. Spandau Prison
5. Brandenburg Gate
6. Lichterfelde South

E A S T
G E R M A N Y

REINICKEN-DORF

PANKOW

WEISSENSEE

WEDDING

SPANDAU

Tegel R.

Tegel

Wall

Wall

Spree R.

TIERGARTEN

PRENZLAUER
MITTE BERG

FRIEDRICHS-HAIN

LICHTENBERG

E A S T B E R L I N

CHARLOTTEN-BURG

W E S T B E R L I N

KREUZBERG

TREPTOW

WILMERSDORF

GATOW

SCHÖNEBERG

NEUKÖLLN

Spree R.

KÖPENICK

L. Müggel

Havel R.

DAHLEM

TEMPELHOF

ZEHLENDORF

STEGLITZ

Wall

LICHTERFELDE

WANNSEE

Berlin Wall
(concrete)

Berlin Wall
(barbed wire)

E A S T G E R M A N Y

BERLIN IN THE 1980s

Germans used to have a word to describe what happened to people in West Berlin. The word was *hängengeblieben*. A friend went to Berlin for a year in 1968, but then he stayed longer—*hängengeblieben*. A daughter departed for Berlin to study for four semesters in 1983, and now she still lives there, *hängengeblieben*. *Hängen* means "to hang," and *hängengeblieben* calls up an image of a city of figures caught in a net, transfixed, gently floating, perhaps, an inch or two above the ground. "Stuck" in Berlin, though, is what the Germans meant. The phrase fit because it described more than people. It also described the ex-capital itself, a city "stuck" in time, reflecting on its past, wondering what might come next, and comfortable in its suspension.

When East Germany opened its gates, Berliners on both sides of the city massed along the city's internal border to watch the wrecking balls destroy the Wall. They watched with the same wonder with which people watched a volcano erupt or a river flood: the change seems natural, but it is also unexpected and amazing. Berliners hadn't liked their Wall, but they had learned to live with it, even to appreciate its graffiti-covered face. A city of ironists and aesthetes, Berlin had been proud to possess what legitimately could be called the world's most intensely satisfying piece of political art. Change, coming after close to thirty years, brought a new brand of discomfort and a new set of worries. Even more, though, and in particular for the "stuck" people, change brought real joy. One such "stuck" person is Karin.

The Berlin I encountered in 1982, the year I met Karin, didn't seem stuck. Foreigners who thought about Berlin in those days thought of the Wall and of a city trapped like a hostage in an international cage. But the first impression I got when I arrived to spend a year studying there was that Berlin was big. Even in its halved state West Berlin had 2 million citizens. It had highways, shabby factory buildings, and 100 subway stations stretched over 480 square kilometers, an area bigger than Cologne, or Munich, or Frankfurt, or Stuttgart. Grand, I thought, was the adjective to describe this city—not grand like Paris, not grand like New York, but late-nineteenth-century industrial grand, grand like Chicago. My second day in the city I took the subway to Kreuzberg, a downtown neighborhood I'd been told was Berlin's version of New York's East Village, its version of the Marais in Paris. The ride started out underground, in a clean, empty station. As we traveled east the car rose aboveground onto elevated tracks and into a summer evening. Old Turkish ladies in scarves stood by teenagers dressed in leather at rusty high-ceilinged stations where pigeons dove around the rafters. Kreuzberg didn't feel like a neighborhood in a squeezed half-city. It didn't even feel like airless West Germany. It felt friendly, anonymous, and free.

West Berlin's problems, too—problems that, indirectly, brought me to Karin—didn't seem like geopolitical ones. Berlin was still technically an occupied city, but the Allied troops seemed to spend most of their time tucked away in their headquarters in far corners of the city. In the early 1980s, West Berlin and its citizens did not appear preoc-

cupied with their geopolitical situation. They were worried
about a more standard urban problem: an acute housing
shortage meant that the city didn't have room to house all
the 81,000 students attending its universities. The universities did not have enough dormitories, and many students
in any case preferred the off-campus, inner-city glamour of
Kreuzberg, or its charming and grubby neighbors, Wedding
and Neukölln.

The unlucky students who were unable to find their own
downtown apartments turned, reluctantly, to a remaining
option—the landlady. A full quarter of West Berlin's population was more than sixty-five years old, and many of these
senior citizens let rooms cheaply. I, too, wanted to live in
Kreuzberg. After a fruitless hunt I, too, dialed a telephone
number I'd copied down from a note posted on a university
bulletin board. The note had read: "Furnished room available. Call between 10 and 4." Wilmersdorf, the neighborhood I found when I arrived for my appointment, made my
heart sink a bit. Instead of cafés and sidewalk artists, the
subway stairs led to a barren spur of autobahn and the "Cosy
Wasch" car wash. The address I'd noted was just as un-
promising: a baker occupied the ground floor of a quiet
building with a dark hallway. As I climbed the stairs, I pic-
tured a short bosomy *Wirtin* and furniture draped in grimy
doilies.

My first surprise came when Karin opened her door: Karin
didn't look "stuck." She was tall and wore glasses that sat
halfway down a diminutive nose. She was more than fifty, I
later learned, but her gray hair looked blond—she seemed
young. The walls of the apartment she led me through were
lined with dictionaries and encyclopedias, and instead of the
predictable stuffed furniture there were a lot of light modern
pieces and what looked like antiques. A chair and a couch,

upholstered in white linen, took up a corner with yet more books. A scratchless mahogany Biedermeier secretary stood next to a pole wrapped in carpeting—a pole designed, it turned out, to give some climbing exercise to Karin's two seal point Siamese cats. A small gold-and-white clock ticked over a yellow memo sticker warning "Nicht berühren," "Don't touch." After forty-five minutes of polite exchange —did I smoke? could I get along with cats?—Karin told me she herself was a born Berliner and she hoped I would like it here. Then she wordlessly handed me a set of keys in what seemed a wonderfully unlandladylike gesture of trust.

My first days at Karin's I spent studying and touring Berlin. Berlin was an old city—some 750 years old—that had originally been little more than a sandy outpost for Prussian princes on the eastern side of the Spree River. When it grew, it grew west over the river. After Wilhelm became Kaiser, in 1871, the new national capital turned into a big industrial crossroads. Even in its halved state, West Berlin was big— it may have been an island, but it took hours to find the island's limits. From the last stop of the university subway line, Krumme Lanke, a bus ride took travelers to the Wannsee, where sailboats and ferries loaded and unloaded Germans in September sunshine. To reach the city border the traveler had to go even farther, down to a park and a little Spartan castle decorated with seashell-style ornaments designed by Berlin's most cherished Prussian architect, Karl Friedrich Schinkel. Up north, in Lübars, at the end of another long ride, there were even Berlin farms—in the fields, I was lucky enough to spot a grazing heifer. Nearly half the island half-city was parks, countryside, and water.

However large the Berlin of my experience, though, Karin's Berlin proved far larger. One September morning when the weather was still hot, she took me and her grandson in

the car downtown to a flea market by the Wall at Potsdamerplatz—the same Potsdamerplatz that would later be
the site of a Berlin–Berlin reunion. On this Saturday morning, the rubber tires, mud, and wire of this empty fairground
had something permanent about them. But as Karin passed
from a leather-jacket vendor to a stall for used books, she
described how this bald lot had been the downtown of her
childhood, her Times Square. The charm of Karin was that
she remembered life in an unedited way. She was true to
her old memories, and her recollection of Potsdamerplatz
was a childish one. "We came here shopping," she said. "I
got an ice cream."

After inspecting the flea market, she drove through the
Tiergarten and pointed out the closed-up remains of the old
Axis embassies, the old German headquarters of the Italians
and the Japanese. At the market Karin had pulled a prewar
Berlin phone book from a vendor's pile of junk. Later, when
I inspected it at home, I found it contained amazing things:
under "N," for Nazi, whole columns of telephone numbers
for Hitler's political apparatus. (Hitler's own phone number
was 120054. The number for his propaganda deputy, Goebbels, was 660603.) But Karin had bought the book because
it contained something special of *hers* from that time: her
family's old address in southern Lichterfelde—a kind of
proof to herself that her childhood and the Berlin of long
ago had really existed.

Beyond artifacts, though, living evidence of Karin's other
Berlins began to pop up. Her second Berlin was the Berlin
she had returned to after the war, a Berlin that had just been
through the Soviet blockade and the Airlift, a Berlin whose
streets still contained a lot of empty spots and a lot of rubble.
One of the rougher voices that asked for Karin when the
telephone rang was that of her friend Bernd, who had

charged West through barbed wire in a truck at a time, Karin explained, "when the Wall still had holes in it." The upholstery of one of her cars had been ruined, she recounted in another moment, because nearly every time she returned from East Berlin the People's Police had pulled up seats to look for hiding adults or children. Karin's family had always lived in West Berlin, like much of the city's middle class. But her former maid and her seamstress both lived in East Berlin. In the early 1980s, the Wall was more than twenty-one years old—it seemed an adult structure whose integrity was unquestionable. But she was still making periodic trips over, coffee as a gift on the seat beside her, to have pants made at her seamstress's. Her reasons for these voyages were not political. She had to go, she said. No matter where she looked, a woman couldn't find something decent that fit when she was six feet tall.

Karin was a good storyteller—even people who had never met her before became transfixed by her small face and her gray-blond hair when she started to tell a story—and she had lots of stories to tell about the Berlins of her past. Many of them involved the days when relations between East and West made travel to, from, and in the Berlins unpredictable and messy. Mostly, she laughed when she told these stories. Even recently, with the Wall crumbling, the drive on the transit road between West Germany and Berlin was a tricky one—only one sign pointed the Westerner to the road for West Berlin, and woe to those who missed it and found themselves stuck heading toward Poland. In earlier days, when things were even less clear, Karin once missed the vital turnoff and found herself cruising illegally through East German countryside. "Of course, the police caught up with me right away," she reported. "But I charmed the man. He wanted to know why I didn't turn around and go to the right road. 'But,' I told him, 'I thought we aren't permitted to turn around.' And the man laughed."

Karin's Berlin even showed up in her worries about her unwitting foreign tenants. After I'd inspected West Berlin, I began making occasional excursions "over." At eight, or nine, or ten in the morning, I'd take the train to the city's subway crossover point, a yellow-tiled monster of a train station whose name is Friedrichstrasse but which East Berliners, trapped on the other side, referred to as the Palace of Tears. In the Palace of Tears I'd hand my passport over, pay DM 30 for a visa and an obligatory exchange of currencies, and wander into a second city. I took blurry photos of the guards goose-stepping at the Memorial for Victims of Fascism and Militarism, a gloomy structure on Unter den Linden. Better pictures generally resulted when I photographed the Pergamon Altar inside one of East Berlin's impressive museums. To the outsider, East Berlin seemed built on a grander scale than its modest postwar twin. Museums and churches lined its center, and Unter den Linden, its grand avenue, was more elegant than West Berlin's neon-dotted Ku'damm. Seeing East Berlin, I understood for the first time how the city had evolved—that it had started here and spread west to where I lived with Karin. The police, waiters, and shopkeepers with their copies of Karl Marx and their posters of Fidel Castro seemed surly. But the place was not frightening.

Karin saw the city differently—as one that really was still occupied by armies, as one where Berliners still lived under surveillance in an abnormal situation. In some ways, Karin liked her city's occupiers. She was used to them, and she talked about them. The British were good people—once, when a British soldier had "confiscated" her mother's good carpet, her mother had written to Winston Churchill himself to complain and had received a letter back. Karin herself had been good friends with an American soldier, who had taken her to the army PX to get her favorite brand of T-shirt, Fruit of the Loom. The Russians were more difficult. She still saw all the Allies, though, regardless of how gentle, as intruders on her city. When I made phone calls, Karin warned me about tapping. I could be certain, she said, that someone, somewhere, was listening. And one evening when I failed to return from an excursion to the capital of East Germany by ten o'clock, she panicked and called a friend to ask what to do. "Amity may be lost *im Osten!*"—"Amity may be lost in the East!"

In general, though, the city seemed to produce in Karin a form of agreeable inertia. Once, early in her life, Karin had had been a child in Berlin in a family with money, and she was waiting for that Berlin and that money to come back again. She had a part-time job in a textbook publishing house that didn't pay for her apartment, but rather than forsake elegance and move, she took in boarders. She had a husband who had lived in a town in West Germany for years, but she was not divorced and still referred to the fellow as *mein Mann*—my husband. Before she sailed into her bedroom at twelve each night we agreed we would get up *früh*, early. But often, when morning came, I found her standing in her bedroom before pictures of her family pinned onto her white bulletin board, lost in contemplation of her two blond daughters in a snapshot where they were still small. She started work at ten—an hour that, to a nine-to-five American, seemed a bit late considering she had no children or husband to look after. Unlike the sloth of the students at the city's Free University, who acknowledged without embarrassment that they hadn't attended a class in half a semester, Karin's slow life had something noble about it. "I have to work all the time," she liked to say with a smile. "But what I'd most like to do is to lie down." "Laziness is our family disease," Karin told me, "and it's ruined my daughters."

Her daughters didn't seemed ruined. Isabelle, nearing thirty, was a thin pretty girl with a five-year-old son and blond bobbed hair. She was confident and funny, and lived *fein*—in a high-ceilinged old apartment in the Mommsenstrasse, an elegant street near many of the designer-clothing shops in West Berlin. There, in one and a half rooms decorated with some of the same inexpensive pine furniture to be found at Karin's, she issued orders to her son and boyfriend, a mumbling Yugoslavian. Isabelle was certainly poor. Her daytime life outside the apartment seemed to consist of rounds of visits to the social welfare offices, her son's nursery school, and the Bewag, the electricity company. But she spoke an elegant German that Karin's foreign boarders, like the Yugoslavian slouched at her kitchen table, could only hope for. There was a kind of authority in Isabelle that was European—the same confidence is visible in young Russian women—that made all others seem lightweight, ten years younger than they really were.

Isabelle's apartment was around the corner from the Bleibtreustrasse, the street with the Jewish School, but Isabelle didn't have much to do with the school. She spent more time in the cafés, many of whose names made reference to the street's name: literally translated, *bleibtreu* means "stay loyal." The most straightforward of these was the Café Bleibtreu, named after the street, but there was also the Café Untreu—Café Untrue. Isabelle occasionally waited tables at one called Reste Fidèle, a name to which she, being monolingual, added several syllables, pronouncing it Rest-e-Fidel-eh.

Isabelle's mother and her sister regarded the afternoons

and evenings Isabelle spent over coffee and cigarettes in
Reste Fidèle as signs of her downfall. As a teenager she'd
dropped out and fallen into what all the family termed "the
world of gastronomy." Her son had been born, her husband
had left, and she met her Yugoslavian. Whenever I called
on Isabelle, she had time to sit, smoke, and chat. Sometimes,
when she was working, she let me take her son shopping for
oranges. Once I picked him up at kindergarten and took him
to the shallow section of a public swimming pool at Halensee.
In the water, he gripped my bathing-suit straps like a mon-
key.

Amélie, the other daughter, had more hidden vulnera-
bilities. She, too, lived with a Yugoslavian—Karin's daughters liked having someone they could dominate, at least
linguistically. Amélie's *Freund* had a profession: he was
a bossy, self-employed architect. Amélie was apprenticed
to a fancy tailor who made clothes to order for "the real
Spiesser"—the real bourgeois—in southwest Berlin. Like her
mother and her sister, Amélie didn't really know why she
was in Berlin. Actually, Amélie told a boarder when she came
to feed the cats while Karin was away, she really ought to
have gone elsewhere—making *Mode* perhaps in Hamburg,
where Germany's most famous woman designer, Jil Sander,
was, or perhaps in Munich. And she, too, stayed in Berlin.

Berlin's odd shape had a different effect on Karin's daughters than it did on Karin. The daughters had something in
common with most students at West Berlin's universities—
they didn't go to East Berlin. This was a form of provinciality
that could be held against the political ones, who spent much
of their days talking to each other—lecturing each other—
about Gramsci, Marx, and economics. More than once I sat
down at a table in a café near the university expecting to
talk about literature and found the topic switching to eco-

nomics. For Americans, these conversations with their old-fashioned description of a world divided into capitalist oppressors and worker victims were frustrating. Once, at the café by the university subway stop in Dahlem, I even amazed myself by delivering a vehement counter-lecture that included a graphic demonstration of where supply crosses demand—as drawn on a cardboard beer coaster. Berliners' ideological emphasis brought out a new and not altogether pleasant side in my own character. For the first time in my life, I was startled to hear what seemed to be reactionary questions coming from my own mouth, Cold War questions like "If you like Communism so much, why don't you go over there?" None of the West Berlin students ever seemed to do it, although the Berlin papers once told about a group of protesters who escaped from West Berlin's police by climbing over the Wall.

The Wall question didn't seem a fair one to pose to Amélie and Isabelle, who were apolitical. Amélie and I were once invited out for dinner at a friendly, garlicky restaurant called Lusiada on the west end of the Ku'damm by an American newspaper correspondent who was writing a story about youth in Germany. We ate chicken and drank red wine. The reporter asked Amélie whether she had been to East Berlin. Not lately. He asked her what she thought of the Wall. "The Wall is something so familiar to me I don't even think about it." She used the word *vertraut*—familiar—but in a comforting, friendly sense. Later Amélie did go to East Berlin —not because it was part of her hometown, but because she, like me, found it strange, otherworldly, and amusing. She was a bit excited when she reported on her visit. She preferred East Berlin's eighteenth-century Staatsoper to the Miesian concrete cube that is West Berlin's opera house. "There, the opera looks like an opera. Here, the opera looks like nothing." The main thing Amélie liked to do in the pre-1989 East Berlin, though, was shop. She talked about some garters in the Kaufhaus on Alexanderplatz, and the old-fashioned school notebooks that had long disappeared from the West but still were available there.

Berlin, nevertheless, seemed to produce a kind of urban insularity in the daughters. Neither daughter drove—they had no reason to. Both of them referred to the Western part of Germany as West Germany, Westdeutschland, the name non-Germans used but not the one used by West Germans, who generally called their country the Federal Republic. When the daughters traveled with their mother, they went abroad, to places like Ibiza. When they traveled alone, they went far, too. Isabelle went to Yugoslavia with her boyfriend. Amélie went to Sylt, northern Germany's answer to Nantucket, with her employer for a week. Since they had never seen the suburbs on the other side of the Wall, they couldn't miss them. They were provincial, but no more so than Manhattanites who report with pride or indifference that they've never been to Queens.

Economically, too, the daughters did seem a bit backward. German *Gymnasium* teachers like to have their students memorize a quotation from Immanuel Kant, the famous philosopher. What is the Enlightenment? Kant asked. "The departure of mankind from his self-imposed minority"—his self-imposed immaturity. The advice offered with these words came in the imperative mode: "Have courage to serve yourself through your own reason." In Berlin, the first definition seemed a good description for Karin's family. They still lived in a mental "minority"—her two daughters on unemployment, herself working only part-time. Both daughters, for example, were adults, but still possessed reduced-rate passes for the public transport system, passes granted them on account of their low economic status. To be sure, the years in which they were unemployed, the 1980s, were years when Germany went through a long period of high unemployment. When the number hit 2 million, the government of Helmut Schmidt fell and the conservatives assumed power. But Berlin in particular had helped to keep Karin's family in "minority." As the Federal Republic's special child—or aged grandparent, really—the city benefited from up to a 50 percent subsidy from the government. That money went directly into the leather handbags of Amélie, Karin, and Isabelle. It paid for an afternoon in a bar, it paid the electricity bill, and it paid for Karin's grandson's milk.

Beyond this family, I found a whole city of "stuck" Berliners. One set of such people lived with Gerlinde, a Dutch girl who, like me, had come to study for a year in Berlin. Gerlinde shared rooms with a writer, a literary scholar, and some other people whose status wasn't clear, in a big, dark apartment near Tempelhof, the old airport that had saved the city during the Berlin Airlift. One afternoon Gerlinde invited guests—with a measure of fanfare—to a soirée whose theme was E. T. A. Hoffmann, a Romantic writer whose dreamy work inspired the opera *Tales of Hoffmann*. The guests arrived with their entrance fee, one bottle of champagne, to find their hosts dressed in white and an ensemble playing E. T. A. Hoffmann's music on strings. As the champagne was consumed the evening lightened up—someone put on "Some Girls" by the Rolling Stones. This was a scene from the 1980s, but one that really seemed to fit more in the 1960s, or better yet in the 1930s, for it was a Weimar-style evening. A guest who asked another what his work was received an answer that seemed worth writing down for its pretension alone: "I write."

Another Berliner from this world was Werner, the editor

at a young Berlin weekly called *Zitty*, a mock-German spelling for the English word "city." Werner liked to get in his car, a diesel Mercedes, and drive around the city, and while he drove he talked—about how he hated Berlin. Werner said he really wanted to get out—not to Hamburg or Frankfurt, but to somewhere really away, like Portugal or Sri Lanka. He had a good life, an apartment in an Art Nouveau apartment house of the sort treasured by people of class in the city, which he shared with a dour instructor of women's studies named Marlies. Marlies and Werner didn't get along, Werner would whisper to a visitor as he got drinks in the kitchen. Marlies, Werner reported, said his cleanliness mania terrorized her. He also took great pains to point out that theirs was a platonic relationship. He did have a girlfriend named Sigi, but she had an apartment in another district, Steglitz—because, Werner emphasized, "I have to live alone."

What was striking about these drifters was their age. Most of them were at least ten years older than the usual student—they were thirty-five, or forty—but still lived in what seemed to an outsider to be studenty arrangements. All the cities in Europe, and some cities in the United States, have their share of "old sixty-eighters," people who seem never to have abandoned habits they picked up years ago and stick to those habits in protest against yuppiedom. The difference in Berlin was that, even in the 1980s, these people represented the majority in the intellectual and academic worlds. They still dressed like people in their twenties—or, to be precise, like people now in their thirties had dressed when they were in their twenties. Although they were a lot different from Karin, with her compulsive vacuuming and her cats, they did share something with her and her daughters—they seemed suspended.

Berliners of this age got "caught" in part because of straightforward things like laws and economic policies. West Germany's university system granted students a tuition-free education and provided generous health and transportation subsidies that were strong incentives to remain a student. Some of the situation was specific to West Berlin. Berlin was still an occupied city, even recently, and not technically 100 percent part of sovereign West Germany. The Allies kept their fortresses in their corners of the city. The United States, for example, quietly carried out military maneuvers in southwest Berlin at a mock mini-Berlin all their own that they had dubbed "Doughboy City." As a result, its citizens had a special status. Germans in the 1960s, 1970s, and 1980s could evade the draft simply by moving to Berlin, just as young American men once moved to Canada or Sweden. The Berlin subsidy from which Karin's family benefited made it a tolerable place to live for a lot of people. The Berlin I first met, the Berlin of the early 1980s, seemed to offer as much as or more than most other cities: the stores were full, Berliners water-skied on the Wannsee, certainly there were as many films, concerts, and theatrical productions available to the populace as in any other German city. People who worked in Berlin nevertheless got an automatic, substantial tax credit because of the "hardship" of living "occupied," as well as bonuses to wages or salaries. They ignored the Wall, they liked West Berlin, and they saw no reason to change or leave. Why should they?

Through Karin I learned that young people were not the only "stuck" ones, the only casualties of the Berlin situation. Most of Germany profited from the nation's economic miracle, and many Germans recalled how, within one day in 1948, the government put an end to bread lines and black-market cigarettes by issuing a fresh currency that turned an

undernourished nation into one of happy shoppers. Many
Germans—in particular conservative Germans—liked to
talk about the cigar-smoking Ludwig Erhard, who played a
leading role in orchestrating the switch and brought the nation the *Wirtschaftswunder*, the economic miracle. (Later,
after the Wall broke and West Germany set to work planning
economic union with East Germany, the Erhard model came
up again and again. What had happened in the Western
zones in 1948, the West German government argued, would
happen again now in East Germany.) But the *Wunder*
seemed to have bypassed Karin and her husband. For years,
she, with his help, had kept books and worked to keep alive
a heating business started by her father. Never, though, was
there a period when there was enough money. When Karin's
husband turned up for a visit in Karin's living room in November, he was elegant in an ascot scarf and double-ply
cashmere. But he was also skinny, nervous, and almost em-
barrassingly arrogant.

It became clear in conversations around the apartment that
Karin's husband was not just a difficult husband or a draw-
ing-room dilettante; he was someone damaged by the war.
Karin's husband, she said once before he arrived, came from
Königsberg, where in the last days of the war he'd been
drafted as a fifteen-year-old into Hitler's *Volkssturm*. He'd
been a reconnaissance aide, a *Nachrichtenhelfer*—had laid
cable for field telephones—and been taken prisoner by the
Russians, who kept him two years until he nearly starved to
death. After the war he worked in various jobs and then
lapsed into unemployment. For years, Karin's daughters reported, he sat around and did nothing: a depressive but also
one who was recovering from a real event, the war, who was
suffering from a form of belated shell shock. In the early
1960s Karin learned to drive and started working at her

current job, in the textbook publishing house. Finally, after not being able to find something in Berlin—or not choosing to find something—her husband went off to Westdeutschland, "Wessieland," to work. Berlin was big, and had 170,000 workers employed by industrial giants, but it was still limited. Once the city itself had been exhausted, it was not possible to find a job in the suburbs or in the next town. The family decided Karin's husband had to go to Westdeutschland. "We said," a daughter reported, "he was just going there to work. And then he didn't come back again."

As a rule, Karin was reticent about her past, more out of modesty than embarrassment. In the days after her husband's visit, though, she started to recount her own story. Over tea, she told me: Karin's father had been an important Nazi. When he first married Karin's mother, a concert pianist who'd played the Bechstein that still stood in Karin's front room, they'd been poor. They'd summered on the Baltic Sea, in Estonia, Karin's mother's home. On her bulletin board Karin had a picture of her father, a tall, handsome man, dipping a naked toddler, Karin, into the Baltic Sea. Through Hitler, her father had fallen into a wonderful career. He was one of those young men—like Albert Speer—whom the new regime lifted into light, to whom the Reich provided professional challenges. Hitler had made Karin's father a director of Strength Through Joy, the social works program that built the Volkswagen Beetle and promised to put one in every worker's garage. As the child of the director, Karin had been entrusted with a splendid toy: a small black VW about the size of a bread box, a VW that really ran. To this day she remembers her disappointment when, one April day in 1938, the toy disappeared. It had only been a loan, it turned out. The car was a present to the Führer for his birthday.

Karin told all this matter-of-factly, and that seemed the

way to take it. Anyone who knew Karin well would not have thought to ask whether she had been a child Nazi—the question would have embarrassed them both, and people who really did know Karin well already knew the answer was no. From what Karin said, it could be gathered that, privately at least, her parents kept their distance from the Nazi movement. Once when Karin was in a good mood—when she wanted to describe something ludicrous—she told me how she'd learned to cheer for Hitler. The instruction didn't come at home. Karin had learned it when she'd been the guest of another little girl. The child's mother had placed the two of them on the balcony and they'd waved and shouted *"Heil!"* along with the rest of the crowd. "Can you imagine?" Karin asked, and laughed her deep laugh.

The Third Reich was nevertheless, for Karin, the first government of her life, and a government that had existed in happy times for her. Karin had enjoyed the typical upbringing of an upper-middle-class child. A lady who came twice weekly to speak French with her. She'd even had a chance to practice her French with prisoners of war who'd collected the garbage at her family's Lichterfelde house. Once, in a pedagogic discussion on how people learn to read, I told Karin how surprised I'd been as a six-year-old to learn that the phrase was written "this morning," and not, as my ear had heard, "thi smorning." Karin said she'd had the same kind of discovery. It came back in 1937, when she'd learned that the Führer actually had a first name and a last name. She had thought the name would be written the way it was spoken, in one excited breath: "Adolfitla."

Children of Nazis have often reacted to their parents' extremist past by searching for a new form of extremism: Albert Speer's daughter Hilde, whom Karin knew, had, for example, become a representative for a local chapter of the ecologist Green Party in West Berlin's Parliament. In the adult Karin, though, the Hitler regime had produced a tolerant person, one with sympathy for labor and the left wing. Karin, and practically every German who ever promenaded through her living room, voted for the Social Democratic Party, Germany's large, left-leaning, union-backed party. In the 1960s, as a young mother, Karin had been friends with many of the leaders of the German version of America's 1960s protest movements. Traces of that time lay around her apartment. One of the funniest ones I found was a picture of naked men lined up against a wall—a snapshot of the members of "Horror Kommune I," a commune formed by a literary friend of Karin's. Karin regarded this era with enough nostalgia to make those she told about it wish they, too, had been communards in a cell in 1968 Berlin.

One of Karin's nicest stories from that Berlin was of how in those days she'd overcome an iron rule of German apartment life—the eight o'clock lockup. Many buildings in Germany bolt their front door at eight o'clock, a safety measure that originated in the days when the *Portier*, the German concierge, was around to open up in emergencies. In Karin's lifetime, though, and mine, buildings no longer had a *Portier* and there was no one to answer the door. The evening lockup, to us, seemed designed to squash spontaneity. The system makes unannounced visits nearly impossible—the bells are behind the closed front door. So Karin put the house keys in a little basket and lowered it on a string to the sidewalk, a bit, it could be imagined, the way Rapunzel in the castle lowered her hair. By the 1980s the basket had disappeared, but Karin had adopted a method also used to combat a similar problem in New York's downtown loft buildings—she leaned over the edge of her balcony and dropped the keys, protectively balled in a pair of thick wool socks.

Karin wasn't a member of a party, and she didn't give money to any party. Her main charity contributions went to the Circle of Cat Friends and to the Graves of the War Dead. But she did know how to point out political danger when she saw it. When the Republikaner, the far-right party, began popping up in German Parliaments in 1989, Karin worriedly advised me to buy and *read* the autobiography of its leader, Franz Schönhuber. You had to know what such people thought if it looked like they might get political power, she warned. "Everyone had a copy of *Mein Kampf*," she said. "But no one read it."

In general, Karin's political statements came in connection with her experiences. One evening as Karin was watching television, a man with a big nose came on the screen to conduct classical music. "That's my brother," she said, agitated. I was confused. Earlier, she'd told me that she was an only child. The sight of this unknown brother produced an explanation of how the war had intruded on Karin's life. In 1943, around the point the Eastern Front began to present a serious challenge to Hitler, around the time the death camps were in full swing and German soldiers started freezing in the Russian snow, Karin's father had found another love—through Nazi society. He was having an affair with a grandchild of Richard Wagner. He had to marry her. What else would the Führer have allowed? In 1943, Karin's father started a new family. For Karin, the event was a personal tragedy—her father abandoned her. It also had a place among the footnotes on Nazi kitsch. For a wedding present, Hitler gave the couple a white Mercedes.

Karin continued to love her father—like any abandoned

child—and kept in touch with him after the war, when she was a teenager and when he was denazified. To explain that process, one afternoon she went to her Biedermeier secretary and retrieved a few papers from a red leather envelope. In the denazification process the Allies had devised various categories. Those who were tried at Nuremberg were in the highest category. The lowest comprised the *Mitläufer*—fellow travelers. The Spruchkammer, the denazification court, wanted to put Karin's father in this category—he was a distinguished gentleman who, the Allies saw, could help build the new Germany. But her father wouldn't accept this—it seemed a form of degradation or dishonesty. "Fellow traveler he certainly wasn't," Karin said. Later, Karin became pregnant and planned to marry, but she was in her seventh month by the time her father could find the time to come to the wedding. At that postwar point she was so poor, she later reported, that "I was happy to have a maternity dress to wear to the mayor's office."

When I started to look I found records of these past times all over West Berlin. For starters, there was the Berlin Museum, a building that stood among vacant lots and weeds along my beloved Kreuzberg subway line. Not far away was the Bauhaus Archiv, a friendly white structure that housed the rickety first models of tubular chrome furniture that we know today as standard office issue. The favorite of most of my guests from abroad was the Haus am Checkpoint Charlie, a touristy museum devoted to the ingenious methods Germans have devised to get across the Berlin Wall. One room showed the tiny trunk of a tiny car in which a woman had hidden during the ride "over." Another showed photos of a rope on which a family had put a wheel—and then ridden, trolley style, to freedom.

My own favorite structure in these years was the Reichstag,

a massive monument that stands just in front of a spot that used to be occupied by the Berlin Wall. Today, the old Weimar—and pre-World War I—Parliament houses a photo exhibit with sound and light called "Questions about German History." The show conducts visitors through German history, from Bismarck and German unification at Versailles, through the querulous Weimar Republic, through the Nazis (dummies in uniforms), and on to the bland Federal Republic that now governs West Germany. The new unified Berlin will certainly find a different use for the Reichstag. But at that time, a friend and I liked to hang out there. We spent an hour one afternoon in a video cubicle that showed Goebbels preaching to the masses after the major defeat at Stalingrad. Goebbels was instructing the Germans to hold out—to continue their fight against the enemy with "total war."

Whenever I didn't discover such places on my own, Karin and my other Berlin friends did their best to show them to me. The same drifters who filled the city in the early 1980s often also had a private mania: they were obsessed with explaining German history. One example of the touring phenomenon was a secondary-school teacher whose telephone number had been given to me by an American professor when he heard I was moving to Berlin. The teacher was a conservative-looking fellow with hangdog eyes and a mustache. He was born in North Rhine–Westphalia, but lived in Kreuzberg—in part out of principle, he informed visitors, because it was near the site of Germany's division, the Wall. After he retrieved his car from the protective garage-cage it required in his wild neighborhood, the teacher drove me past the remains of the Anhalter Bahnhof, a grand old Berlin train station that had once served 40,000 travelers a day. All that was visible was part of a ruined entrance, standing alone among bricks and rubble, but it was on a scale so large it again reminded me that Berlin had been a big crossroads city, the German Chicago. The teacher also told me to visit Plötzensee, where German officers in 1944 hung on S-shaped hooks until they died as punishment for their assassination attempt on the Führer.

Ulrich, another history buff, was cheerier. Ulli was a journalist who knew Russian and liked anything that had to do with "East-West"—in honor of guests to his home he invariably brought out Stolichnaya vodka, or Russian cigars, or caviar. In boxes stored side by side with his daughter's toys he had slides of Königsberg, the old Baltic Sea city that today is Kaliningrad, and he mused about how we could write a story around them to sell to a magazine. Ulli's other mania was the *Wirtschaftswunder* of the 1950s and 1960s. He collected old VWs, motor scooters, and motorcycles from that period. He waited until his wife's back was turned to admit to guests that he owned thirteen such vehicles, all of which slumbered quietly in various parking spots around his neighborhood, Charlottenburg. When he learned that I knew Karin, he asked for an introduction, because he wanted to describe her father in a book he was writing about the history of the Volkswagen.

At Karin's the discussion of these themes was less direct, in part because she was older, and actually remembered, and in part because for her the national defeat of the war coincided with a personal tragedy, the breakup of her family. When bombing made Berlin too dangerous, Karin's father arranged a refuge farther west for his estranged family at a cloister in a town called Mariental. Tall Karin still remembered how "tiny Italian men" employees under her father at the Volkswagen factory in nearby Wolfsburg carried her mother's giant grand piano up the steps of their home and

moved them in. Mariental was a little village near a small
town called Helmstedt, a name Karin pronounced with the
horror some city sophisticates reserve for rural life. Karin
told how she, her mother, and the remaining female relatives
of her clan—her aunt, her cousin—had waited out the war's
end here with other refugees. They slept in dark rooms connected by a big corridor. Hot water was hard to come by.
Karin learned to peel potato skins so thin that none of the
food was wasted—a skill which later caused her to forbid
me to prepare her potatoes, for I always cut away too much
of the potato. The walls in the cloister were cold and in the
winter ice formed on them. As usual, though, Karin's description of her "poor" time in Mariental contained some
incongruous signs of wealth. Her voice still ringing with
disappointment—but not with bitterness—she told how a
special staircase to provide a separate entrance for her family
was to have been built. Her father had ordered it. But like
so many things, the staircase was a victim of the war and
was never built.

According to Karin, these were the years she got into her
bad habits of "grand laziness." She was supposed to go to
school in Helmstedt, seven kilometers up the road, but for
a long time the school was closed. By the time the school
did open again, many months after the end of the war, Karin
had become skilled at avoiding spending much time there.
She used to arrive hours late every morning, she reports,
with the excuse that she hadn't been able to get a ride from
Mariental—an excuse that was often legitimate. She left
early, telling her teachers she "had to get the last bus." For
the teachers in Helmstedt the Berlin girl had little respect.
In particular she remembers one little lady who was the last
instructor to continue the Hitler greeting—the stiff-armed
"*Heil!*"—well after more dubious or opportunistic colleagues

had returned to "*Guten Tag*." When the school opened after the war, Karin remembered, "she didn't do it anymore."

On vacation in Paris, in 1989, Karin sat in a café near St.-Germain-des-Prés with me and Claus, a lifelong friend of hers from the Helmstedt time. Claus lived in Spain and was an architect, a tan man in a bright white shirt with a small gray pigtail that hung over his collar. The two drank coffee and talked about the renovations going on in Barcelona, where Claus lived and which was being prepared for the Olympics.

It was a June afternoon, quite hot, and by our feet street cleaners were spraying the pedestrian walk, covering it with a thick white layer of soap and water. Karin talked about the mass arrests of students and the death sentences that had been the Chinese regime's response to the student demonstrators in Beijing's Tiananmen Square. "Those *Schweinehunde*, those *Schweinekerle*," she kept repeating. She and Claus both grew mirthful as Claus reported on the news clips Karin and I had missed of Mikhail Gorbachev's reception on a recent trip to West Germany. "The Germans wouldn't let him go, they wouldn't stop cheering him," Claus said. He used the verb *zujubeln*, which can be translated roughly as "celebrate," a verb that brings to mind the massive parades and joy fests of the Third Reich. "Well, you can understand them," Karin said. "They've been waiting so long. You can't exactly bring yourself to *zujubeln* West German politicians." She and Claus both laughed at the prospect of cheering Helmut Kohl, the giant, rotund, lisping Chancellor of West Germany. "Der Gorbachev is the first chance they've had to celebrate someone like this since Hitler."

Claus had gone to school with Karin in Helmstedt, but when I asked him if he was from there, he gave the same horrified response: "*Nein!*" He'd actually come north from

Blankenburg. Unlike Karin, he didn't seem fond of reminiscing, and preferred to discuss the news of the prohibitive real estate prices in San Diego, California, he'd just heard about from a friend. Claus was a bit of a dandy, and during this break Karin and I were thinking how much he'd like the present she'd brought him—a red silk dressing gown her daughter Amélie had finished sewing for him around midnight the night before Karin departed. For my benefit, he and Karin reminisced a bit about their time together in Helmstedt, when no one was certain whether the Russians would advance. Karin recalled a cousin of hers, a male and therefore by default the head of the family, who was convinced the Russians would move into Mariental. "Every time a rumor came along that this was so, he'd pack all his belongings onto his bicycle."

Once, the same year, Karin took her family and me to see the Mariental where these gruesome events had transpired. We had somehow expected to be transported back in time, and we all walked around in shock at how modern and peaceful this former war scene seemed. The Cistercian cloister had been founded, a small exhibit at the cloister informed one, in 1138. Inside the cool Romanesque church tourists inspected the altar and collected postcards. Outside, in the cloister garden, a band played Dixieland music—the tenant and the guardian of the cloister told us that they were a group organized at the VW factory, still in nearby Wolfsburg.

The biggest shock, though, was provided by Karin's wartime quarters, which turned out to be a swank exercise in the innovative use of alternative space. Instead of dripping walls we found a whitewashed structure full of massive wardrobes—*Schränke*—and elegant couches. "I imagined it small and dark, not like this," said Amélie. The house had been restored by a schoolteacher—new walls, wider windows—and she showed Karin's family each room. In the large kitchen all paused to sniff the fresh aroma of a newly baked cake. The schoolteacher had baked it for her husband's friends, the musicians playing outside in the courtyard. "Usually, when you visit a place where you once lived, it looks smaller than you remember it, more run-down," said Karin. The schoolteacher herself had been displaced during the war, just like Karin—the furniture in Karin's old refuge came from her parents' old apartment in Jena, now part of East Germany. She in her turn had paid a return visit—"but when I saw the rooms I cried," she said, seeming a bit disappointed at Karin's serenity.

It was back in Berlin, another time, that Karin showed me a bit of jewelry that told the story of the first loss in her family history of losses: the loss of their Baltic home. After Karin's parents' marriage broke up, she told me, she took their rings and wore them on a chain around her neck. Later, she'd had them melted into a ring for herself. This seemed morbid, until Karin explained what the rings were made of: a golden ruble Karin's mother had from the Czar's time. Most weekends, and sometimes during the week, Karin went to visit her mother, a Baltic German who lived in a special old people's home for Baltic Germans. Karin's mother didn't like to receive strangers, but another lady in the home was receiving—a Frau Thiling. Frau Thiling regaled visitors with stories of the town where she and Karin's mother came from; a place called Reval. Today Reval is the Estonian capital, Tallinn. As a girl Frau Thiling had made snowy expeditions on sleds to the country—an image hard for a Westerner to conjure, the closest one comes being a picture of wintry New Hampshire with sledders singing "Over the hills . . . to Grandmother's house we go." Frau Thiling had lived in a big German community "where most people were educated and most people knew each other." Frau Thiling's husband was a *Nervenarzt*—a neurologist—and he'd gotten a job in Berlin. She'd stayed in Reval until Hitler made his pact with Stalin, and then all Germans had been called *Heim ins Reich*—home to the Reich.

A few years later, both Karin's mother and Frau Thiling were dead, but Karin still came back to the neighborhood, to visit a small cemetery where her mother was buried. Berliners take care of their graves. Sometimes Karin brought her grandson and they plucked weeds from graves that seemed to have no keepers. Berlin is an old city—more than 25 percent of the population is over sixty-five, compared with the average of 15 percent in the rest of the Federal Republic. Because of the crowding, citizens of Berlin can't reserve graves. Karin felt lucky to have gotten this plot, the demand was so great. From the trunk of her car she pulled out plastic gloves and scissors and walked to her mother's grave to clean it up. The arrangement looked exotic, not at all like the usual sterile arrangement. That's right, Karin said, when I asked her. She'd made her mother an eco-grave.

It was this Karin, a woman stuck in the late-middle-age groove of tending a parent's grave, who greeted the "return" of Berlin. On the famous Thursday evening when East Berliners began pushing their way through the crossing points, I telephoned an excited Karin, who could only croak a single order to me: "Turn on your television." She spent the first historic weekend of the Wall's opening, the weekend the East Berliners first came over, wandering from corner to corner, inspecting. Sheer exhaustion brought her down with the flu the week after, but she wasn't down for long: her office needed her. Every day East German teachers poured into the publishing house's small offices looking for copies of West German textbooks to replace their old Communist ones. Karin spent hours leaning on the counter explaining to these teachers, bewildered by the vast Western selection of texts, which ones they ought to take and how to pay for them.

For the "stuck" people, the boomtown, the capital that Berlin is becoming, also brings disadvantages. The opening of the Wall has thrown Berlin's left-leaners, the city's Marxists, into a state of confusion. With the Eastern bloc abandoning socialism, how can they fight for it in West Berlin? When she's not visiting her new Germany, Karin sits at her dining-room table and works out numbers with a pen. What if the city's bull market means the end to the rent control on her apartment? The East German teachers who come to her publishing house often steal stock samples and rarely have cash. What if her publishing house spends so much money on helping East Germans that it goes bankrupt? A house in Potsdam would be nice, but no one in Karin's family will be able to afford one. Nevertheless, Karin gets in her Volvo, and drives into the city, and explains the Wild West to her East German customers.

The first Saturday, thirty-eight hours after the Wall came down, Karin took me on an inspection of Berlin border crossings. She wrapped herself in a white raincoat and a blue scarf and set out down the Blissestrasse, past the supermarket, past a stationery store, and turned the corner for the Bundesplatz subway stop. With me and another American in tow, she made her way down the packed subway stairs and onto a platform so crowded that only Karin, the tallest of us three, could see the train doors. After a change to an equally crowded elevated train, we disembarked at Lehrter Bahnhof to watch arrivals make their first entry to West Berlin at the Invalidenstrasse crossover.

The first thing we saw was a long queue of people—at

least a hundred—lining up for a welcome gift of coffee and chocolate from Kaiser's, the supermarket chain. The next thing we saw was some new graffiti, sprayed on an empty billboard between an advertisement for the Wienerwald restaurant chain and another for laptop computers, reading: "German Unity Now! But Which Unity?" Then we saw the snub-nosed East German cars, Trabanten, rolling across the border to the bemusement of confused East German police and the excitement of Westerners, who dumped confetti on the square cars' small hoods.

The calmest person in this confusing reunion scene was Karin. She watched the cars a bit, she smiled embarrassedly at a policeman—in general, she is not fond of policemen—she pushed her glasses further up on her diminutive nose. Soon she was devoting her energy to East Berliners who were stepping for the first time into unknown parts of their own city. She helped a blond girl with a blue baby carriage orient herself—together they pored over a Berlin map until the girl understood that she really was on a West Berlin street. Later, Karin and her crew marched along the Wall past the Reichstag, Germany's old Parliament building. But this day's inspection wasn't enough for Karin. The next morning she raced off to the Potsdamerplatz, the flea-market area where she and her mother had once, in another era, done their shopping. Karin got there in time to watch the mayors of the two Berlins, East and West, open a slice of the Wall there. What did the weekend feel like to her? "I'm no political scientist," was her first answer. Her second answer, after she'd thought about it, was a different one. Now that Berlin was back, Karin said, Berliners like her knew that World War II was finally ending.

Acknowledgments

Many people and institutions contributed to this book. Only a few of them can be named here. The West German Ministry of the Interior and the staff of Grenzdurchgangslager Friedland were kind enough to introduce me to the beginning of this long story. Hartmut Koschyk, the Bund der Vertriebenen in Bonn, and the Sudeten Germans in Munich were especially helpful on the exile issue.

Everyone at the Führungsakademie in Hamburg, but in particular Axel von Claer, Manfred Backerra, and their families, extended extraordinary hospitality. Alexander Friedrich Paulus provided some important background as well. The Luftwaffe Academy in Fürstenfeldbruck, Bavaria, was also a fine host.

On Bavaria, many people gave advice. Among them: Klaus Seidel and August Everding, the staff of the Prince Regent Theater, Munich architects and professors. Beatrice Heuser and Hagen Schulze also provided some wise insights.

Marina Wolff-Bühring, Marion Gräfin Dönhoff, and Jeannette Hesse devoted a week explaining Barbara, the charity organization, to a stranger. The East German refugees who took time to speak with me were extraordinarily kind, Kerstin Meinke in particular. Mike Naumann gave one golden tip. Thanks, too, to Karl von Schwarzenberg, who allowed me to tag along on an exciting Prague tour, as well as Wulf Hauser in Vienna.

To Josef Joffe and Christine Brinck, my gratitude for help on the Jewish chapter as well as help on all the others. To the Bodemann family and the Jewish School and to Heinz Galinski, warm thanks. General advisers on Berlin, and friends, have included: Ulrich Kubisch, Amy Alving, and Christian Caryl. Above all, thanks to my Berlin family, Karin and her children.

A talk with Arnulf Baring in Berlin helped in the conception of this book. So did conversations with Michael Stürmer. John Kornblum, who knows everything about Germany, has been a special help. So has Enno von Loewenstern. Dominic Lawson of the *Spectator* in London has been a good editor and friend. Paul and Daniel Johnson helped the project along. Particular thanks to my editor at *The Wall Street Journal*, Robert Bartley, who first sent me on the stories that led to this book, then tolerated my absence while I completed it. Additional *Journal* support, gratefully accepted, came from George Melloan, Peter Keresztes, and Esther Bourrée.

Dennis Bark, the co-author of *A History of West Germany*, had the kindness to review the manuscript and saved me from a few major blunders.

Finally, there are a few people who got me to Germany in the first place. They are my aunt and uncle, Marylea and Rolf Meyersohn, who took me to the Starnbergersee and first spoke German to me there, and my parents, who taught me to love language.

Most translations and all errors are my own.

New York, July 1990

Notes

INTRODUCTION

"A clean sweep will be made . . ." Winston Churchill, December 15, 1944, in Parliamentary Debates, quoted in Alfred M. de Zayas's *Nemesis at Potsdam*. In general, de Zayas's book proved a great aid in the construction of the early chapters. The volume is one of the few published in English to give a relatively sympathetic portrait of the Germans expelled from Central Europe. It offers a revision of the question of the Sudeten Germans. Rather than portraying them as a kind of fifth column, a people who unabashedly supported Hitler so loyally they "deserved" their violent expulsion after the war, it presents a more varied picture. To de Zayas, the Sudeten Germans, like other expellees, were a mixed group, some of whom backed Hitler and some of whom didn't. To support this thesis de Zayas provides considerable historical evidence—for example, documentation of Social Democratic Germans in the Sudetenland who feared Hitler. De Zayas also traces discriminatory behavior by the Polish and Czech governments against their German populations between the wars. At the Paris Peace Conference, which created the League of Nations, countries with large German minorities signed a treaty guaranteeing those minorities autonomy and equal rights with their fellow citizens. The Permanent Court of Justice in The Hague subsequently ruled in favor of Germans who charged violations by the Polish government of this treaty.

"In fact, both Konrad Adenauer . . ." Henry Turner calls attention to this phenomenon of dates in his *The Two Germanies Since 1945*.

CHAPTER 1: "In the bookshops of nearby Göttingen . . ." A most useful explication of this history told from the German point of view is *Die Russland-Deutschen*, by Sven Steenberg. This section draws heavily on the book.

Notes

CHAPTER 2: "In March, 1919, Czech soldiers fired . . ." Sudeten literature documents this. For an English-language version, see de Zayas.

"All these young people feel . . ." Joint Relief Commission quote from de Zayas, p. 107.

CHAPTER 3: "Sarajevo . . ." David Large, a historian at Montana State University, reviewed this history in an article in *The Wall Street Journal*, April 25, 1990.

"There was 'no heel clicking' . . ." This quote is cited in Gordon Craig's *The Germans*. His chapter on soldiers provides an informative and accessible tour of the history of the German military.

"Historian Golo Mann . . ." This account comes from *The History of Germany Since 1789*.

"The count died . . ." The quote comes from Golo Mann as well.

"In Bonn, Adenauer . . ." Bark and Gress describe this in *A History of West Germany*, Vol. I, p. 286.

"National tolerance of thunderous low-level flights . . ." Bark and Gress detail the air disasters on page 506 of *A History of West Germany*.

CHAPTER 4: "A witness in 1885 described the scene . . ." This description is reprinted in the Merian guide to Munich.

"The *Bayerische Kurier*, a local paper, mourned the transformation . . ." Karl Köwer's excellent chapter in the commemorative volume *Das Prinzregententheater in München* provided this bit of information, as well as many others mentioned in the description of the history of the Prinze.

CHAPTER 6: "Who could imagine . . ." Golo Mann gives a lucid explanation of 1848, on which this section relies heavily.

"History books" . . . Schwarzenberg holdings. This list comes from William Johnston's *The Austrian Mind*.

CHAPTER 7: Map at start of chapter is based on Map 6 in Martin Gilbert's *Atlas of the Holocaust*.

"Heine, of Jewish background himself . . ." The quotes are from S. S. Prawer's *Heine's Jewish Comedy*, pages 61–62. The volume links Heine's ironic humor to that of more modern Jewish humorists such as Woody Allen.

Bibliography

Bald, Detlef. *Der Deutsche Offizier*. Munich: Bernard and Graefe Verlag, 1982.

Bark, Dennis L., and David R. Gress. *A History of West Germany*. Oxford, Eng., and Cambridge, Mass.: Basil Blackwell, 1989.

Bauer, Curt. *München, Ein Stadtführer*. Munich: Heinrich Hugendubel Verlag, 1989.

Broszat, Martin, and Klaus Schwabe, eds. *Die deutschen Eliten und der Weg in den Zweiten Weltkrieg*. Munich: Beck'sche Reihe, Verlag C. H. Beck, 1989.

Burleigh, Michael. *Germany Turns Eastwards: A Study of Ostforschung in the Third Reich*. Cambridge: Cambridge University Press, 1988.

Carr, William. *A History of Germany: 1815–1985*. 3rd ed.; London: Edward Arnold, 1987.

Craig, Gordon A. *The Germans*. Harmondsworth, Eng.: Penguin Books, 1982.

————*Germany: 1866–1945*. New York and London: Oxford University Press, 1978.

Dagerman, Stig. *Automne Allemand*. Trans. from the Swedish into French by Philippe Bouquet. Actes Sud, Hubert Nyssen Editeur, 1980.

de Zayas, Alfred M. *Nemesis at Potsdam: The Anglo-Americans and the Expulsion of the Germans*. Rev. ed.; London and Boston: Routledge & Kegan Paul, 1979.

Dönhoff, Marion Gräfin. *Namen die keiner Mehr Nennt:*

Bibliography

Ostpreussen—Menschen und Geschichte. 3rd ed.; Munich: Deutscher Taschenbuch Verlag, 1985.

Frenzel, H. A., and E. Frenzel. *Daten deutscher Dichtung: Chronologischer Abriss der deutschen Literaturgeschichte.* Munich: Deutscher Taschenbuch Verlag, 1962.

Gay, Peter, and R. K. Webb. *Modern Europe to 1815.* New York: Harper & Row, 1973.

Gilbert, Martin. *Atlas of the Holocaust.* Oxford, Eng., and Elmsford, N.Y.: Pergamon Press, 1988.

Grosser, Alfred. *Geschichte Deutschlands Seit 1945: Eine Bilanz.* 13th ed., Munich: Deutscher Taschenbuch Verlag, 1987.

Heine, Heinrich. *Reisebilder.* Frankfurt am Main: Insel Verlag, 1980.

Hubensteiner, Benno. *Bayerische Geschichte: Staat und Volk, Kunst und Kultur.* 5th ed.; Munich: Richard Pflaum Verlag, 1967.

Johnston, William M. *The Austrian Mind: An Intellectual and Social History, 1848–1938.* Berkeley: University of California Press, 1972.

Koch, H. W. *A History of Prussia.* London: Longman, 1978.

MacDonogh, Giles. *A Good German: Adam von Trott zu Solz.* London and New York: Quartet Books, 1989.

Large, David Clay. "Sarajevo and Its Causes." *The Wall Street Journal,* April 24, 1990.

Mann, Golo. *The History of Germany Since 1789.* Trans. by Marian Jackson. Harmondsworth, Eng.: Penguin Books, 1974.

Ostow, Robin. *Jüdisches Leben in der DDR.* Frankfurt am Main: Athäneum, Jüdischer Verlag, 1988.

Prawer, S. S. *Heine's Jewish Comedy: A Study of His Portraits of Jews and Judaism.* Oxford: Clarendon Press, 1983.

Reich-Ranicki, Marcel. *Über Ruhestörer: Juden in der deutschen Literatur.* Stuttgart: Deutsche Verlags-Anstalt, 1989.

Raschhofer, Hermann, and Otto Kimminich. *Die Sudetenfrage: Ihre völkerrechtliche Entwicklung vom Ersten Weltkrieg bis zur Gegenwart.* Munich: Olzog Verlag, 1988.

Shirer, William L. *The Rise and Fall of the Third Reich: A History of Nazi Germany.* New York: Simon & Schuster, 1960.

Sichrovsky, Peter. *Schuldig geboren: Kinder aus Nazifamilien.* Cologne: Kiepenheuer & Witsch, 1987.

Bibliography

Steenberg, Sven. *Die Russland-Deutschen: Schicksal und Erleben.* Munich: Langen-Müller, 1989.

Steimel, Robert. *". . . im vordersten Gefecht!": Kleine Geschichte des deutschen Adels.* Cologne-Zollstock: Steimel Verlag, 1959.

Turner, Henry Ashby, Jr. *The Two Germanies Since 1945.* New Haven: Yale University Press, 1987.

Additional documentation:

Werkbesuch bei der Oper. Bayerischer Rundfunk, 1987.

Portrait on the occasion of August Everding's 60th birthday. "Mosaik," Zweites Deutsches Fernsehen, 1988.

Der Spiegel, September 14, 1955.

Manfred Wörner, NATO secretary-general, in an interview with the author for *The Wall Street Journal*, Spring 1989.

Flüchtlings-Starthilfe e. V. Hamburg. "Tätigkeitsbericht 1988." Also: "30 Jahre Flüchtlings-Starthilfe e. V. Hamburg: Bericht mit Rückblick," 1982.

Seidel, Klaus-Jürgen, ed. *Das Prinzregententheater in München.* Nuremberg: Drei W. Druck und Verlag J. Schoierer KG, 1984.

Ranft, Ferdinand, ed. *Munich.* Merian Reiseführer. 3rd ed.; Munich: Deutscher Taschenbuch Verlag, 1987.

Köwer, Karl, and Manfred Mayer, eds. *Rund Ums Prinzregententheater*, a pamphlet produced by the Generalintendanz der Bayerischen Staatstheater, April 1989.

Finkenzeller, Roswin. "Helft dem Prinzregententheater." *Münchner Stadtanzeiger*, No. 58, July 29, 1983.

"Nicht wahr, aber gut und schön." *Frankfurter Allgemeine Zeitung*, Jan. 17, 1988.

"Wie es 1990 weitergeht, weiss jetzt noch keiner." *Abendzeitung*, Jan. 26, 1988.

"Das 'Prinze' soll bald wiederverschwinden." *Münchner Merkur*, Jan. 13, 1988.

Linkenheil, Rolf. "Der Generalintendant in der Rolle des Schnorrers." *Stuttgarter Zeitung*, No. 298, Dec. 28, 1987.

Eichholz, Armin. "Und huldvoll neigt Bavaria ihre Stirn." *Die Welt*, Dec. 28, 1987.

Bibliography

Göhl, Hans. "Wie sieht die Zukunft aus?" *Münchner Merkur*, Jan. 26, 1988.

Hénard, Jacqueline. "Aus nächster Ferne; Neue Bindungen, Tschechloslowakei und Österreich." *Frankfurter Allgemeine Zeitung*, April 1990.

Schmemann, Serge. "A Prince, His Castle, and the Tenants." *The New York Times*, April 29, 1990.

Christian, Shirley. "Pinochet Irks Bonn with Potshots at Army," *The New York Times*, Sept. 8, 1990.

Index

Adenauer, Konrad, 10–11, 25, 31,
  39, 83
Adolfs, Dieter, 35
Albanians, 7, 66–67
Alternative list, 195
American vs. German citizenship
  (territorial vs. personal), 20
Anglo-American private charity
  tradition, 140, 143
anti-militarism, in West Germany,
  74–75, 93–95, 98–99
anti-Semitism, 202; of political right,
  211–13
appeasement (Munich 1938), 46
Arendt, Hannah, 193
aristocracy, German, *see* nobility
Armenians, 7, 32
arms control, 74–75, 93, 99
army, West German, 7, 71; *see also*
  Bundeswehr
arts, private funds vs. state subsidies
  for, 106–7, 109–11, 124–25, 126–
  27, 129
Asylanten, 36
asylum, political, 19, 36, 154, 155,
  204
Attlee, Clement, 56, 60
Augstein, Rudolf, 86
Auschwitz, 55, 58
Ausländer (foreigners), 36
Aussiedler (settlers), 18–28, 30–36,
  37–39, 128, 153–54; benefit
  entitlement, 20, 25–26, 34;
  citizenship, 20, 23–25, 26, 32;
  defined, 18, 36; postwar exiles'

welcome to, 64–65; statistics, 25,
  39, 43–44
Aussig (Sudetenland) massacre, 54
Austria, 50, 66, 89, 111, 163, 169,
  178; Hungarian border opening to,
  10, 34
Austro-Hungarian empire, 7, 46, 163;
  see also Habsburg empire
authoritarianism, 95, 98, 129, 147,
  192

Baden-Württemberg, 56, 105
Baltic Germans, 7, 29, 44–45, 177,
  243
Barbara (Refugee Start Help), 133–
  43, 145–46, 147–53, 156–58
"Barbara Requests" notices, in *Die
  Zeit*, 134, 142–43, 146
Barkol, Micha, 189
Basic Law (*Grundgesetz*), 122
Bavaria, 59, 62, 113–14, 118, 122,
  125–27; culture and its funding,
  103–18, 120, 124–25, 126–29; and
  Sudeten Germans, 56
Bayreuth, 115, 116
Beck, General Ludwig, 82, 83, 134
benefits entitlement: Eastern-bloc
  Germans, 20, 25–26, 34; East
  German refugees, 155
Beneš, Eduard, 50, 60
Berchtold, Leopold von, 80
Berenberg-Consbruch, Jutta von, 146
Berlin, 5, 13, 104, 124, 130, 200, 217–
  46; Allied occupation of, 218, 223–
  24, 231; as capital, 11, 220, 245;

Index

Berlin (*cont.*)
descriptions of, 183, 218–24, 227–
32, 237–39, 244; descriptions of
past in, 198–200, 232, 233–37,
239; government of, 195; Jewish
community, 184–98, 203–5, 206–
7, 209–10, 213–14; Jewish
population of 1930s, 184; refugees
in, 155; Republican party in, 195,
211; *see also* East Berlin; West
Berlin
Berlin Wall, 4, 12, 33, 39, 135, 150,
151, 217–18, 227, 231; Checkpoint
Charlie, 237; escapees, 222, 237;
fall of, 10, 11–12, 96, 213, 217,
232, 244–46
Bernhard, Thomas, 130
Bernstein, Leonard, 123
Bernstorff, Albrecht von, 87
Bethmann-Hollweg, Theobald von,
80
Biermann, Wolf, 171
Bismarck, Otto von, 91
Bismarck family, 179
Bitburg, as symbol, 87–89
black-market activities, 190, 206,
207; immediate postwar, 231–32
Blank, Theodor, 84
Bodemann, Michal, 191–92, 209
Bohemia, 50, 162, 166, 176–77
Bonn, 104; as capital, 10, 76
Borchmeyer, Dieter, 114–15
border question, Poland-Germany, 9,
13, 45, 65–66
Börner, Holger, 201
*Born Guilty: Children from Nazi
Families* (Sichrovsky), 202
Brandt, Willy, 39
Bräunlich, Helmut, 48
Breslau (Wroclaw), 32
Buchenwald concentration camp,
170, 176
Bücklein, Klaus, 98–99
Bundestag, 177; Kristallnacht address
of Jenninger in, 202, 211;
representation of exiles in, 48, 56
Bundeswehr, 72, 73–78, 81, 84–87,
90, 92, 94–100; citizen attitudes
toward, 98–99; shift in identity, 95,
98; and unification, 74–75, 96–98,
100
Burckhardt, Jakob von, 144

Burda brothers, 125–26
Burleigh, Michael, 63
Bush, George, 57

Cambodia(ns), 36, 55
campus unrest, late 1960s, 8, 183
capitalism, 227; 1968's critics of, 8–9
Carpathian Germans, 63
Castorf, Frank, 112
Catherine the Great, Czarina, 8, 28–
30
Chamberlain, Neville, 10, 46, 82
charity, private, 134–35, 140–49,
150–51; *see also* Red Cross;
Refugee Start Help
Christian Democratic Union (CDU),
66, 127, 139, 212
Christian Social Union (CSU), 66
church and state, German lack of
separation of, 198, 208
Churchill, Sir Winston, 6, 18, 223
church taxes, 208
citizenship: Eastern-bloc Germans,
20, 23–25, 26, 32; Nazi
(Reichsbürgergesetz), 4; territorial
vs. personal concepts, 20
"citizen soldiers," 98
Civic Forum, Czechoslovakia, 52,
164, 167, 173, 174, 176
Claer, Alexander von, 79
Claer, Axel von, 71–72, 75, 78–85
passim, 89–94, 96–97, 100
Claer, Carl-Gideon von, 81–82, 83–
89, 94
Claer, Eberhard von, 78, 80
Claer, Helmut von, 89–90
Claer, Otto von, 71, 78–79
Claer, Sitta von, 90, 93–94
Claer, Susanne von, 90–91, 93–94,
96
Cohn-Bendit, Daniel, 212
Cold War, 10, 66, 150, 227; in
Berlin, 221–22
Common Market, 49, 96, 178
concentration camps, Nazi, 35, 55,
60, 119, 121, 176, 194, 199
conscientious objectors, 99
conservatives, 212, 229, 232; anti-
Semitic views among, 211; in the
military, 96; ties to expellees, 44,
56, 64–66, 128
Cuban Missile Crisis, 39

Index

currency reform of 1948, 124, 231–
32
Czechoslovakia, 46, 57, 61, 164–67;
Communist, 52, 165, 167, 173;
German minority in, 7, 45, 50, 52,
61, 62; German minority denied
self-determination, 46, 60–62;
1968 revolt, and refugees from,
151–52, 176; post-Communist, 12,
52, 164, 180; prewar, 46, 50, 58–
60, 170; velvet revolution of 1989,
164, 173; see also Sudeten
Germans; Sudetenland

Dachau concentration camp, 119
Dagerman, Stig, 122
Daladier, Edouard, 46
Danzig, 6, 32
decolonization, 13–14
democracy: lack of German tradition
of, 10; tradition built in West
Germany, 14, 86, 94
denazification, 37, 237
détente, 44–45
Deutschkron, Inge, 198–200, 201,
205
displaced persons, see refugees
Dönhoff, Marion, 134, 146–47
draft, military, 231
Drang nach Osten, 63
Dresden, 13, 96, 115

eagle, as national emblem, 77
East Berlin, 222–24, 227–28, 244–
46; Jews of, 184, 191, 209–10
Eastern-bloc Germans, 6–8, 17–39,
44–68; adjustment problems, 33;
benefit entitlement, 20, 25–26, 34;
citizenship, 20, 23–25, 26, 32;
statistics, 6, 25, 34, 39, 43–44; see
also Aussiedler (settlers); exiles
(expellees); and see specific groups
Eastern European Jews ("Ostjuden"),
205–6; see also Soviet Jews
East Germany (German Democratic
Republic, DDR), 3, 14, 135, 162,
194; army of, 76, 96–97; glimpses
of life in, 136–40 passim, 148,
149–50, 157, 222–23; Jews of, 184,
191, 209–10; opening of (1989),
10, 11–12, 74, 155, 213, 217, 244–
46; refugees from, 10, 12, 19, 26,

33–34, 133–40, 141–42, 147, 148–
58; refugee statistics, 34, 135, 151
East Prussia(ns), 44, 147
economic miracle
(*Wirtschaftswunder*), 3, 124, 231–
32; exiles participating in, 44; role
of guest workers in, 19, 36
education, 186; tuition-free, 231
Eichmann, Adolf, 210
Eisner, Kurt, 118
Erhard, Ludwig, 232
Espelkamp, North Rhine–
Westphalia, 38
Estonia(ns), 29, 32, 243
Ethiopians, 19, 36, 154
ethnic resettlement, 6–7, 55; see also
exiles (expellees)
Europe: disarmament, 74–75, 93; of
1990s, 67; postwar reshaping of
map of, 6–7, 18, 65
European Community, 49, 177–78
Europeanism, of Germans, 9, 150; of
exiles, 49, 66–67; of military, 96,
97
European Parliament, 62, 163, 177–
78, 211
Everding, August, 103, 104, 106,
107–11, 112–13, 117, 126–27,
129–30
exiles (expellees), postwar, 6–7, 17–
18, 43–45, 54–55, 63–66, 128,
142, 147; annual conventions of,
43, 47–48, 63–68; campaigns for
vote of, 64–66; Europeanism of,
49, 66–67; ranks swelled by
Aussiedler, 64–65; second
generation, 46, 53–56, 64;
statistics, 6, 18, 39, 43–44, 57; see
also Silesians; Sudeten Germans
Extra-Parliamentary Opposition, 90
extremism, 13, 212–13, 234–35

Falz-Fein family, 29
Fassbinder, Werner, 138
Federal Republic of Germany, see
West Germany
Fischer von Erlach, Johann
Bernhard, 168
Fischer von Erlach, Josef Emanuel,
168
Flegel, Otto, 39

Index

foreigners, German attitudes toward, 19–20, 34, 153–54, 155, 207, 212, 213; terminology, 36
Franco-Prussian War of 1870–71, 4, 71, 77, 78, 80, 114, 170
Frankfurt: Jewish community of, 206, 212; refugees in, 155
Frankfurter Allgemeine Zeitung, 179, 201
Frankfurt National Assembly of 1848, 111, 169
Franz Ferdinand, Archduke, 163
Frederick II, the Great, King of Prussia, 13, 45–46, 63
freedom, lack of German tradition of, 10–11, 14
Fremde (strangers), 36
Freud, Sigmund, 50
Friedland *Aussiedler* camp, 18–19, 20–25, 26–28, 30, 32–33, 34, 37–40, 44, 133; administration of, 35–36; statistics, 39
Friedland monument, 17, 38
Friedmann, Michel, 202, 212–13
From Today On, Your Name Is Sara (play), 200
Führungsakademie, Bundeswehr, 75–78, 80, 92, 95–99

Gabert, Volkmar, 59–61
Galinski, Heinz, 192, 194–98, 203, 207, 211
Gastarbeiter, 36; *see also* guest workers
Gdansk, 6, 32
Geisler, Klaus, 54, 55, 56, 66
German Democratic Republic, *see* East Germany
German language, 5
"German Question," 9, 150
German Reich of 1871–1918, 4, 72, 79–80, 114
Germany Turns Eastwards (Burleigh), 63
Gestapo, 11, 170
Giessen *Aussiedler* camp, 133
Gleichenstein, Leonore von, 146
Goebbels, Josef, 221, 238
Goethe, Johann Wolfgang von, 27, 107
Gop, Ilja, 207

Gorbachev, Mikhail, 10, 25, 57, 72, 74, 105, 241
Göring, Hermann, 76
Graham, Kay (Katherine), 147
Grass, Günter, 6
Great Britain, 79–80, 96; arts funding, 110; citizenship concept, 20
Green movement, 8, 13, 212, 235
grossdeutsch solution, 111, 169
guest workers, 8, 19, 36
Gysi, Gregor, 210

Habsburg, Otto von, 61–62, 68, 163–64, 178
Habsburg, Regina von, 48
Habsburg empire, 7, 46, 47, 50, 62, 67, 79–80, 162, 163, 168–70; ethnic minorities of, 170
Hamburg, 71, 96, 125, 151; cosmopolitan atmosphere and civic participation in, 134, 143–45; recent refugee waves in, 152–55; social unrest in, 155
Hamburger Morgenpost, 152
Haniel, Elly, 151
Haus der Kunst, Munich, 120
Havel, Václav, 52, 54, 164–65, 167, 172–75, 180
Heimatpfleger (homeland caretakers), 52, 56
"Heim ins Reich," 30, 38, 50, 244
Heimkehrer, 38
Heine, Heinrich, 3, 4, 14, 205–6
Helsinki Federation, 166, 167
Henlein, Konrad, 46, 58
Herrenchiemsee, 114
Hesse, George, 143, 146
Hesse, Jeannette, 134, 140, 143–46
Himmler, Heinrich, 88
history, German attitudes toward, 4, 10–11, 62; Sudeten German distortions of, 50, 58
Hitler, Adolf, 4, 10, 11, 20, 59, 61, 72, 76, 82, 88, 91, 106, 111, 119–20, 128, 162, 170, 175, 232, 233, 236; assassination attempt on, 82–83, 87, 89, 176, 239; eastward expansionism, 36, 46, 63; *Heim ins Reich* program of, 30–31, 50, 244; *Mein Kampf*, 236; mentioned, 5,

Index

81, 104, 108, 121, 134, 201, 221,
234
Höger, Fritz, 143–44
Högner, Dr., 122
Holocaust, 12, 63, 185, 202, 210; and
Wiedergutmachung for survivors,
208
Holy Roman Empire, 62, 163; *see
also* Habsburg empire
Home of the Gentry (Turgenev), 29
Honecker, Erich, 10, 135, 194, 196,
210, 213
Honecker, Margot, 140
Hotter, Hans, 122
housing of refugees, 34, 152–55
Hungary, 54, 57, 164, 178; border
opening of 1989, 10, 12, 34, 138;
1956 uprising, 90; post-
Communist, 12, 62, 67
Hus, Jan, 176
Hussein, Saddam, 75

Ibsen, Henrik, 117
Ilsemann, Marie-Luise von, 146
INF (intermediate nuclear forces)
debate, 74, 75, 93, 99
International Helsinki Federation,
166, 167
International Red Cross Joint Relief
Commission, 54–55
intifada, 209, 210
Ireland, 55
Iron Curtain, 25, 33; *see also* Berlin
Wall
Ismay, Lord Hastings, 73–74
Israel, 20, 185, 208–9, 210
Italian guest workers, 8, 19, 36
I Wore the Yellow Star (Deutschkron),
200

Jenninger, Philipp, 202, 211
Jewish Community Center, West
Berlin, 193–94, 196, 204, 208
"Jewish Question," German attitudes
toward, 184, 185, 199–200, 201–2,
210
Jewish School, West Berlin, 185–93,
194, 196, 201, 208, 213–14
Jews, 20, 123, 184–214; attitudes
toward German reunification, 11–
12, 185, 197, 213; Berlin

community, 184–98, 203–5, 206–
7, 209–10, 213–14; Berlin
population of 1930s, 184; black-
market activities, 190, 206, 207;
Nazi persecution of, 11, 50, 57,
121, 184, 194, 199–202; in postwar
Germany, 6, 7, 13, 184–85, 191,
198–201, 203–14; prewar
population in Germany, 198;
Soviet, 18, 25, 28, 32, 184–85,
190–91, 194, 203–5, 206–7, 213

Käfer, Gerd, 125
Kafka, Franz, 50
Kant, Immanuel, 228
Karajan, Herbert von, 200
Karsch, Iris, 23, 25
Kazakhstan, Germans of, 22, 31
Kennedy, John F., 39
Khrushchev, Nikita, 39
Killing Fields, The (film), 55
Kirgizia, Germans of, 28, 33
Kir Royal (TV show), 126
Klee, Paul, 117
Klein, Hans, 56, 64
kleindeutsch solution, 111, 169
Kleinschmidt, Mascha, 213
Knappertsbusch, Hans, 122, 123
Kohl, Helmut, 56, 64–65, 97, 156,
197, 202, 241; and eastern border
question, 65
Koschyk, Hartmut, 45, 56
Krabler, Inge, 53–54
Krauss, Barbara von, *see* Oster,
Barbara
Kristallnacht (1938), 4, 11–12, 184;
1988 Jenninger address, 202, 211
Kultur (culture), 112, 130; private vs.
public funding of, 106–7, 109–11,
124–25, 126–27, 129
Kundera, Milan, 174

Lager (camps), 35; *see also* Friedland
Aussiedler camp; resettlement
camps; transfer camps
Lambsdorff, Otto von, 177
land claims, for confiscated
properties, 179
Landovsky, Pavel, 174
Laski, Harold, 60
Latvia, 29

Laufzettel, 35–36
League of Exiles, 45, 56
Lebanon war of 1980s, 209, 210
Lebensraum, 36
left-wing groups, 8, 13, 183, 212, 235, 245
Lenin, Vladimir Ilytch, 30
Le Pen, Jean-Marie, 128, 197
Lessing, Gotthold Ephraim, 112
Lindermeier, Elisabeth, 121–24
Lithuania, 29
Littmann, Max, 116
Ludwig I, King of Bavaria, 113
Ludwig II, King of Bavaria, 103, 104, 106, 107, 108, 114–16
Ludwig III, King of Bavaria, 118
Luitpold, Prince Regent of Bavaria, 104, 106, 116–17
Lummer, Heinrich, 34
Luther, Martin, 167, 176, 187

Mann, Golo, 10, 80, 114, 169–70
Mann, Thomas, 104, 117
Maria Theresa, Empress, 45–46
Marxists, 8, 209–10, 223, 226–27, 245; *see also* left-wing groups
Masaryk, Tomáš, 50
Matuschka, Count, 109
Mauthausen concentration camp, 194
Maximilian I, King of Bavaria, 106
Mazowiecki, Tadeusz, 65
Meinhardt, Sabine, 190–91, 192, 214
Mein Kampf (Hitler), 236
Meinke, Kerstin, 137–39, 155–56
Meir, Golda, 209
Mendelssohn, Moses, 193
Mideast crisis of 1990, 75
military tradition, German, 71–73, 75–76, 78–85, 87; authoritarianism, 95, 98; changes in, 74–75, 95, 98–99
minorities, German, in Eastern Europe, 7; *see also* Eastern-bloc Germans
Miss Sara Sampson (Lessing), 112–13
Mitläufer (fellow travelers), 237
Moltke, Helmuth James von, 82, 87
Moltke, Helmuth von (of Franco-Prussian War), 71, 72, 77, 78, 80, 87
Moltke, Helmuth von (of World War I Schlieffen plan), 79–80

monarchism, remnants of, 163, 177
Mössel, Ludwig, 126
Mozart, Wolfgang Amadeus, 107
Munich, 56, 117, 144; culture and its funding in, 103–18, 120, 124–25, 126–27, 129–30; and Nazism, 119–21, 128; postwar, 121–30
Munich agreement of 1938, 46

Nachmann, Werner, 208
Names No One Mentions Anymore (Donhöff), 147
Napoleon I, Emperor, 161, 168
Napoleon III, Emperor, 78
national anthem, German, 77
nationalism, 66; of East European minorities, 7, 13, 18; German, 36–37, 211
National People's Army (East German NVA), 76, 96–97
NATO (North Atlantic Treaty Organization), 73–75, 91; two-track decision, 99
Nazism (National Socialism), 4, 11, 50, 58, 63, 119–21, 170, 232–35, 236–37; aristocrats and, 82–83, 175–76; persecution of Jews, 11, 50, 57, 121, 184, 194, 199–202; records of, used in resettlement, 24, 26; Sixty-Eighters' revolt as protest against, 8–9, 202, 234–35; *see also* Third Reich
neo-Nazi skinheads, 13, 213
Neubauer, Franz, 57, 58, 60
Neuschwanstein, 114
New York Times, The, 95
1968 generation, 8, 183, 212, 230, 235; and Nazi crimes, 8–9, 202, 234–35
nobility, German, 162–63, 178–80; international traditions of, 177–80; military tradition of, 78, 163; and Nazis, 82–83, 175–76; in private charity work, 146; role in modern Europe, 62, 163–64, 166–67, 170, 177–80
North German Confederation, 113–14
November 9, as date in German history, 11–12
nuclear weapons in Europe, 74, 77, 86, 93, 96, 99

Nuremberg race laws, 199
Nuremberg war crimes trials, 89, 98, 237

Orff, Carl, 124, 126
Oster, Barbara, 134–35, 142, 143, 145
Oster, Hans, 134
Ostforschung, 63
Ostow, Robin, 192, 209
Ostpolitik, 44; of Brandt, 39

Pamyat, 213
Paulskirche National Assembly of 1848, 111, 169
Paulus, Axel, 92, 93, 94
Paulus, Field Marshal Friedrich von, 92
Pazderski, Georg, 99
Peters, Heinrich, 27–28, 29
Peter the Great, Czar, 29
Pinochet, Augusto, 95
Pirandello, Luigi, 130
Placak, Petr, 177
Poland, 39, 54, 142; demise of Communism in, 10; expulsion of Germans from, 6, 17, 57, 60; former German provinces incorporated in, 6, 13, 32, 45; German border with, 9, 13, 45, 65; German minority of, 7, 18, 32, 45; Hitler's expansionism into, 63; loss of eastern parts to USSR, 6; opening of borders, 12; post-Communist, 65
Poles, in Berlin, 213
Polish-German *Aussiedler*, 18, 21–24, 27, 32–33, 34, 36, 39, 153–54
Polish Jews, 205–6
Pomeranians, 44, 55
Possart, Ernst von, 109, 118
Potsdam Conference and Agreement of 1945, 6, 18, 57, 60
POWs in USSR, 31–32, 39
Prague, 47, 58, 60, 152, 165–67, 173–77, 180
Prahl, Hildegard, 39
Precan, Vilem, 173
Prinzregententheater, Munich, 103–12, 115–19, 120–27, 129–30
Proebst, Gertrud, 110
property claims, 179

Prussia, Prussian tradition, 10, 45, 95, 114, 122, 147, 170, 175; army, 71–72, 75, 95

racism, 211–12; Third Reich, 4, 11, 20, 50, 57, 162, 184, 199–200
Ramstein air show disaster, 98
Reagan, Ronald, 74, 88
Red Army Faction, 8
Red Cross, 18, 20–23 *passim*, 39, 133, 143
refugees: *Aussiedler*, 18–28, 30–36, 37–39, 128, 153–54 (*see also* *Aussiedler*); Czech, in 1968, 151–52; East German, 10, 12, 19, 26, 33–34, 133–40, 141–42, 147, 148–58; hierarchy of, 34, 153–54; postwar, all Europe, 57; postwar German exiles, 6–8, 17–18, 39, 43–44, 54–55, 57, 63–66, 128, 142, 147 (*see also* exiles; Silesians; Sudeten Germans); statistics, 39; statistics for early postwar years, 6, 18, 39, 43–44, 57; statistics for East Germans, 34, 135, 151; statistics of 1988–89, 18, 25, 34, 135; terminology, 36; Third World political-asylum seekers, 19, 36, 154, 155; West Germany overwhelmed with, 152–55
Refugee Start Help ("Barbara"), 133–43, 145–46, 147–53, 156–58
regionalism, 67
Reich-Ranicki, Marcel, 5, 200–1, 205, 206
Reichsbürgergesetz of 1935, 4
Reichswehr, Weimar Republic, 81, 83
repatriation law of 1953, 20, 25
Republikaner (political party), 13, 65–66, 89, 154, 195, 197, 211–12, 213, 236; in Berlin, 195, 211; in Munich, 128–29
resettlement camps and centers, 26, 33–34, 142, 205; Schnelsen, 152–54, 155
Resistance, German, in World War II, 11, 82–83, 87, 176, 239
reunification, 109–14, 134–35; attitudes of exiles (expellees) toward, 9, 45, 47, 67, 150; attitudes of Germans toward, 9, 13, 128, 150; attitudes of non-Germans

reunification (*cont.*)
 toward, 11–12; and border
  question, 9, 13, 65; economic, 232;
  emotional problems of, 12–13;
  Jews and, 11–12, 185, 197, 213;
  military issues of, 72, 74–75, 96–
  98, 100; ten-point plan for, 156;
  treaty, 197
revolutions of 1848, 4, 169
Richter, Franz Xaver, 48
Richter, Walli, 56
right-wing groups, 13, 211–12; *see
 also* conservatives; Republikaner
Rilke, Rainer Maria, 117
Romania: German minority in, 7;
 German refugees from, 17–18, 63,
  153; Hungarian minority in, 62
Rommel, Manfred, 43, 49
Roosevelt, Franklin D., 18
Russia, Czarist, Germans in, 28–30
Russians, in Berlin, 213; *see also*
 Soviet Jews, in Berlin
Russland-Deutschen, Die, 37

Sander, Jill, 226
Sarajevo, assassination at, 72, 79, 163
Scheven, Werner von, 82
Schiller, Friedrich, 49, 112
Schinkel, Friedrich, 75, 220
Schlieffen plan, 79, 80, 163
Schmidt, Helmut, 127, 146, 229
Schneider family of refugees, 23, 31
Schnelsen mobile-home camp, 152–
 54, 155
Scholl, Geschwister (siblings), 119
Schönhuber, Franz, 89, 128–29,
 211–12, 236
Schreger, Klaus, 124
Schwarzenberg, Felix zu, 168–70
Schwarzenberg, Heinrich von, 170,
 176
Schwarzenberg, Johann von, 167
Schwarzenberg, Prince Karl I von,
 161, 168, 171–72
Schwarzenberg, Karl Johannes von,
 161–62, 164–77, 180
Schwarzenberg, Teresa von, 171
Schwarzenberg family, 161–62, 166,
 168–72, 175–77
Seidel, Klaus, 109, 117, 118–19, 120,
 126
self-determination, Wilsonian, 46, 59;

denied to Sudeten Germans in
 Czechoslovakia, 46, 50, 60–62
Semper, Gottfried, 115
"settlers," *see Aussiedler*
Shakespeare, William, 130
Siberia, Germans in, 7, 23, 31, 37
Sichrovsky, Peter, 202
Siebenbürger Saxons, 63
Siemens (firm), 103, 109, 124
Silesia, 13, 45, 66
Silesians, 9, 13, 44–45, 64; attitude
 toward reunification, 9, 45; Polish
 border as election issue for, 65–66
Sixty-Eighters' movement, 8; *see also*
 1968 generation
skinheads, neo-Nazi, 13, 213
Slavs, German views of, 63
social class, 94, 162–63; *see also*
 nobility
Social Democrats, 199, 212, 235;
 attitudes toward reunification, 9; in
 Berlin, 195, 196; and expellees, 59,
 64
socialism, 179, 245; Jews and, 199,
 209–10; 1968 movement, 8
soldier identify, shift in, 95, 98
Solidarity (Poland), 6, 39, 142
Solti, Georg, 123
Soviet-German *Aussiedler*, 7–8, 17–
 18, 22, 26, 27–28, 30–32, 33, 34,
 36, 37, 38, 39, 153
Soviet Jews, 18, 25, 28, 32; in Berlin,
 184–85, 190–91, 194, 203–5, 206–
 7, 213
Soviet Union, 38, 72, 100; ethnic
 minorities of, 7, 67; German
 minorities of, 7–8, 18, 28–32; and
 German reunification, 100; Pamyat
 anti-Semitism in, 213; westward
 expansion into Polish and German
 territories, 6
Späth, Lothar, 56
Speer, Albert, 233, 234
Speer, Hilde, 234–35
Spiegel, Der (magazine), 73, 85–86,
 91
Springer (Axel) publishing house, 64
Sri Lankans, 19
SS (Schutz-Staffel), 82, 83, 88, 89,
 91, 121
Stalin, Josef, 6, 18, 23, 28, 29, 30, 44,
 57, 244

Index

Stauffenberg, Claus Schenck von, 82–83, 87, 176, 178
Stauffenberg, Franz Ludwig Schenck von, 178
Straus, Henning, 99
Strauss, Franz-Josef, 56–57, 59, 86, 104, 105–6, 125–26, 127–28
Strauss, Richard, 117, 126
Strength Through Joy, 120, 233
student revolt (late 1960s), 8, 183
students, in Berlin, 183, 219, 226–27, 231
Stuttgart, 43, 47
Sudeten Germans, 6, 13, 43–54, 56–64, 66–68; attitude toward reunification, 47, 67; distortions of historical facts by, 50, 58; eastward orientation of, 47, 63; expulsion from homeland, 43–44, 49–50, 54–55, 57; and Nazism, 46, 50–51, 58–59, 60–61, 64; preoccupation with past and "roots," 49–54, 56, 62–63; second-generation expellees, 53–56
Sudeten German Society, 49
Sudetenland, 13, 43, 49–52; area, 50; as part of Third Reich, 6, 43, 46, 47, 50, 66, 176
Sudeten Youth Group, 53, 56, 66
Süsskind, Artur, 196

Tamils, 36, 154
terrorism, 8, 185
Thatcher, Margaret, 57, 66, 111, 147
Third Reich (1933–45), 4, 10, 11, 63, 77, 81–83, 88–89, 119, 175–76, 234; racism, 4, 11, 20, 50, 57, 162, 184, 199–200; Resistance, 11, 82–83, 87, 176; Sudetenland as part of, 6, 43, 46, 47, 50, 66, 176; see also Nazism
Third World refugees, in Germany, 19, 36, 154, 155
Thurn und Taxis, Johannes and Gloria von, 163, 179–80
Times, The (of London), 55
Tin Drum, The (Grass), 6
transfer camps, 34–35, 133; see also Friedland
Treblinka concentration camp, 55
Trotsky, Leon, 72
"Trud Army" ("labor army"), 31

Truman, Harry S., 6, 57
Turgenev, Ivan, 29
Turkish guest workers, 8, 19, 36

Übersiedler ("trans-settlers"), 36; see also East Germany, refugees from
Ukraine, Germans of, 23, 28
Ulbricht, Walter, 11, 12, 135
Unbearable Lightness of Being, The (Kundera), 174
unemployment, 105, 154, 228–29
unification: attempt of 1948–49, 4, 111, 169–70; of 1871, 4, 72, 91, 114, 170; see also reunification
United States, 96, 204; arts funding in, 110; citizenship concept, 20; West Germany and, 75, 84
university system, German, 140, 231

Versailles, Treaty of, 46, 62
Vienna, 46, 47, 62, 162, 163, 167–69, 171–72
Vietnam(ese), 55, 147
Vigotsky, Edi, 207
Volga Germans, 30–32, 33, 38
Volkssturm, 232
volunteer work, in West Germany, 134–35, 140–49, 150–51; see also Red Cross; Refugee Start Help
von Claer family, 78–94
Voroshilov Academy, Moscow, 96

Wackernagel, Christof, 8–9
Waffen-SS, 88, 89
Wagner, Cosima, 116
Wagner, Richard, 103, 104, 106, 107, 108, 114–15, 116, 117–18, 121
Wagner family, 121
Waldheim, Kurt, 89
Walesa, Lech, 6
Wall, the, see Berlin Wall
Wandsbeck Barracks, 134, 143, 145
Warthegau, 30
Wedekind, Frank, 117, 118
Wehrmacht, Nazi, 24, 26, 81–82; Resistance fighters in, 82–83, 87, 89, 239
Weimar Republic (1919–33), 4, 12, 81, 83, 118–19
Weiser, Gerhard, 48
Wellershoff, Dieter, 96
Welt am Sonntag (weekly), 113

Werfel, Franz, 118
Werthern, Etta von, 146
West Berlin, 4, 184, 217;
  demographics of, 218–19, 233,
  244; of 1980s, 217–24, 227–31,
  237–39; subsidies to, 229, 321; *see
  also* Berlin
West Germany (Federal Republic of
  Germany), 3, 4, 10, 76, 122, 162,
  228; anti-militarism in, 74–75, 93–
  95, 98–99; asylum for foreigners
  in, 19, 36, 154, 155, 204;
  citizenship, 20; democratic
  tradition built in, 14, 86, 94;
  eastern displaced persons as "war
  ghosts" in, 7–8 (*see also* refugees);
  expenditures for *Aussiedler* by, 26;
  guest workers in, 8, 19, 36;
  national anthem of, 77; press
  freedom vs. national security, 86;
  rearmament within NATO, 73–74,
  77, 83–84 (*see also* Bundeswehr);
  recent refugee waves to, 18, 25, 34,
  135, 152–55; repatriation law of
  1953, 20, 25; social benefits for
  East Germans, 155; social net for
  Jewish arrivals, 204, 208; social
  welfare for *Aussiedler*, 25–26, 34;
  subsidies to West Berlin, 229, 231
Wiedergutmachung, 208

Wilhelm I, Kaiser, 78–79, 91, 220
Wilhelm II, Kaiser, 4, 79–80, 163
Wilson, Woodrow, 46, 59–60, 61, 62
Wirtschaftswunder, see economic
  miracle
Wittelsbach dynasty, 103, 104
Wittmann, Franz, 48
Wolff-Bühring, Marina, 136–40, 142,
  146, 156
World War I, 72, 73, 76, 78, 79–80,
  81, 82, 118, 163, 176
World War II, 6, 13, 46, 55, 73, 77,
  78, 81, 82–83, 98, 121, 210, 232,
  236, 239–40
Wörner, Manfred, 74
Wroblensky, Vincent von, 209

Young Generation of Exiles, 64
youth, West German: exiles, 45, 53–
  56, 64; Jewish, 203, 206–7; 1968
  movement, 8–9, 183, 202, 212,
  230, 235; protest against Nazism of
  their parents, 8–9, 202, 234–35;
  "roots" search of exiles, 54
Yugoslavia, Albanian minority in, 7,
  66–67
Yugoslavian guest workers, 19, 36

Zeit, Die (weekly), 134, 142, 146–47

WITHDRAWN

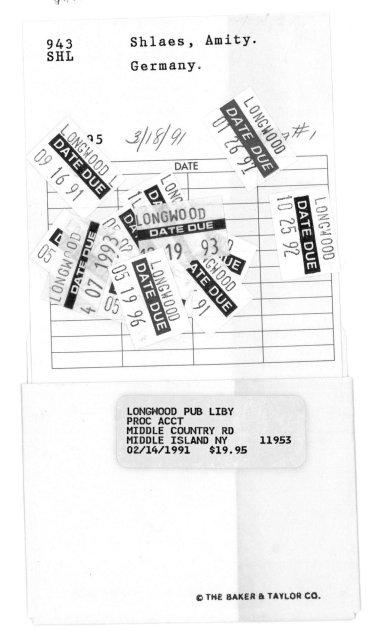